The Windows Textbook

Stewart Venit

California State University,
Los Angeles

Scott/Jones, Inc., Publishers

P. O. Box 696
El Granada, CA 94018
(415) 726-2436
(415) 726-4693 Fax

The Windows Textbook
Stewart Venit

ISBN 1-881991-31-8

Book Production: The Canfield Bookworks
Text Design: V & J Enterprises
Composition: Stewart Venit
Book Manufacturing: Malloy Lithographing, Inc.

V W X Y   4 5 6

ADDITIONAL TITLES OF INTEREST FROM SCOTT/JONES

Quickstart in Windows
by Stewart Venit

The DOS-6 Coursebook
by Forest Lin

Quick Start in DOS (120 pages)
by Forest Lin

The DOS Coursebook
(covers versions 3 and 4)
by Forest Lin

The DOS-5 Coursebook
by Forest Lin

The DOS Primer (covers versions 3 and 5)
by Dorothy Calvin

**The 1-2-3 Coursebook: Beginning and
Advanced Topics**   by Forest Lin

**Modern FORTRAN 77/90: Alternate
Edition**   by Gary Bronson

**Assembly Language for the IBM PC
Family**   by William Jones

C by Discovery, Second Edition
(emphasizing ANSI C)
by L. S. Foster

WordPerfect 6.0 for Windows
by Rolayne Day

Visual Basic
by Forest Lin

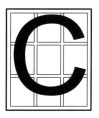

Contents

Test 3/22 & 3/24

 # Preface

There is now little doubt that Microsoft Windows and other graphical user interfaces are the wave of the computing future. From its shaky beginnings about ten years ago, Windows' importance has grown to the point where the ability to work in this environment is now a necessity for business-related computing of all kinds. It is the purpose of this text to provide students with proficiency in the use of Windows 3.1.

Organization of the Text

There are probably as many different courses on Windows as there are schools that teach them. With this in mind, we have organized the text to provide a great deal of flexibility in choosing topics and the order in which they are presented. An instructor can use this textbook to teach courses ranging from short ones concentrating on the basics to extended ones covering Windows in considerable depth.

A pictorial representation of the text's organization is shown in the Chapter Dependency Flowchart on the next page. Here is a more detailed description:

- An Introduction provides general information about computer hardware and software. It is intended for those students who have little or no experience with computers, but it could be given as a reading assignment to others.

Chapter Dependency Flowchart

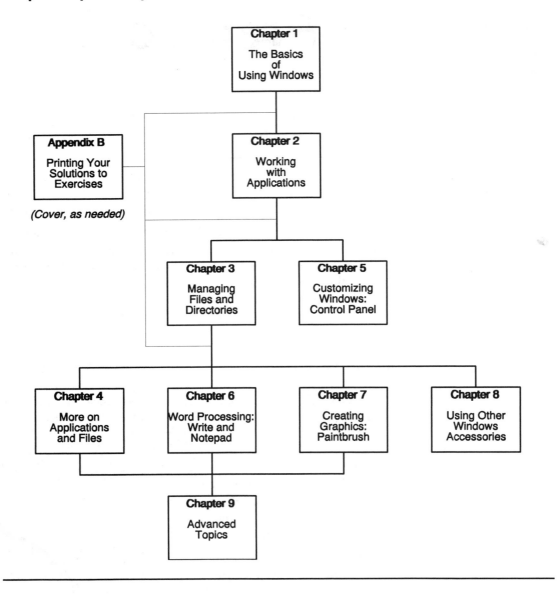

- Chapter 1, covering the basics of Windows, is the normal jumping off point for students who have some familiarity with computers, but none with Windows. The terminology and techniques discussed here are used throughout the text.

- Chapter 2 also covers some fundamental material. Chapter 1 and the first three sections of Chapter 2, which deal with Program Manager, should be considered prerequisite material for all other Windows' topics. The rest of Chapter 2 provides students with the tools they need to begin working with Windows and non-Windows applications.

- After completing Chapter 2, there are two alternatives. One option is to continue in sequence to the File Manager material in Chapter 3. A second alternative is to skip to Chapter 5, which deals with Control Panel, and then return to Chapter 3.

- Once Chapter 3 has been completed, the remaining chapters, except for Chapter 9, can be covered in any desired order. Moreover, the Windows "accessories" in Chapter 8 are independent of one another, as well, and can be dealt with as time permits.

- Chapter 9 contains some relatively esoteric material. We suggest that students become comfortable with Windows and a few of its applications before tackling it.

Features of the Text

Hands-on approach

1. Certainly, the best way to learn Windows is to use Windows. With this in mind, we have written this text in a way that encourages students to follow along at the computer. This approach is reinforced by Hands-On exercises at the end of most sections and all chapters.

No delay in starting up

2. The text introduces Windows' terminology and techniques immediately; we start up Windows on the first page of the first chapter. For those courses that require it, the Introduction provides material on using personal computers and an appendix supplies information about installing Windows.

Chapter integrity

3. We have tried to integrate the material within each chapter as much as possible, so that it forms a cohesive whole. To help in this respect, every chapter begins with a brief overview and statement of objectives, and ends with a fairly comprehensive summary.

Variety of exercises

4. The text contains a large number and variety of exercises. At the end of most sections, a Hands-On exercise asks the student to carry out the techniques that were just introduced. This provides an immediate review of the section material. There are also several types of end-of-chapter exercises:

- Short Answer drill exercises (completion, true/false, and multiple choice) test the students' knowledge of facts presented in the chapter.

- Hands-On exercises (like the end-of-section ones) require the students to perform the kinds of tasks they will encounter in using Windows on an everyday basis.

- Creative Writing exercises help the students to learn by writing. Some are straightforward ("Describe a technique that..."); others are more thought-provoking ("Why do you think that ...").

Printed solutions

5. Appendix B shows students how to produce a printed copy of the text and screens that make up their solutions to the exercises. Ideally, a student will be able to follow these instructions after completing Chapter 1; realistically, the material in Section 2.4 on switching and transferring data between applications makes Appendix B more accessible to the average student after Chapter 2 is completed.

6. TIPs appear periodically throughout the text (identified by the logo shown at the left). These provide insight into, or specialized knowledge about, the topic at hand. A fact or technique may be called a TIP because it is especially important or just because it is interesting or unusual.

Margin notes

7. Occasional short notes in the left margin of the text make it easy for the reader to locate subtopics and important procedures.

Interface options

8. As befits a graphical user interface, the text emphasizes the use of the mouse in performing operations within Windows, but it also provides some keyboard alternatives:

- Important keystroke combinations, such as common "shortcut keys," are described in the main body of the text.

- More obscure keyboard alternatives are deferred until later and set off from the rest of the text (to facilitate skipping) by the logo shown at the left.

Flexibility

9. The text is flexible; it lends itself to courses of varying lengths and content. (See the section entitled "Organization of the Text.")

Supplements

10. The text is accompanied by supplementary material to aid the teaching process. This material is described in the next section.

Supplementary Material

The following material is provided with the text or available to instructors directly from the publisher:

- A 3½-inch Lab Projects diskette is included with every textbook. (If you need a 5¼-inch version, ask your instructor to contact the publisher*.) This diskette contains some files that are referenced in Hands-On exercises and others that are used in the body of the text.

- An Instructor's Resource Guide is available from the publisher*. It contains sample course syllabi, additional test items for each chapter plus a midterm and final exam, transparency masters, and answers to the even-numbered exercises (answers to the odd-numbered exercises are in the text itself).

Acknowledgements

I would like to thank the many people who helped bring this project to fruition. First and foremost, Richard Jones proposed that I write this book, suggested numerous improvements to the developing manuscript, and gave me enthusiastic support from start to finish. The following instructors, through their critical reviews and thoughtful comments, also had a profound effect on the resulting text:

Clifford Appleby
Treshold Software Training Systems

Ronald Burgher
Metro Community College

Joan Flood
St. Paul Area Vocational College

Judy Graff
Red Wing Area Vocational Institute

Wayne Horn
Pensacola Junior College

Frank Myers
Cabrillo College

Kathy Blicharz
Pima Community College

Susan Finch
Pima Community College

Janet Gerth
Essex Community College

Cathy Hall
Aims Community College

Young Kim
Porterville College

Dennis Olson
Pikes Peak Community College

---

*The address and telephone number of the publisher appear on the back cover.

John Parker   Tony Rhode
Santa Barbara City College   *Northeast Metro Tech College*

Nancy Webb
City College of San Francisco

I am especially indebted to Kathy Ponti. She read the entire manuscript, scrutinized every aspect of the text, and improved it in countless ways.

Finally, I would like to thank my wife Corinne and my daughter Tamara, not only for their encouragement and support, but also for understanding that a project of this sort requires the author to spend seemingly endless periods of time planted in front of a computer.

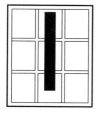

Introduction

OVERVIEW   We are living in a world that is becoming increasingly dependent on the electronic computer. Computers help run our businesses and institutions, design and build manufactured products, provide instantaneous worldwide communication, publish our newspapers, magazines, and books, and supply all sorts of educational and recreational activities. Many forms of employment now require some kind of **computer literacy** — an understanding of how to use a computer effectively.

In this introduction, we will describe, in general terms, the computer's *hardware* and *software* — the components and programs that make it work. Although this material is not essential for an understanding of Microsoft Windows, it may help with certain topics and will probably increase your computer literacy. More specifically, you will learn about:

1. Computers in general and personal computers in particular.

2. The components of a computer: its central processing unit, internal memory, mass storage, and input and output devices.

3. Types of computer applications.

4. The function of an operating system.

5. Microsoft Windows — what it is and why it's important.

6. The history of personal computers.

Personal Computers

Everyone who uses a computer on a daily basis becomes accustomed to dealing with special computer-related terminology. Yet, to a beginner, many of these terms can be confusing and even intimidating. There are floppy disks and hard disks, kilobytes and megabytes, mice and monitors, and much, much more. In this section, we will try to take some of the mystery out of computer terminology.

What is a Computer?

As with any evolving technology, precisely defining the term *computer* is not easy. Computers can take many different forms and their capabilities are constantly expanding. Yet, all computers do the same basic things. Every **computer** can input, store, manipulate, and output vast quantities of data at very high speed. Moreover, all computers are *programmable* — they can follow a list of instructions (a **program**) and act upon intermediate results without human intervention.

A **personal computer** (also called a **microcomputer** or a **PC**) is a relatively small type of computer, usually intended for use by one person at a time. (Larger computers — known as *minicomputers*, *mainframes*, and *supercomputers*, in order of increasing size and power — can be simultaneously shared by many users, connected to the computer by cables or telephone lines.) All personal computers are small enough to fit on a desktop; portable PCs are even smaller — usually no larger than a looseleaf binder. A drawing of a typical PC is shown in Figure 1.

Components of a computer

As the definition implies, a computer must have the ability to input, store, manipulate, and output data. These functions are carried out by the five main components of a computer system:

1. The central processing unit.

2. Internal memory (primary storage).

3. Mass storage devices.

4. Input devices.

5. Output devices.

In a personal computer, the first two of these components (and usually the third as well) are housed in the **system unit** (see Figure 1).

FIGURE 1   A Typical Personal Computer

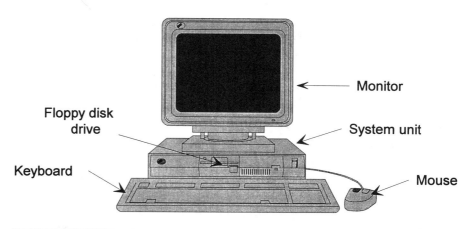

The input devices, such as the keyboard and mouse, and output devices, such as the monitor, are housed in their own enclosures and are connected to the system unit by cables. Devices like these, that are used by a computer but located outside the system unit, are sometimes called **peripherals**. All the physical equipment that makes up the computer system is known as **hardware**.

The Central Processing Unit

The **central processing unit** (also called the **processor** or **CPU**) is the brain of the computer. It receives all program instructions, performs the arithmetic and logical operations necessary to execute them, and controls all the other computer components. In a personal computer, the processor consists of hundreds of thousands of transistors residing on a single *chip* the size of a large postage stamp and plugged into the computer's main circuit board, the *motherboard*.

More then any other component, the CPU distinguishes one computer from another. In the kind of computer you will be using (which is known as *DOS-based* or *IBM-compatible* for reasons we will discuss later), the processors are usually referred to by their part numbers; for example: 80286, 80386, or 80486 — the larger the number, the more powerful the CPU. The 80286 is called a *16-bit chip* (a **bit** is either a 0 or a 1) because it can process 16 bits of information at a time. The 80386 and 80486 are 32-bit processors. The latest, most powerful CPU for IBM-compatible computers, the Pentium, is a 64-bit chip.

Processors are also distinguished from one another by the speed (in *megahertz*, MHz) at which they can process information. Thus, in an ad for an IBM-compatible computer, you may see it referred to as "a 33 MHz 486DX" machine. This is shorthand for a computer equipped with an 80486 processor running at 33 megahertz; the suffix DX designates a variant of this CPU. This is a very common, relatively fast PC.

Internal Memory

A computer uses its **internal memory** to store the instructions and data to be processed by the CPU. In a personal computer, memory resides on a series of chips either plugged directly into the motherboard or into one or more smaller circuit boards connected to the motherboard.

RAM and ROM

Internal memory is divided into two types: ROM and RAM. **ROM** stands for *Read-Only Memory*. It contains an unalterable set of instructions that the computer consults during its start-up process and during certain other basic operations. **RAM** (*Random-Access Memory*), on the other hand, can be both read from and written to. (Think of ROM as a reference sheet, while RAM is a scratchpad — a very large scratchpad.) RAM is used by the computer to hold program instructions and data. Whereas ROM is a permanent form of memory storage, all the information stored in RAM is lost when the computer is turned off.

Memory is usually measured in *kilobytes* and *megabytes*, where one **byte** consists of eight bits and is the amount of memory used to store one character of information. (Loosely speaking, a *character* is any symbol you can type, such as a letter, a digit, or a punctuation mark.) One **kilobyte**, abbreviated **KB**, is 1,024 (= 2^{10}) bytes and one **megabyte** (**MB**) is 1,024 kilobytes. Thus, a computer with four megabytes of RAM, a typical amount nowadays, can store 4,194,304 (= 4 × 1,024 × 1,024) characters of information.

Mass Storage Devices

In addition to ROM and RAM, a computer needs **mass storage**, another form of memory, which stores programs and data semi-permanently. (They remain in mass storage until you decide to erase them.) However, to make use of any information stored on a mass storage device, that information must first be *loaded* (or copied) into RAM.

Disk drives

On personal computers, the primary type of mass storage device is the **disk drive**. Most PCs contain a **hard disk drive** housed within the system unit and one or two **floppy disk drives**, also housed within the system unit but accessible from the outside (see Figure 1). To store information, the hard disk drive makes use of a constantly spinning magnetic platter — the **hard disk** — which is sealed within the drive. **Floppy disks** (or **diskettes**), on the other hand, are stored away from the computer and, when needed, are inserted into the floppy drive.

Floppy disks and their drives come in two sizes: 3½ or 5¼ inches in diameter. (Figure 2 shows the two sizes of disks.) Surprisingly, the smaller 3½-inch disk has a greater storage capacity than the larger one. *High density* 3½-inch diskettes hold up to 1.44 MB of data; high density 5¼-inch diskettes hold up to 1.2 MB. *Low density* diskettes, which are used in older machines, hold less data. Hard drive capacities nowadays range from 40 MB to 500 MB or more.

FIGURE 2   Floppy Disks

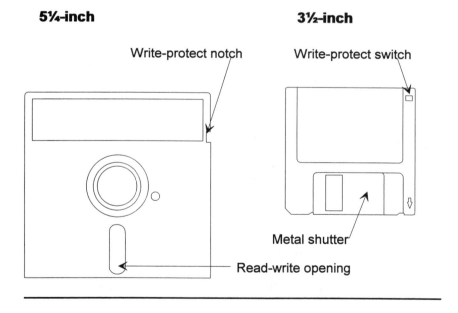

5¼-inch   **3½-inch**

Write-protect notch   Write-protect switch

Metal shutter

Read-write opening

Caring for diskettes   Floppy disks, especially the 5¼-inch variety, are relatively fragile and need to be handled with care. In particular:

■   Don't touch the surface of the diskette (for example, the part of the 5¼-inch floppy that shows through the read-write opening).

■ Keep diskettes away from magnets; data on them can be erased by exposure to a magnetic field.

■ Extreme heat can damage diskettes. Don't, for example, expose them to direct sunlight.

■ Dust is also an enemy. Although, 3½-inch diskettes are protected by their metal shutters, 5¼-inch floppies should be kept in their paper sleeve when not in use.

If you want to avoid the possibility of accidentally overwriting or erasing data on a floppy disk, you can *write-protect* it. A write-protected diskette can be read from, but not written to. To write-protect a 5¼-inch floppy, cover its write-protect notch with a small piece of tape; to write-protect a 3½-inch diskette, throw its write-protect switch.

You may be wondering why a computer needs both hard and floppy drives. (In fact, a relatively small number of computers contain only floppy drives and an even smaller number contain only hard drives.) Typically, the hard drive is used to store almost all the programs and data to be used by a PC. Floppy drives, which are much slower in operation, are typically used in the following ways: to transfer newly purchased programs from the distribution disks to the computer's hard disk; for *backup* purposes — to make copies of valuable hard disk information; to help transfer information from one computer to another; and for *archival* purposes — to move hard disk data that is not likely to be needed in the future to diskettes.

Other mass storage devices   Some personal computers are equipped with additional types of mass storage devices. A **tape drive**, which uses media that resemble audio cassettes, can be used to copy (backup) the entire contents of a hard disk. Should the hard disk become inoperable — should it *crash* — its data could then be retrieved from the backup tape. A tape drive works slowly, but this isn't too important, given its intended role. A **CD-ROM drive** uses disks that are similar to audio compact discs (hence the "CD" in its name). These disks, like floppies, are removable and portable, but, unlike floppies, hold huge amounts of information — about 500 MB. Because CD-ROM drives are read-only devices (hence the "ROM" in the name), they are used primarily to hold reference material such as encyclopedias, dictionaries, and the like.

Input Devices

The computer uses its **input devices** to receive data from the outside world. For this purpose, every computer includes a typewriter-like **keyboard** (see Figure 3). To enter information into the computer, you simply type it at the keyboard in the same way you would using an ordinary typewriter. The characters you type will simultaneously appear on the computer's display screen.

FIGURE 3   A Common Keyboard Layout

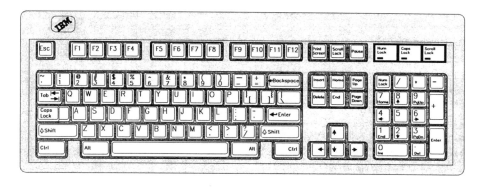

Special keys   Computer keyboards contain quite a few keys not found on a typewriter. (Figure 3 shows the most common keyboard layout for IBM-compatible machines.) These "extra" keys include:

- Twelve *function keys* labeled F1 through F12 are arrayed across the top of the keyboard. They perform special tasks that vary depending on the program you are using.

- Just to the right of the large block of typewriter-like keys are ten *cursor control keys*: the four *Arrow keys* (↑, ↓, ←, and →) plus Insert, Home, and so on. These keys allow you to move the *cursor*, which indicates the current typing position, around the screen. (We will say more about this in Chapter 1.)

- A *numeric keypad*, at the far right of the keyboard, allows you to enter numbers quickly. If the *Num Lock* light in the upper right is off, these keys will not input numbers; the secondary function indicated on the key (for example, Home or ↑) is performed instead. To turn the Num Lock light on or off, press the Num Lock key.

You may notice a few other special keys (such as Esc and Print

Screen) here and there on the keyboard. We will explain their functions in later chapters. Two of the special keys, labeled Ctrl (for Control) and Alt (for Alternate) are worth mentioning now. Holding down Ctrl or Alt, each of which appears twice in the bottom row, while pressing a character or function key performs a special program-dependent task.

Another common input device is the **mouse**, a hand-held object containing one, two, or three buttons, which (together with the cable connecting it to the computer) vaguely resembles a very long-tailed rodent. When you roll the mouse around on the desk top, a pointer moves correspondingly on the screen. For example, if you roll the mouse to the left, the pointer moves left. Once the pointer is positioned appropriately on the screen, pressing a mouse button (*clicking the mouse*) performs a program function. The mouse can speed up certain input operations, but lacks the versatility of the keyboard.

Output Devices

Whereas input devices allow us to communicate with the computer, **output devices** make it possible for the computer to "talk" to us. The most common output devices are *monitors* and *printers*.

A **monitor** is a high resolution television-like screen enclosed in a case and controlled by circuitry — the *video adapter* — within the computer. (The screens on portable computers use an entirely different technology; they are usually *LCD* — liquid crystal display — *panels*.) As is the case with televisions, monitor size is measured along the screen's diagonal. The most common screen size for desk top computers is 14 inches, but they vary from 12 inches to 20 inches or more. Another characteristic that affects the quality and cost of a monitor is its *resolution* — the number of *pixels* (tiny dots of light) it uses to create its images. Nowadays, screen resolutions of 1024×768 — 768 horizontal rows, each containing 1,024 pixels — are becoming increasingly common. This kind of resolution puts even the finest of TVs to shame.

Unfortunately, output to the screen is both impermanent (it disappears when the power is turned off) and not terribly portable (you'd need a pretty long extension cord to take your screen output home from school). If you want to make a permanent copy of a program's output on paper, you need to use a **printer**.

The text and pictures produced by virtually all printers are composed of tiny dots of ink or an ink-like substance. The size of these dots and how closely they are packed together determines the quality of the output. Here are the most common types of printers in use today, in order of increasing price and quality of output:

- *Dot matrix printers* produce the "tiny dots" by rapidly striking an inked ribbon against the paper with a row of small pins. They are relatively inexpensive (usually costing from $200 to $500) and are very reliable. Moreover, these printers usually have an adjustment that allows the pins to strike harder if you want to print on multipart forms. Some dot matrix printers also work with multicolored ribbons, although their color output tends to be somewhat dull.

- *Ink jet printers* spray incredibly tiny drops of ink on the paper producing finer images than their dot matrix counterparts at a slightly higher speed and price. On the negative side, ink jet printers are relatively expensive to operate and aren't of much use with multipart forms. (Think about it!) Color ink jets are the most common of color printers and produce fairly good output at a reasonable price.

- *Laser printers* produce the best output at the highest rate of speed. They are also remarkably reliable. However, laser printers are more expensive than dot matrix and ink jet printers, ranging in price from about $500 to $5,000. (Color laser printers, which are relatively rare, cost more than $10,000.) Nevertheless, as prices steadily drop, it seems clear that laser printers will soon dominate the market. Then, almost everyone will be able to create documents with print quality that rivals that produced by professional typesetting equipment.

Software, Operating Systems, and Windows

The most powerful hardware cannot accomplish anything by itself. It needs **software** — computer programs — to bring it to life. Software provides instructions for the central processing unit and, in so doing, allows the computer user to write letters, calculate loan balances, draw pictures, play games, and perform countless other tasks.

Applications Software

Software is divided into two general categories: applications and system software. **Applications software** (or more simply, *applications*) are programs you use to enhance your productivity, solve problems, supply information, or provide recreation. To be able to use programs like these is the reason why you learned (or are learning) to use a computer. The most commonly used applications include:

- *Word processors* help you create, edit, and print documents such as letters, reports, memos, and so on. We will discuss the use of a word processor called *Write* in Chapter 6.

- *Database managers* allow you to enter, access, and modify large quantities of data. You might use a database program to create a personal phone directory. A business can use this kind of program to maintain customer lists and employee records.

- *Spreadsheet programs* simplify the manipulation and calculation of large amounts of tabular data (spreadsheets). These programs are heavily used by the business community to try to foresee the effect of different strategies on their bottom line.

- *Drawing and painting programs* allow one to use the computer to (you guessed it) draw or paint pictures — *graphics* — on the screen and print them on paper. Chapter 7 discusses the use of a graphics-creating program called *Paintbrush*.

- *Desktop publishing programs* provide the user with a high degree of control over the placement of text and graphics within a document. These programs are used to produce flyers, newsletters, brochures, and even entire books.

Applications are developed and published by many different companies and sold through retail stores and mail order firms. Each application package consists of an instruction manual (or *user's guide*) together with one or more diskettes that contain the application *files* — programs, data, and documents needed by the application. Although some applications can be run directly from the diskettes supplied, most must first be *installed* — copied (by the computer) from the floppies to the hard disk.

The Operating System

The second general software type is **system software**, the programs used by the computer to control its hardware. System software includes:

- The **operating system** is the computer's master control program; it coordinates the interaction among the computer's hardware, applications, and user.

- **Programming languages** allow users (in this case, *programmers)* to write applications.

- **Utility programs** perform basic tasks such as managing files, destroying computer *viruses* (programs designed to wreak havoc with your computer), and making more efficient use of memory and disk space.

A lot of system software is written by the developer of the operating system and included with it. Additional system software is produced by other companies.

The operating system has two general functions:

1. It helps the application you are using to communicate with the computer hardware. Applications are written to run under a specific operating system, which supplies easy ways for the programmers to access the computer's disk drives, memory, and so on.

2. It provides an *interface* — a link — between you and the computer that allows you to install and start up applications, manipulate disk files, and perform other very basic tasks.

DOS   The central processing unit may be the brain of the computer, but the operating system gives the computer its personality. Most IBM-compatible computers use the MS-DOS operating system developed by Microsoft Corporation or its near twin, PC-DOS, which is a product of International Business Machines Corporation (IBM). Both MS-DOS and PC-DOS are often just called **DOS** (which stands for *disk operating system*) and IBM-compatible computers are sometimes referred to as *DOS-based* machines. DOS dates back to the original IBM Personal Computer introduced in 1981 and, although major changes have been made to it over the years, DOS still retains much of the awkwardness of its distant past.

An immediate clue to an operating system's personality is its *start-up screen*, the one you see after you turn on the computer and it has gone through its preliminary functions. With pure, unadorned DOS, you are presented with a few lines of mysterious-looking text ending with the *DOS prompt* (most likely, C:\>) followed by a blinking underline (the *cursor*). This is DOS' way of asking you to enter a command. For example, if you wanted to start up your word processor, you might type the following two lines (pressing the Enter key at the end of each):

```
CD \WP51\DATA
\WP51\WP
```

User
interfaces

This kind of **command line interface** is classic DOS. In order to direct DOS to perform a function, the computer user must memorize (or have a handy list of) a large number of arcane commands. This is certainly not a *user-friendly* system.

More recent versions of DOS have included an optional **menu-driven interface**. Although this interface is not very visually exciting, it *is* more user-friendly. Typically, its start-up screen (Figure 4) contains a list — a **menu** — of available applications. In order to start one of these programs, the user presses an Arrow key until the desired program is highlighted (stands out) and then presses the Enter key. Operations on files, such as copying or deleting them, can also be done by selecting the desired files from a list and then selecting the appropriate operation from another list.

FIGURE 4   A Start-up Screen for a Menu-driven Interface

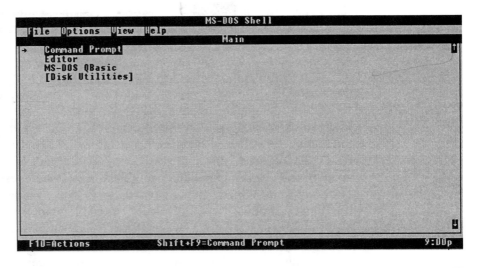

The **graphical user interface** (**GUI**, pronounced "gooey") provides a further improvement in ease of use. Here, the opening screen consists of a collection of small titled pictures called **icons** (see Figure 5) together with a list of available menus (File, Options, Window, and Help in Figure 5). With a graphical user interface, you can start up applications and perform other operating system functions as easily as moving the mouse pointer to the corresponding icon or menu item and pressing a mouse button. The keyboard can also be employed to select functions, but using a GUI is much easier with a mouse.

FIGURE 5   The Windows Start-up Screen

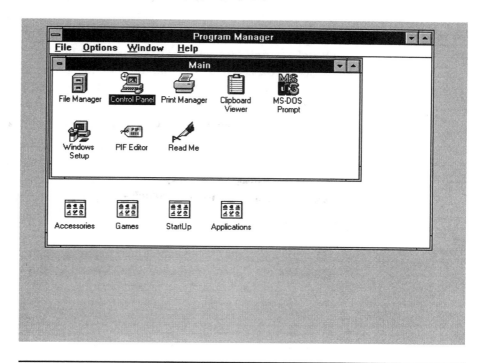

Microsoft Windows

Windows is a very sophisticated program developed by Microsoft Corporation to make IBM-compatible computers easier to use. Microsoft refers to Windows as an operating system, and it acts like an operating system in all respects but one — it cannot be used unless DOS has already been loaded into memory. For this reason, most knowledgeable computer users refer to Windows as an *operating environment*.

Windows has many advantages over plain old DOS:

■   Its graphical user interface (Figure 5 shows a typical screen) is much easier to use than DOS' command line or menu-driven interfaces.

- Windows has **multitasking** capabilities — you can run more than one application at a time, each occupying its own area on the screen. For example, you can start up a paint program to draw a picture without closing down the word processor that is already running.

- You can easily transfer data from one application to another. For example, the picture you've just completed in the paint program can be inserted by Windows into your word processing document.

- Windows provides uniform standards for the look and feel of applications developed to run under it. (Such programs are called *Windows applications*; those not designed specifically for Windows are called *DOS applications*.) This is of great benefit to the computer user, making it easier to learn and use new applications.

- The Windows user interface is highly customizable; you can exert a great degree of control over the way that it looks and acts. For example, you can design your own start-up screen, choose your own screen colors and fonts (typefaces), position and size the areas on the screen in which your applications are running, and much, much more.

- Windows supplies a large number of useful small and medium-sized applications. These include an on-screen clock and calculator, a simple database manager, a word processor, a paint program, an easy-to-use file manager, and even a couple of games.

- Windows provides modules that control a wide assortment of different monitors, printers, mice, and other peripherals. As a result, applications software programmers don't have to worry about writing their own software to communicate with the huge variety of input and output devices.

Does Windows have any disadvantages? Absolutely. In general, Windows applications run more slowly (on some computers, *much* more slowly) than their DOS counterparts. Consequently, Windows needs more powerful, more expensive hardware in order to run effectively. Realistically speaking, Windows requires at least a fast 386 processor, a 100 MB hard disk, and 4 MB of RAM. Nevertheless, Windows has become a phenomenally successful program; it and its descendants appear to be the wave of the future for IBM-compatible computers.

A Brief History of Personal Computers

The electronic computer is a relatively modern invention; the first fully operable computer was developed about 50 years ago, at the end of World War II, by a team at the University of Pennsylvania's Moore School of Engineering. This team was headed by John Mauchly and J. Presper Eckert, who named the new machine *ENIAC*, for Electronic Numerical Integrator and Calculator. ENIAC was hardly a *personal* computer, occupying a large room and weighing about 33 tons. By today's standards, ENIAC was extremely slow, unreliable, and expensive to operate. In 1945, on the other hand, it was considered a marvel.

Over the next 30 years, computers became smaller, faster, and less expensive. However, most of these machines remained isolated in their own air-conditioned rooms, tended by specially trained personnel. By 1975, computers were in great demand at universities, government agencies, and large businesses, but relatively few people had ever come face-to-face with an actual computer. This all began to change in the late 1970s.

To understand why, let's take a closer look at the early computers. ENIAC and its immediate successors were large, slow, and unreliable primarily because they used thousands of large, slow, and unreliable *vacuum tubes* in their electronic circuits. The vacuum tubes were glass cylinders, typically about four inches high and an inch in diameter, which generated a lot of heat and thus could not be placed too close together. Then, in 1947, a momentous event occurred at Bell Labs — William Shockley, John Bardeen, and Walter Brattain announced the invention of the *transistor*. Only about an inch long and a quarter inch across, a transistor produced very little heat, and did the same job as a vacuum tube.

The downsizing of computers began in the 1950s as transistors replaced vacuum tubes, and continued into the 1960s with the introduction of the *integrated circuit* (IC) — an ice cube-sized package containing hundreds of transistors. By the late 1960s, *microchips*, consisting of thousands of electronic components residing on a piece of silicon the size of a postage stamp, had begun to replace ICs. At this time, some mini-computers occupied a space no larger than a small filing cabinet and cost less than $25,000. Then, in 1970, Marcian Hoff, Jr., working at Intel Corporation, invented the **microprocessor**, a central processing unit on a chip. The technological world was now ready for the personal computer.

The first personal computer

The first personal computer to be successfully marketed to the public was built in 1974. It was designed by Micro Instrumentation and Telemetry Systems (MITS), a small electronics firm located in New Mexico, which named it the Altair 8800. The Altair was a very primitive machine about the size of a bread box; it contained 256 bytes (not kilobytes) of RAM, had no ROM, and its input and output devices consisted of rows of toggle switches and lights, respectively. It was also quite inexpensive — $395 in kit form. Sales of the Altair took off after an article about it appeared in the January, 1975 issue of *Popular Electronics* magazine.

Although add-on products for the Altair 8800 (such as memory boards and paper tape readers) gradually appeared over the next couple of years, it's questionable whether anyone ever did any useful work on this machine. Nevertheless, the Altair is of major historical significance because it inspired thousands of computer hobbyists and professionals to become interested in personal computers.

Two of those inspired by the Altair were Paul Allen and William Gates, both about twenty years old and living in the Boston area at the time. They joined together to write and sell a version of the BASIC programming language for the new computer. With the easy-to-use BASIC available, Altair owners no longer had to write programs in low-level, mind-numbing machine language. Soon thereafter, Gates and Allen formed Microsoft Corporation, which is now the world's largest software company (and the publisher of Windows).

Another Altair aficionado was Stephen Wozniak, who joined forces with his friend and fellow Californian, Steven Jobs, to form Apple Computer, Inc. In 1977, they brought the now legendary Apple II personal computer to market. The Apple II was an instant hit and for the next few years, Apple was the fastest growing company in the United States.

The IBM PC   By 1980, there were dozens of companies manufacturing personal computers, but the major producers of the larger minicomputers and mainframes had not yet entered the fray. This changed dramatically in 1981, when IBM brought out its first personal computer (not so imaginatively named the *IBM Personal Computer*). Although it wasn't much more powerful than most other personal computers of the time, the IBM PC (Figure 6) was a milestone in the history of personal computers for two basic reasons:

1. For many businesses, especially the larger ones, it "legitimized" personal computers. If IBM was selling them, the reasoning went, then maybe PCs really could be a useful business tool. As a result, the IBM PC became wildly popular; IBM could not produce them fast enough to keep up with the demand.

2. It was built with generic parts and used an operating system (PC-DOS) developed by Microsoft and virtually identical to MS-DOS, which was sold by Microsoft. The IBM PC also used *open archi-*

tecture — IBM published detailed specifications so that anyone could build circuit boards for it to expand its capabilities. These features enabled enterprising companies to "clone" the PC — to build their own IBM-compatible personal computers.

FIGURE 6 Two Historic Computers

IBM PC   **Apple Macintosh**

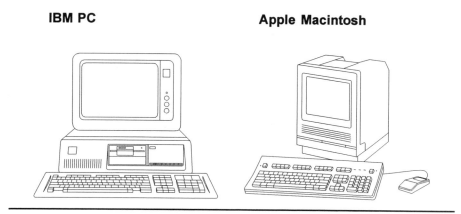

The Apple Macintosh

For the next few years, the personal computer industry evolved as a few IBM clones and dozens of non-IBM compatible PCs were brought to market. Then, in 1984, Apple introduced the Macintosh (Figure 6), which it advertised, with a decidedly anti-IBM slant, as "the computer for the rest of us." With its small size and integral screen, the "Mac" certainly *looked* different, but what really made it stand out was its easy-to-use, mouse-driven, graphical user interface. (This GUI is similar, broadly speaking, to the Windows interface developed later by Microsoft. Both interfaces, and the mouse as well, trace their roots back to work done about 1980 at Xerox Corporation's Palo Alto Research Center.) The Apple Macintosh was not at all compatible with the IBM PC. Nevertheless, after a slow start, it became increasingly popular. Today, the Macintosh and its descendants are the only reasonably popular alternatives to IBM-compatible personal computers.

In 1984, IBM also introduced a new microcomputer, the IBM PC/AT, which used the more powerful 80286 processor. This event set off a flurry of activity by other manufacturers who quickly cloned the new machine and introduced improvements of their own.

Recent developments

From this point on, the increased competition for the PC buyer's dollar brought forth more powerful computers at an ever-accelerating rate. This boom was fueled by Intel Corporation, which introduced new generations of microprocessors in 1986, 1989, and 1993 (the 80386, 80486, and Pentium, respectively). In each case, microcomputer manufacturers quickly brought out machines designed around the new chip and software developers used the greater speed to create more sophisticated programs.

Microsoft Windows was one of the major beneficiaries of the more powerful computers. When it was first introduced in 1985, Windows ran sluggishly on the existing hardware (graphics-intensive programs require relatively fast computers), and it did not have much success. However, by the time the much improved Version 3.0 was brought to market in 1990, hardware had caught up with the demands of the software and this version of Windows was an immediate hit. Then, when an even better Version 3.1 was introduced in 1992 in the midst of a computer price war that made top-of-the-line machines affordable, Windows became the standard operating environment for IBM-compatible microcomputers.

Summary

Key Terms

Applications (software) [page I-9]	Bit [I-3]
Byte [I-4]	CD-ROM drive [I-6]
Central processing unit, CPU [I-3]	Command line interface [I-12]
Computer [I-2]	Computer literacy [I-1]
Disk drive [I-4]	Diskette [I-5]
DOS [I-11]	Floppy disk [I-5]
Floppy disk drive [I-5]	Graphical user interface, GUI [I-12]
Hard disk [I-5]	Hard disk drive [I-4]
Hardware [I-3]	Icon [I-12]
Input device [I-6]	Internal memory [I-4]
Keyboard [I-7]	Kilobyte, KB [I-4]
Mass storage [I-4]	Megabyte, MB [I-4]
Menu [I-12]	Menu-driven interface [I-12]
Microcomputer [I-2]	Microprocessor [I-15]
Monitor [I-8]	Mouse [I-8]

Topics Covered

Components of a Computer

Central processing unit (CPU, processor, microprocessor)

Internal memory — ROM and RAM

Mass storage devices — such as floppy and hard disk drives, CD-ROM drives, and tape drives

Input devices — such as the keyboard and mouse

Output devices — such as the monitor and printer

Types of Software

Applications software	Word processors, spreadsheet programs, database managers, drawing programs, desktop publishing programs, and so on.
System software	Operating system, programming languages, and utilities.

Windows

Advantages over DOS	More user-friendly, multitasking, more consistent "look and feel", supplies more mini-applications.
Disadvantages	Slower, requires more expensive hardware.

History of the Personal Computer

1945 — The first fully-operable computer, ENIAC, is built.

1947 — The transistor is invented.

1970 — The microprocessor, a CPU on a chip, is invented.

1974 — The first personal computer, the Altair 8800, is built.

1977 — The Apple II makes its debut.

1981 — The IBM PC is introduced.

1984 — The Apple Macintosh, with its GUI interface, is introduced. The IBM PC/AT, with its 80286 chip, hits the market.

1985 — Microsoft rolls out the first version of Windows.

1986 — Intel introduces the 80386 microprocessor.

1989 — Intel introduces the 80486 microprocessor.

1992 — Windows 3.1 is brought to market.

1993 — Intel introduces the Pentium microprocessor.

Exercises

Short Answer

Complete each of the statements in Exercises 1 through 15.

1. The physical components of a computer system are referred to as its _Hardware_

2. A computer's main circuit board is called its _Motherboard_

3. One byte of memory consists of _8_ bits.

4. One megabyte is equal to _1024 k_ bytes.

5. Some examples of mass storage devices are floppy disk drives, hard disk drives, and _CD-Rom_ drives.

6. Of the various types of printers, the highest quality output is produced by a _Lazer_ printer.

7. Software is divided into two broad categories: _Applical_ software and system software.

8. The master control program that oversees the computer's operations is called its _Operating System_

9. The generic name for the operating system used by most IBM-compatible computers is _DOS based machine_

10. Windows makes use of a GUI, which stands for _Graphic User Interface_

11. The first fully-operable electronic computer was named _ENIAC_ .

12. The _Microprocessor_, a CPU residing on a single computer chip, was invented in 1970.

13. The first personal computer received national attention in the year _1974_ .

14. The first microcomputer built by International Business Machines Corporation was called the _1981_ .

15. The first widely-used computer to make use of a graphical user interface was the _The Apple Macintosh._

In Exercises 16 through 30, determine whether each statement is true or false.

16. Computer components housed outside the system unit are called peripherals.

17. One megabyte of RAM can store more than 1,000,000 characters of information.

18. The contents of a computer's ROM are lost when the power is turned off.

19. Floppy disk drives access data more slowly than hard disk drives.

20. A CD-ROM drive can be used for backup purposes.

21. Computer keyboards contain fewer keys than a standard typewriter.

22. Laser printers are especially good for printing on multipart forms.

23. Computer programs are also known as software.

24. Most computer users find it easier to use a command line interface than a graphical user interface.

25. Most IBM-compatible personal computers use the DOS operating system.

26. One of the advantages of Windows over DOS is the speed with which it runs applications.

27. The invention of the transistor led to smaller, cheaper, more reliable computers.

28. The first personal computer was manufactured by Apple Computer, Inc.

29. The Apple Macintosh makes use of the Windows operating environment.

30. Computers have not increased appreciably in speed and power since 1984.

In Exercises 31 through 40, choose the correct answer.

31. Which of the following components is *not* contained within the system unit of a typical PC?

    a. The motherboard.
    b. A floppy disk drive.
    c. Random access memory (RAM).
    d. None of the above answers is correct.

32. The computer's central processing unit

    a. Processes program instructions.
    b. Performs arithmetic and logical operations.
    c. Controls the other components of the computer.
    d. Performs all the above functions.

33. Which of the following is an input device?

    a. A monitor.
    b. A keyboard.
    c. A printer.
    d. Read-only memory (ROM).

34. One advantage of a floppy disk over a hard disk is that

    a. It can be used to transfer data between computers.
    b. It holds more data.
    c. Data can be retrieved from it more quickly.
    d. None of the above answers is correct.

35. Which of the following is an example of system software?

    a. The computer's RAM.
    b. The computer's operating system.
    c. A computer game.

d. A word processor.

36. One advantage of DOS over Windows is that

a. It can run several programs at once.
b. It is easier to learn to use.
c. It requires less powerful hardware.
d. All of the above are correct.

37. Microsoft Windows

a. Requires DOS to be running before it can be started up.
b. Requires a mouse to use.
c. Runs on both IBM-compatibles and the Apple Macintosh.
d. Was the first graphical user interface.

38. The first *personal* computer was

a. ENIAC.
b. The Altair 8800.
c. The Apple II.
d. The IBM Personal Computer.

39. Microsoft Corporation was founded by

a. Stephen Wozniak and Steven Jobs.
b. Richard Rogers and Oscar Hammerstein.
c. J. Presper Eckert and John Mauchly.
d. Paul Allen and William Gates.

40. In the 1990s

a. Intel Corporation introduced the 80286 chip.
b. Microsoft Corporation brought out Windows.
c. Apple Computer, Inc. introduced the Macintosh computer.
d. None of the above is correct.

Creative Writing

41. In your own words, define the term *computer*. Then, using your definition, explain why the following devices are not computers: a simple calculator, a programmable calculator, a video game, a TV set.

42. Describe the qualities that make a computer a *personal* computer.

43. Briefly describe the function of each of the five major components of a computer.

44. Explain the difference between applications and system software, giving examples of each.

45. Contrast DOS and Windows, explaining why the latter is considered a more user-friendly environment.

46. It has been about 50 years since the first computer was built. What do you think a personal computer will be like in another 50 years? What new uses will it have?

The Basics of Using Windows

OVERVIEW In the introduction to this text, we discussed the *what* and *why* of Windows. Recall that the primary goal of this powerful operating environment is to make IBM-compatible computers easier to use. In this chapter, you will begin to see some of the things that Windows can do and how easily they are done. More specifically, you will learn to:

1. Start up Windows.

2. Use the mouse to perform various Windows operations.

3. Choose items from menus.

4. Move, resize, and close windows.

5. Move around within windows.

6. Use dialog boxes to indicate preferences.

7. Obtain on-screen help related to the particular task you are trying to accomplish.

8. Exit Windows.

1.1   Starting Windows

After you turn on the computer, you will see some messages flash across the screen. Then, depending on how this particular computer has been set up, one of two things is likely to happen; either:

- Windows will start up automatically, displaying its colorful logo and, eventually, a screen similar to the one in Figure 1.1.

or

- The *DOS prompt* will appear, indicating that you should type a command. (The DOS prompt will probably display as `C:>` or `C:\>`.) To start Windows if this occurs, type `WIN` in uppercase or lowercase letters and press the Enter key. The Windows logo will be displayed and, after a short time, a screen like the one in Figure 1.1 will appear.

FIGURE 1.1   A Typical Windows Start-up Screen

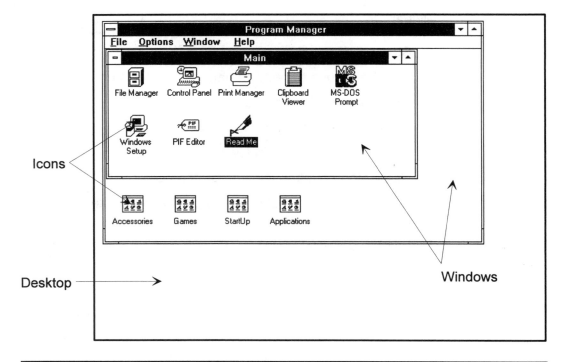

Windows, icons, and the desktop

Let's take a closer look at the screen in Figure 1.1. (Your Windows start-up screen may look somewhat different than this one, which is the screen that appears when Windows is started for the very first time.) It contains two **windows** — boxed areas of the screen — one (entitled "Main") inside the other ("Program Manager"). The stylized pictures within these windows with names below them reading File Manager, Accessories, and so on, are called **icons**. As you will see, these icons represent **applications** (programs) or groups of applications. The entire screen area is referred to as the Windows **desktop**. Just like a regular desk top, it's the place on which you do your work. In Figure 1.1, the region outside the Program Manager window is the part of the desktop not obscured by the two windows. Usually, when you are working within Windows, the various applications in use completely cover the desktop.

We will have a lot more to say about windows, icons, and the desktop in the remainder of this chapter.

1.2   Of Mice and Menus

As you know, one of the primary advantages of Windows is that it is easy to use. It accomplishes this, in part, by extensive use of the mouse and menus.

Using the Mouse

Recall that when a *mouse* is moved around on the (actual) desk top, it causes a pointer to move correspondingly on the screen. In Windows and its applications, the mouse can be used to select items displayed on the screen, initiate actions, and move and resize objects on the desktop. Before we illustrate these uses, let's discuss some important mouse terminology.

Mouse terminology

- To *point at* an object is to move the mouse so that its on-screen pointer is positioned over the specified object. Be aware that the mouse pointer takes on different shapes depending upon the application and the use to which it is being put. It may be an arrow, a double-headed arrow, an I-beam, or a hand, among other things.

- To **click** means to press and release a mouse button. If no particular button is mentioned, the *left* button is the one to press.

- To *click on* an object means to point at that object and click the mouse.

- To **double-click** on an object means to point at that object and click the mouse button twice in rapid succession.

- To **drag** an object with the mouse means to point at the object, press (but not release) the left mouse button, move the mouse pointer to a new location, and then release the button.

Read Me

To illustrate these actions, let's return to the computer screen in Figure 1.1. If, in the Main window, you double-click on the Read Me icon (or on the text *Read Me*), the window pictured in Figure 1.2 will **open** — be displayed on the screen. Here, the double-clicking action has started up an application program, Windows Write, and also opened the ReadMe file, displaying its first few paragraphs in a window.

FIGURE 1.2   Write Application with ReadMe Document

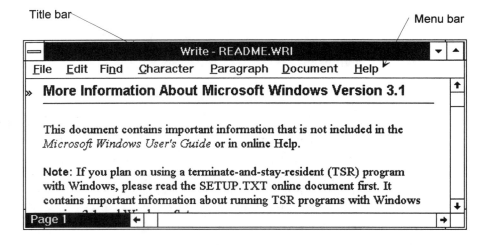

If you double-click on an object and it doesn't initiate an action, it may be that you moved the mouse slightly between clicks or that you didn't follow the first click by the second one quickly enough. Try double-clicking again!

As an alternative to double-clicking, you can use the Arrow keys on the keyboard to *highlight* (darken) and select the Read Me icon. Then, press Enter to initiate the action of starting up Windows Write and opening the ReadMe file.

Using Menus

Notice that the first line of this new window contains a **title bar**, which provides the name of the application running within the window (Write) as well as the name of the file whose contents is displayed (README.WRI). Below the title bar is the **menu bar**, which for the Windows Write application looks like this:

File   Edit   Find   Character   Paragraph   Document   Help

These words are the names of **menus** — lists of commands — for this application. To display (or *open*) one of these menus, simply click on its name. For example, if you click on the word *File*, the menu pictured in Figure 1.3 appears. Because these menus look as if they were pulled down like a window shade unrolling from the word *File*, they are called **pull-down menus**.

FIGURE 1.3   A Typical Pull-down Menu

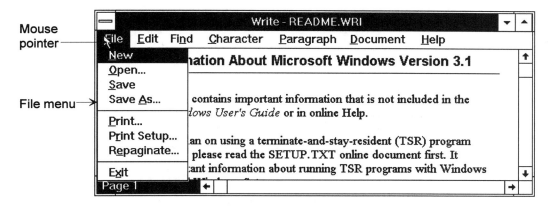

Keyboard Alternatives

If you prefer, the pull-down menus for an application can be accessed by using the keyboard. In Windows, it is usually easier to use a mouse (assuming your computer has one!), so in describing how to perform a task, we will normally discuss the mouse technique first and provide the corresponding keystrokes later. If the keyboard technique is somewhat complicated, we will set it off from the rest of the text and identify it by a keyboard icon (like the one at the left) in the margin.

Notice that each of the menu names on the menu bar has one letter underlined; for example, the F in File and the n in Find. To display a pull-down menu, hold down the Alt key, press the key representing the underlined letter, and then release the Alt key. For example, to open the File menu, hold down the Alt key, press the key labeled F, and release Alt. (We will write this keystroke sequence as Alt+F.)

You can also pull down a menu using the following keystrokes. First, press and release the Alt key, which will highlight the left-most entry on the menu bar — File. Now, either press the key that represents the underlined letter of the desired menu or use the Right Arrow key (→) to highlight the desired menu and press Enter.

Once a menu has been opened, you can *choose* one of the items listed in several ways:

- Click on the desired item.

or

- Type the letter that is underlined in the desired item.

or

- Press the Down Arrow key (↓) until the desired item is highlighted, then press the Enter key.

For example, to choose the New option from the File menu in Figure 1.3, pull down this menu using the mouse or keyboard, as already described. Then, choose New by either clicking on it, or pressing the letter N, or just pressing Enter (since New is already highlighted). Henceforth, we will describe these actions simply as *choose New from the File menu*. Whether you use the mouse, keyboard, or the power of positive thinking to accomplish this is entirely up to you. (As you can see if you are performing these operations yourself, the New command *clears the document window* — the current document, in this case, the ReadMe file, is closed; it "disappears" from the screen.)

Still another, quicker, way to choose an item from a pull-down menu makes use of the *drag* mouse operation. As an example, to choose the Save option from the File menu of Figure 1.3, point at File on the menu bar and drag the mouse to the Save entry (which will highlight it). When you release the mouse button, this command will be executed.

Occasionally, you will open a pull-down menu, or the wrong pull-down menu, by mistake. To close it and return to your document without performing any action, either click anywhere else on the screen, press and release Alt, or press the Escape key twice.

Types of Menu Items

Before we close this section, let's take a closer look at some special types of items that can appear on a pull-down menu. Most of these are illustrated on two other Windows Write menus: the Edit and Paragraph pull-down menus, which are shown next.

Edit Menu

Undo Editing	Ctrl+Z
Cut	Ctrl+X
Copy	Ctrl+C
Paste	Ctrl+V
Paste Special...	
Paste Link	
Links...	
Object	
Insert Object...	
Move Picture	
Size Picture	

Paragraph Menu

Normal
✓Left
Centered
Right
Justified
✓Single Space
1 1/2 Space
Double Space
Indents...

Notice that some menu names are preceded or followed by a symbol, such as a check mark (✓), an *ellipsis* (...), or a keystroke combination, such as Ctrl+Z. Still other menu items are *dimmed* — the letters are gray instead of black. These symbols tell us something about what will happen if we choose these kinds of menu items. Specifically:

■   A keystroke combination (like Ctrl+Z) attached to a menu item is called a **shortcut key**. It gives you a quick way to select that option while working in your application. For example, pressing Ctrl+Z while working in Windows Write has the same effect as choosing

Undo Editing from the Edit menu; it undoes your last change to the document. Memorizing the shortcut keys for tasks you perform frequently can usually save a lot of time. Note, however, that if you press a seemingly appropriate shortcut key *after* a menu is pulled down, nothing will happen!

- If you choose a menu name that is followed by an *ellipsis* (three consecutive periods), a *dialog box* will open requesting additional information. (Dialog boxes will be discussed in Section 1.4.) For example, choosing the Insert Object command from the Edit menu shown on the previous page opens a dialog box requesting the name of the object that you wish to insert.

- A *check mark* appearing before a menu name indicates that this item or characteristic is currently in effect. For example, on the Paragraph menu shown on the previous page, single spacing is currently used between lines. If Double Space is chosen, the check mark is deleted from Single Space and is attached to Double Space.

- Another symbol that sometimes follows a menu name (although not on any of the Windows Write menus) is the *triangle* (▸). The triangle symbol indicates that choosing this item will display a new menu, just to the right of the original menu, containing options related to the item just chosen.

- If a menu item is **dimmed** so that the letters in its name are lighter than normal, it means that that particular option is not available at this time. Usually, some other operation must be performed first; then the dimmed item will appear in normal type. As an example, the last two items on the Edit menu shown on the previous page are dimmed because there is no picture in the current document to move or size.

Hands-On 1.2

Start up Windows (if it's not already running) and try the following exercise. If you have trouble performing a particular task, review the relevant material in the text.

1. If the Write window is open, close it by choosing Exit from its File menu, which will return you to Program Manager.
2. If the Main window is not open, open it by double-clicking on the Main icon or by choosing Main from the Window menu.

3. In the Main window, click (once) on the Print Manager icon. What, if anything, happened?
4. Drag the Print Manager icon to another location in the Main window.
5. Choose Arrange Icons from the Window menu in Program Manager. What happened to the Print Manager icon?
6. Double-click on the Print Manager icon to open its window.
7. Open the Print Manager's pull-down menus one-by-one. On which menus do you find: a shortcut key, a check mark, an ellipsis?
8. Close the Print Manager window by choosing Exit from its View menu.

1.3 Windows within Windows

While working at your desk (say, doing homework), you might have several documents open at once — a textbook, a reference book, your notebook, and so on. This is often the case on the Windows desktop as well. Here, the documents and other related information are contained in separate windows. Windows has a very broad interpretation of the word *document*; a **document window** can contain a letter or report, a picture, a spreadsheet, or even a collection of icons. These windows, in turn, lie within **application windows** belonging to the programs that create or manipulate the documents.

Depending on what you're doing at the moment, you might want to move some windows around, make one of them bigger, or perhaps put some of them temporarily out of sight. In this section, we will describe how to perform these actions — how to move, resize, and close a window.

Operations on Windows

If you've been following our discussion of Windows to this point, you'll recall that there are currently two application windows open on the desktop — Program Manager and Write. Program Manager contains one open document window, Main, and Write also has one open document window which is "Untitled". Our desktop at this point is shown in Figure 1.4 on the next page.

FIGURE 1.4 **Two Application Windows Open on the Desktop**

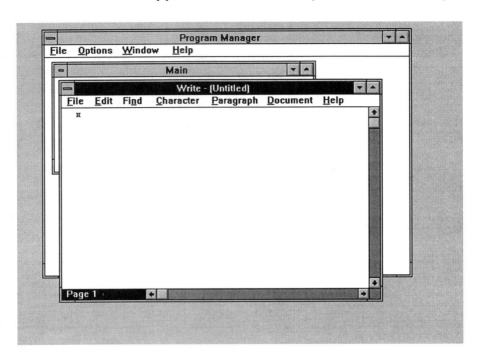

Notice that Write's title bar is highlighted (darkened) while those for Program Manager and Main are not. A highlighted title bar designates the **active window**, the one in which we are currently working. In Windows, only one window within a single application can be active at a given time; all the commands you issue apply to this window. You can switch to another window — make *it* the active one — by clicking anywhere on it, or by using other techniques that we will describe in Chapter 2. For the rest of this discussion, assume that the window you want to manipulate is already active.

Why move or resize a window?
Before we explain *how* to move or resize a window, let's look at a few reasons *why* you might want to perform these operations. For one thing, it is usually easier to use an application when it covers the entire screen; you can view more information and, in some cases, more detail is visible as well. Nevertheless, when some applications start, they occupy only part of the desktop. In such a case, you might want to increase the size of the application's window, perhaps **maximizing** it so that it uses as much screen real estate as possible (often, the entire screen).

The disadvantage of maximizing a window is that it then might obscure everything else on the desktop. Even when not maximized, it might cover vital information in another window (see Figure 1.4). So, at times, you will want to reduce a window in size or even **close** it, which takes it off the desktop. As an alternative to closing a window, which removes the application or document from the computer's memory, you could **minimize** it. Minimizing an application or document replaces its window by an icon on the desktop, but keeps the application in memory. We also refer to this operation as *reducing the window to an icon.*

Manipulating Windows

You can manipulate a window or its contents using either mouse or keyboard. Figure 1.5 identifies some of the parts of a window involved in the process.

FIGURE 1.5 Parts of a Window

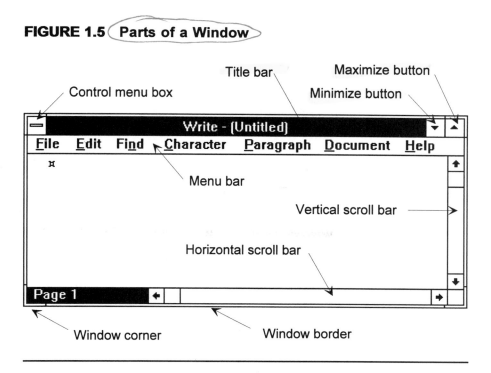

As is often the case in Windows, the mouse provides the simplest way of performing most operations on windows. Using the mouse (without the aid of menus or the keyboard):

Move ■ To *move* a window, drag its title bar to the new location. More specifically, move the mouse pointer to the title bar; it will change to an arrow shape, as shown at the left. Now, press (but don't release) the left button and move the mouse in the direction you want the window to move. As you do this, an outline of the moving window appears on the screen. When the outline is positioned to your liking, release the mouse button.

Resize ■ To *resize* a window, drag its border or corner (see Figure 1.5) to a new position. For example, to increase the height of a window, position the mouse pointer on the bottom border; it will become a two-headed arrow, as shown at the left, when positioned properly. Then, drag the border down and the window outline will enlarge accordingly. When the window outline indicates that you've achieved the desired height, release the mouse button. The window will redraw to its new size. If you drag a window *corner*, both sides attached to that corner move at once.

 If you change your mind while moving or resizing a window and want to cancel the operation, press the Escape key before releasing the mouse button.

Minimize/ ■ To *minimize* or *maximize* a window, click on the **minimize button**
maximize (▾) or **maximize button** (▴) in the upper-right corner of the window (see Figure 1.5). The window will be reduced to an icon in the first case or enlarged to maximum size in the second. You can **also maximize a window** by double-clicking on its title bar. Once a window is maximized, its maximize button is replaced with the **restore button** (♦). Clicking on the restore button returns the window to the position and size it was before it was maximized, and replaces this button with the maximize button. You can also restore a window by double-clicking on its title bar.

Close ■ To *close* a window, double-click on its **Control menu box**, located in the upper-left corner of the window (see Figure 1.5).

All the operations we've just described can be performed by choosing options from the window's **Control menu**. You can open this menu by clicking on the Control menu box (see Figure 1.5). Using the keyboard, press Alt+Hyphen to open the Control menu for a document and Alt+Spacebar to open the Control menu for an application. A typical Control menu is shown in Figure 1.6.

FIGURE 1.6   The Control Menu for an Application

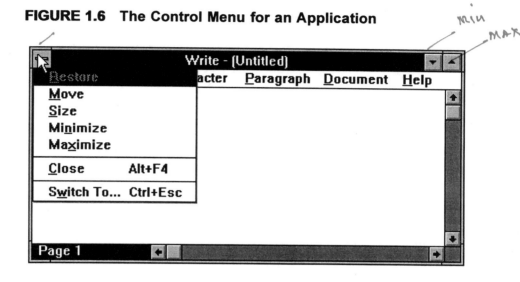

The Control menu options are usually used in conjunction with the keyboard. (The mouse can perform these operations directly, as just described.) We will discuss these options in the following note.

Keyboard Alternatives

To use the keyboard to perform an operation on the active window, you must first open its Control menu (by pressing Alt+Hyphen or Alt+Spacebar).

■ To *move* a window, choose <u>M</u>ove from its Control menu. (A four-headed arrow will appear on the screen.) Then, press the Arrow key or keys that move the window in the desired direction. When you do this, an outline of the moving window will appear on the screen. Continue pressing the Arrow keys until the outline is positioned as you want it. Then, press Enter.

■ To *resize* a window, choose <u>S</u>ize from the Control menu. (A four-headed arrow will appear on the screen.) Now, press the Arrow key corresponding to the window border you want to move. (A double-headed arrow will appear on that border.) Then, repeatedly press the appropriate Arrow key to move that border in the desired direction and an outline of the window will change accordingly. When the window outline is positioned where you want it, press Enter. The window will redraw to its new size.

For example, if you want to increase the width of a window, press either the Left or Right Arrow keys to select the corresponding border. Then, repeatedly press that same Arrow key until the window outline indicates that the proper size has been reached. Now, press Enter to complete the operation.

Note: Both the move and the size operations can be cancelled before completion (before pressing Enter) by pressing the Escape key.

■   To *minimize* or *maximize* a window, choose Mi_nimize or Ma_ximize from the Control menu. The window will be reduced to an icon in the first case or enlarged to maximum size in the second. To return a window to the position and size it was before it was maximized, choose _Restore from the Control menu.

■   To *close* a window, choose _Close from the Control menu. In most application windows, pressing Alt+F4 (without opening the Control menu) will also do the job.

It is certainly easier to perform the move, resize, minimize, maximize, and restore operations using the mouse alone rather than menus or the keyboard. So, if you have a mouse, use it to perform these tasks! On the other hand, you might forget that closing a window can be accomplished by double-clicking on its Control menu box. Choosing _Close from the Control menu is always an easy alternative. Moreover, in many applications, pressing Alt+F4 closes the active application and its window. Here's still another way to close most applications: choose E_xit from its _File menu.

Working within a Window

To view, edit, or select various items or pieces of information within a document window, you have to move a *cursor* around the screen. A

cursor is a symbol that moves on the screen in response to mouse or keyboard input, keeping track of your current position. Depending on the application and situation, the cursor might be represented by a blinking vertical bar, a pointer, cross hairs, or some other symbol. For example, when viewing a pull-down menu, the cursor is a highlight bar, which indicates the currently selected item.

Moving the cursor

You can usually use either the mouse or keyboard to move the cursor to a new point in the document or list you're viewing. If this new position is visible on the screen, just click on it with the mouse or move to it by repeatedly pressing the appropriate Arrow keys. For example, to move to a point on the screen below the current cursor position, click on that location or press the Down Arrow key.

If the material you want to view is not currently visible on the screen, you'll have to **scroll** to reach it. To understand how this works, imagine the active window as a cutout under which the document, in all its entirety, is placed. In order to view various parts of the document, you have to move (scroll) the cutout up, down, left, or right until the desired material is visible.

In actuality, the window stays fixed on the screen and, in effect, the document is moved around. When we say, for example, that "the window scrolls down," we simply mean that the part of the document or list below the current window position becomes visible (and the part at the top of the current window disappears from the screen).

You can use the mouse to scroll through a document by clicking on parts of a **scroll bar** (see Figure 1.5). The *horizontal* scroll bar scrolls the window left or right; the *vertical* scroll bar scrolls it up or down. (If you can view the entire width or height of a document without scrolling, the corresponding scroll bar is not usually present.)

Let's take a closer look at a vertical scroll bar.

A scroll bar

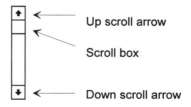

Here's how this scroll bar is used. (A horizontal scroll bar works in an analogous way.)

■ Clicking the up or down scroll arrow scrolls the window up or down one line. Holding down the mouse button while pointing at the up or down scroll arrow moves it continuously up or down until you release the button.

■ Clicking on the scroll bar above or below the scroll box scrolls the window one screen's worth of information up or down.

■ Dragging the scroll box up or down to a new position scrolls the window to that position in the document or list. For example, dragging the scroll box halfway down the scroll bar scrolls the window to a position about halfway through the document.

Keyboard Alternatives

In any application, you can move up, down, left, or right by pressing the corresponding Arrow key. For example, pressing the Up Arrow key moves the cursor up one line. If the cursor is at the top of the window when this key is pressed, then the window will scroll up one line along with the cursor. Pressing, but not releasing, an Arrow key results in a faster, continuous movement through the document or list.

In many applications, the keys listed in the following table have the indicated effect:

Cursor movement keys

Key	Moves Cursor
Up Arrow/Down Arrow	Up/down one line.
Page Up/Page Down	Up/down one screen.
Home	To the beginning of the current line.
End	To the end of the current line.
Ctrl+Home	To the beginning of the document.
Ctrl+End	To the end of the document.

Hands-On

1.3

Start up Windows (if it's not already running) and try the following exercise. If you have trouble performing a particular task, review the relevant material in the text.

1. Maximize the Main window. Does it occupy the entire screen?
2. Restore the Main window.
3. Move the Main window to the upper-right corner of the screen. Can it be moved to the very top of the visible screen area?
4. Minimize the Main window, reducing it to an icon.

5. Restore the Main window by double-clicking on its icon or by choosing Main from the <u>W</u>indow menu.
6. Resize the Main window so that it is as small as possible. Which window components (Control menu box, title bar, etc,) are visible? Are any icons visible within the Main window?
7. Return the Main window to its original size and location.

1.4   Conversing with Dialog Boxes

As you may recall, choosing menu items followed by an ellipsis (...) opens a **dialog box**, a special type of window. Dialog boxes present groups of related options from which you can make selections.

A Simple Dialog Box

To illustrate the basic idea of a dialog box, suppose that in Windows Write you make a change in a document and then immediately try to close that document or the Write application itself. In this case, the following dialog box pops up on the screen:

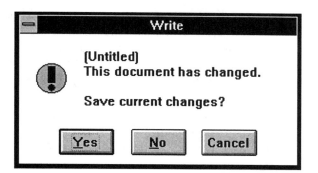

Like most dialog boxes, this one displays a message ("This document has changed.") and requests information (should the changes be saved to disk?). To respond, you have to choose one of the three **command buttons**, the shaded rectangles labeled <u>Y</u>es, <u>N</u>o, and Cancel. (*Cancel* means "Cancel the Save operation and return to the document".) To choose a button, do *one* of these things:

- Click on the appropriate button.

- Press the key corresponding to the underlined letter in <u>Y</u>es or <u>N</u>o, or press the Escape key for Cancel.

- Use the Arrow keys to select one of the three buttons and then press Enter. The currently selected button (<u>Y</u>es, in this dialog box) has a darker border than the others and a faint dotted rectangle around its label.

When you choose one of the options, the dialog box closes.

If you open this dialog box's Control menu by clicking on the Control menu box (see Figure 1.5) or by pressing Alt+Spacebar, you'll see only two options: <u>M</u>ove and <u>C</u>lose. This is typical. You cannot generally resize, minimize, or maximize a dialog box. Moving it may be useful, however, because it might be covering some vital information in the underlying document.

Types of Dialog Box Options

As a more comprehensive example, let's take a look at the Print dialog box (Figure 1.7), which opens if you choose <u>P</u>rint from the <u>F</u>ile menu in Windows Write. The Print dialog box contains virtually all the features you are likely to encounter in dealing with dialog boxes in general.

At the top of this dialog box is the familiar *title bar* which supplies the name of the window. Below this, on the left, is some information concerning the printer connected to the computer (here, an HP Laserjet). The rest of the items in the dialog box involve information to be supplied by you, the user, concerning the Print operation. Notice that these items are arranged in related groups and are often associated with symbols such as shaded rectangles, small circles, small squares, and so on. These groups and their symbols provide different types of options, as described below.

> OK

Recall that the relatively large shaded rectangles in the upper-right corner of the Print dialog box labeled *OK*, *Cancel*, and *Setup...* are called *command buttons*. When you choose a command button by clicking on it with the mouse (or by using the keyboard as described later), it initiates an action or, if the label contains an ellipsis, supplies additional options. Most dialog boxes contain the OK and Cancel buttons, as pictured in Figure 1.7.

- Choosing Cancel cancels any changes you may have made to the

FIGURE 1.7   The Print Dialog Box

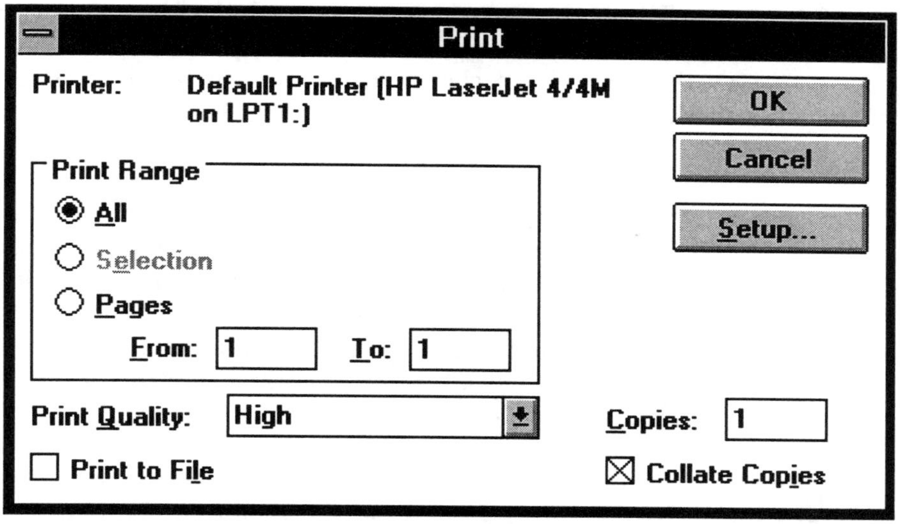

information in the dialog box, closes it, and returns you to the previous window.

■ Choosing OK accepts all changes you have made to the information in the dialog box, closes it, and returns you to the previous window. (Sometimes this button is labeled *Close*.)

Choosing the third command button in this particular dialog box, Setup..., opens another dialog box with additional options.

Option buttons are represented by small circles like those appearing under the Print Range heading in the Print dialog box of Figure 1.7. Option buttons are sometimes called *radio buttons* because they work like the station selection push buttons on a radio — when one of them is *selected* (turned on), the others are automatically *deselected* (turned off). For this reason, in a grouping of option buttons, only one of the corresponding options can be selected at any given time. For example, in the Print dialog box shown, the All option is currently selected, as indicated by the darkened center of its option button. If you select the Pages option, its button will darken, and the All option will be deselected — its button will become an empty circle.

If an option is not presently available, its label will be *dimmed* — its letters will appear in a lighter color, just like an unavailable menu item. (This is the case with the Selection option button in the Print dialog box.) A dimmed label is an indication that you must do something else first before you can choose that option. (In the case of Selection, you first have to select a block of text to print.)

A **check box** is represented by a small square, like the Print to File and Collate Copies options in the Print dialog box. When a check box is selected, it looks like this: ⊠; when it is not selected, it looks like this: □. (In Figure 1.7, the Print to File check box is currently not selected; the Collate Copies box is selected.) To select a check box that is currently not selected, click on it or type its underlined letter. To deselect a currently selected check box, do exactly the same thing.

Sometimes it is necessary to input numbers or names in a dialog box. Windows uses **text boxes** for this purpose. Text boxes are symbolized by rectangles containing the number or name that is the **default value** for that option, the one that is automatically used if you don't change it. For example, in the Print dialog box, there are three text boxes: From, To (in the Print Range section) and Copies. To change a default value, select the appropriate text box, use the Backspace or Delete key to erase the displayed value and then type the desired text. For example, to change the number of copies to 2 in the Print dialog box, select the text box Copies, erase the 1 currently displayed there, and type the number 2.

When Windows wants you to choose from among a list of names, it uses a **list box**. In some dialog boxes, part or all of the list is displayed in a large rectangular box; in other cases, just the default name is displayed followed by the symbol ↓. This kind of list is called a **drop-down list box.** It is used for the Print Quality option in the Print dialog box. (The default value is High.) When a drop-down list box is selected (by clicking on it), the rest of the list appears. To choose one of the names, either click on it, or press the Up or Down Arrow key until it is highlighted and press the Enter key.

The easiest way to choose an option in a dialog box using the keyboard is to type its underlined letter. (In some dialog boxes, you may have to hold down the Alt key while typing the letter.) You can also *select* an

Keyboard Alternatives

option, which places a dotted rectangle around its label, by using the Arrow, Tab, or Shift+Tab keys. Usually, repeatedly pressing the Tab key cycles through the various options in one direction, while the Shift+Tab key cycles in the opposite direction. The Arrow keys operate in a similar manner, but in many dialog boxes, they can only be used to cycle within a group of related items, such as among a list of option buttons.

Hands-On 1.4

Start up Windows (if it's not already running) and try the following exercise. If you have trouble performing a particular task, review the relevant material in the text.

1. In the Main window, double-click on the Clipboard Viewer icon (or use the Arrow keys to highlight it and press Enter).
2. Choose Open from the File menu.
3. In the Open dialog box:
    - In the List Files of Type list box, select All Files. Did any other part of the dialog box change?
    - In the File Name text box, type MYFILE.
    - Select the Read Only check box.
    - Choose the Cancel button (or press Escape). What happened?
4. Close Clipboard Viewer by choosing Exit from its File menu.

1.5 Some Help Getting Help

No matter how experienced you become at using Windows, there will be times when you'll need some help in performing a particular task. At such a time, you can probably find the answer to your questions in this text or in the *Windows User's Guide*, the printed instruction manual that is included with the Windows program. Another alternative is to use the Windows **on-line help** system. This powerful feature provides immediate on-screen information about Windows itself or the Windows application that is currently active on your desktop.

Accessing On-line Help

On-line help can be accessed in several ways:

1. Choosing the Help item from the menu bar at the top of the active

application opens a Help menu. For example, the Help menu for the Windows Write application, which we started earlier in this chapter by choosing the Read Me icon from the Main window in Program Manager, is shown below. (The Write Help system is similar to that of most applications running under Windows.)

A Help
menu

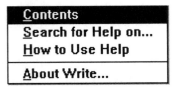

The following table gives a brief description of each of these options:

Items on the
Help menu

Menu Item	Action
Contents	Opens the Help window and lists the topics for which information is available.
Search for Help on ...	Opens the Search dialog box, which allows you to specify a topic you would like to view.
How to Use Help	Opens the How to Use Help window, which provides information about the Help system.
About Write ...	Opens a dialog box that supplies general information about the active application — its name and developer, its version number, and so on.

We will discuss how to use the Help windows and the Search dialog box later in this section.

2. Pressing the Help command button present in some dialog boxes opens the Help window and displays information about how to use that dialog box. We say that pressing the Help button here accesses **context-sensitive help** — information about the current task.

3. Pressing the F1 function key provides help of various types depending on when and where you press this key.

   ■ If you press F1 while using an application, the general Help window opens. Usually, a list of available topics is displayed, just as if you had chosen the Contents option from the Help menu. In some applications, if a menu item or command button is highlighted when you press F1, the Help window opens and context-sensitive information is displayed about that option.

■ If you press F1 while in the general Help window, the How to Use Help window opens; Windows assumes that you need help with Help!

Obtaining Information on a Specific Topic

Both the Contents and Search options on the Help menu can aid you in finding information on a specific topic. Roughly speaking, using Contents is similar to using the table of contents of a book to locate the information; using the Search option is analogous to using the book's index. For example, the Search option usually provides a more detailed list of topics from which you can choose. Search also allows you to enter a word or phrase of your own to trigger the Help system. Thus, you might select the Contents option if you were not sure of precisely what information you were seeking about a topic; you might choose Search if you knew exactly what aspect of the topic interested you.

Choosing between the Contents and Search options really comes down to a matter of preference. Both will eventually display the same information in the Help window. (This is another example of the built in redundancy in Windows, which usually provides more than one way to perform a given task.) After you have gained some experience with the Windows Help system, you will develop your favorite ways of getting the desired information from it.

Now let's see how both Contents and Search help us access a particular topic.

Using the Contents Option   When Contents is chosen from the Help menu or by pressing the F1 function key (or from the Help *window* as described later), the general Help window opens and an alphabetical list of topics is displayed. The screen will resemble the one in Figure 1.8 on the next page.

FIGURE 1.8 A Typical Help Window (Showing *Contents*)

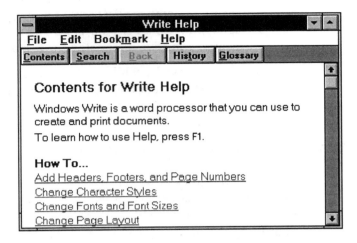

To bring up information about one of the listed topics, just click on that topic or select it using the Down Arrow key and press Enter. (You may have to scroll the window to reach the topic in which you're interested.) When you choose a topic, a new window will open with information about that topic. Often, a list of related topics will appear at the bottom of this window. Choose one of these, if desired, and the Help system will bring up that topic. To return to the Contents screen, choose the Contents button situated below the menu bar.

Using the Search Dialog Box   The Search dialog box (Figure 1.9 pictures the one for Write Help) can be brought up from an application's Help menu or by choosing the Search button in the Help window.

The Search dialog box helps you locate specific information about a certain topic. To do so, *either*

- Type the word or phrase in the text box. This will highlight the corresponding phrase in the list box below. Now choose the Show Topics button, select the desired topic from the list at the bottom of the dialog box, and choose the Go To button.

or

- Select a word or phrase from the list box, choose the Show Topics button, select the desired topic from the list at the bottom of the dialog box, and choose the Go To button.

FIGURE 1.9   A Typical Help Search Dialog Box

```
┌─────────────────────────────────────────────────────┐
│ ▭                        Search                       │
├─────────────────────────────────────────────────────┤
│ Type a word, or select one from the list.  ┌────────┐│
│ Then choose Show Topics.                    │ Close  ││
│                                             └────────┘│
│ ┌─────────────────────────────────────────┐┌────────┐│
│ │ documents, opening                      ││Show Topics││
│ └─────────────────────────────────────────┘└────────┘│
│  ┌────────────────────────────────────────────┬──┐  │
│  │ documents, opening                         │▲ │  │
│  │ documents, repaginating                    │  │  │
│  │ documents, saving                          │░ │  │
│  │ drawings, inserting                        │░ │  │
│  │ editing embedded drawings                  │  │  │
│  │ editing linked drawings                    │▼ │  │
│  └────────────────────────────────────────────┴──┘  │
│                                                       │
│ Select a topic, then choose Go To.         ┌────────┐│
│                                             │ Go To  ││
│                                             └────────┘│
│ ┌───────────────────────────────────────────────────┐│
│ │ Opening Documents                                 ││
│ │                                                   ││
│ │                                                   ││
│ │                                                   ││
│ │                                                   ││
│ └───────────────────────────────────────────────────┘│
└─────────────────────────────────────────────────────┘
```

Using either technique opens the general Help window and displays information about the selected topic.

Accessing Additional Information   Once you locate the information you were seeking about a particular topic, other questions may arise. You might encounter a term or phrase that you don't understand or perhaps you see that to understand the original topic, you need information about a related one. Through the Help system menus, buttons, and other devices, Windows provides several ways to help you get at and view the needed information.

Jumps

1. You may have noticed that certain key words or phrases in the Help window of Figure 1.8 are underlined. These are called **jumps**. When you point to a jump using the mouse or select it using the keyboard, the cursor will change to a hand shape. Then, choosing the jump by clicking the mouse or pressing Enter will display information about that jump. If the jump has a *dotted* underline, the Glossary window will open and display a definition of the term. (We will have more to say about this shortly.) If the jump has a *solid* underline, Windows Help will go to that topic and display information about it.

To use the keyboard to choose a jump, repeatedly press the Tab key to cycle through the jumps in the current topic. Then, when you reach the desired jump (the one currently selected is highlighted), press the Enter key.

Contents
and Search
buttons

2. The Contents and Search command buttons on the button bar perform the same functions as their counterparts on the application's Help menu. So, to display the "table of contents" screen (like the one in Figure 1.8) at any time, choose the Contents button; to open the Search dialog box (Figure 1.9), choose the Search button.

Glossary
button

3. The Glossary command button on the button bar gives you access to a small dictionary of terms related to the active application. Choosing Glossary opens a window containing an alphabetical list of the available words and phrases. Just scroll to the desired term and choose it: click on it or press Enter. This opens a small window containing the definition of that term. To close this window, click anywhere on the screen or press Esc; to close the Glossary window, double-click on its Control menu box or press Alt+F4.

Displaying Previous Help Screens   Occasionally, you may want to return to topics you had accessed in this or previous Help sessions. Of course, you could just use the Contents or Search buttons, as described earlier, to locate the desired topic again. However, Windows provides easier ways:

Back and
History
buttons

1. The Back and History command buttons on the button bar (see Figure 1.8) allow you to backtrack to previous topics in the *current* help session; that is, until you exit Help and return to the active application. (Pop-up windows, such as dialog boxes and Glossary cannot be retrieved.)

Choosing Back brings up the previous topic's screen. By choosing it repeatedly, you can backtrack through all screens of the current Help session.

The History button provides a shortcut to this process. Choosing this button pops up a window that displays a list of all topics already accessed in the current session. To view one of these topics, either double-click on it or select it using the mouse or Arrow keys and then press Enter. (This action also closes the Help History window.)

Bookmarks 2. At times you may want to have easy access to a particular Help topic, even after you've returned to your application. Most applications supply the Bookmark menu item within their Help windows (see Figure 1.8) for this purpose. While reading a book, you might use a bookmark, perhaps a slip of paper, to make it easy to find a particularly important page. Similarly, you can use Help bookmarks to electronically tag an important Help screen.

When you choose Bookmark from the menu bar, a menu similar to the following one appears:

> **Define...**
> **1 Changing Page Layout**
> **2 Copying, Cutting, and Pasting Text**

At the bottom is a list of previously defined bookmarks. These may have been defined in either the current or a previous Help session. To access one of these topics, either click on it, press the corresponding number key (in this case, either 1 or 2), or highlight it with the aid of the Down Arrow key and press Enter.

To add the current topic to the list of bookmarks, or to delete an existing bookmark from the list, choose the Define option from the Bookmark menu. A dialog box will open, allowing you to perform one of these two tasks.

Additional Features of the Help System
In addition to bookmarks, virtually all Windows applications have Help systems that provide the following menu-accessed features:

The File, Edit, and Help menus

- The File menu allows you to (among other things) print the current topic on a printer and to exit the Help system. (You can also exit the Help system by double-clicking on the Control menu box or by pressing Alt+F4.)

- The Edit menu lets you add your own comments to (annotate) a particular topic or to copy the text of the current topic onto the Clipboard. (We will discuss the Clipboard in Section 2.4.)

- The Help menu provides help in using the Help system itself. Choosing How to Use Help has the same effect as pressing the F1 function key at this point — it displays the How to Use Help window. Choosing the Always on Top option allows you to continue viewing the Help window after you have switched back to your application. To discontinue the Always on <u>T</u>op option, just choose it again.

For more information on these features and Help in general, just ask Windows for Help!

Hands-On 1.5

Start up Windows (if it's not already running) and try the following exercise. If you have trouble performing a particular task, review the relevant material in the text.

1. Choose <u>S</u>earch for Help On from Program Manager's <u>H</u>elp menu.
2. Bring up the help screen for Starting an Application (listed under "applications, starting" in the Search list).
3. Choose the <u>C</u>ontents button in the Help window.
4. Use the <u>G</u>lossary button to look up the definition of *scroll bar*.
5. Close the Glossary and jump to the Quit Windows topic.
6. Define a bookmark for the Quitting Windows screen.
7. Now, use the <u>B</u>ack button to return to the Starting an Application screen. How many times did you have to "tap" this button?
8. Retrieve the bookmark for Quitting Windows.
9. Exit the help system.

1.6   Quitting Windows

All good things (in fact, all things in general) must come to an end. At some point, you're going to want to quit (exit) Windows. To do so:

1. Close all open application windows (see Section 1.3). As each application is closed, another one will become active until the only application remaining open is Program Manager.

2. Close the Program Manager window and exit Windows by doing one of the following things:

   ■ Double-click on its Control menu box.

   ■ Open its Control menu and choose <u>C</u>lose.

   ■ Choose E<u>x</u>it Windows from the <u>F</u>ile menu.

   ■ Press Alt+F4.

3. When the following dialog box appears on the screen, choose OK by clicking on it or by pressing the Enter key. (If you choose Cancel, the dialog box closes and you are returned to Program Manager.)

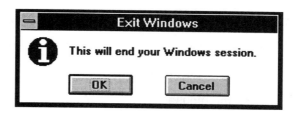

Chapter Summary

Key Terms

Active window [page 10]	Application [3]
Application window [9]	Check box [20]
Click the mouse [3]	Close a window [11]
Command button [17]	Context-sensitive help [22]
Control menu [12]	Control menu box [12]
Cursor [15]	Default value [20]
Desktop [3]	Dialog box [17]
Dimmed item [8]	Document window [9]
Double-click the mouse [4]	Drag the mouse [4]
Drop-down list box [20]	Icon [3]
Jump [25]	List box [20]
Maximize a window [10]	Maximize button [12]
Menu [5]	Menu bar [5]
Minimize a window [11]	Minimize button [12]
On-line help [21]	Open a window [4]
Option button [19]	Pull-down menu [5]
Restore button [12]	Scroll [15]
Scroll bar [15]	Shortcut key [7]

Text box [20]   Title bar [5]

Window [3]

Topics Covered

Starting Windows

To start Windows   Type WIN and press the Enter key.

Mouse Terminology

Click the mouse   Press and release the left mouse button.

Click on an object   Move the mouse pointer over an object and click the mouse.

Double-click   Click twice in rapid succession.

Drag an object   Move the mouse pointer over an object, press the left button, move the pointer to the desired location, and release the button.

Menus

To open a menu   Click on its name; or press Alt+*underlined letter*, or press Alt, use the Arrow keys to highlight the desired menu, and press Enter.

To open the Control menu   Click on the Control menu box; or press Alt+Spacebar for an application or dialog box window, Alt+Hyphen for a document window.

To choose a menu item   Click on it; or type the underlined letter; or use the Down Arrow key to highlight the desired item and press Enter.

Manipulating Windows

To move a window   Drag its title bar to the new location; or choose Move from the Control menu, use the Arrow keys to move the window, and press Enter.

To resize a window   Drag its border or corner to a new location; or choose Size from the Control menu, press an Arrow key to select a border, use an Arrow key to move it, and press Enter.

To maximize/minimize/ restore a window   Click on the corresponding button; or choose the appropriate item from the Control menu.

To close a window	Double-click on its Control menu box; or choose Close from the Control menu. For an application window, choose Exit from the File menu; or press Alt+F4.

Scrolling a Window

Up/down/left/right	Click on the corresponding scroll arrow; or drag the scroll box in the appropriate direction; or press the corresponding Arrow key.
One screen up/down	Click above/below the scroll box; or press Page Up/Page Down.
To beginning/end of line	Press Home/End.
To beginning/end of document	Press Ctrl+Home/Ctrl+End

Dialog Box Options

Command buttons	Perform actions such as close, cancel, etc.
Option buttons	Allow one of several related options to be selected.
Check boxes	Turn a particular option on or off.
Text boxes	Allow text or numbers to be input.
List boxes	Allow an item to be selected from a list.

On-line Help

To access Help	Choose Contents, Search, or How to Use Help from the Help menu; or press the F1 function key.
To locate a topic	Choose a topic from the Contents screen or the Search dialog box; or *jump* to a topic; or choose the Glossary button (for a definition).
To return to previous topics	Choose the Back or History buttons or use the Bookmark menu to define and retrieve bookmarks.

Quitting Windows

To exit Windows	In Program Manager, double-click the Control menu box; or choose Close from the Control menu; or choose Exit Windows from

the File menu; or press Alt+F4. Then, choose OK in the resulting dialog box.

Chapter Exercises

Short Answer

Complete each statement in Exercises 1 through 12.

1. To start Windows (if it does not start automatically), type _____ and press the Enter key.

2. To click on an object on the screen, move the mouse pointer over that object and press the _____ .

3. To open an application's Edit menu using the keyboard, press the _____ key combination.

4. If the name of a menu item is followed by an ellipsis, choosing that item opens a _____ .

5. A highlighted (darkened) title bar indicates that that window is the _____ window.

6. To move a window using the mouse, drag its _____ to the desired location on the screen.

7. To increase the size of a window as much as possible, click on the _____ button.

8. To move the cursor to the beginning of a line of text, press the _____ key.

9. In a dialog box, the item that is currently selected has a _____ around its label.

10. To access on-line help while using an application, press the _____ key.

11. In using on-line help, if you want the definition of a term, choose the _____ button.

12. Windows must be exited from the _____ application.

Determine whether each of the statements in Exercises 13 through 24 is true or false.

13. When double-clicking the mouse, you should pause for a second or

two between clicks.

14. To use a shortcut key to perform a task, open the menu listing that task and press the shortcut key.

15. When a menu item or dialog box option is dimmed, that item or option is not presently available.

16. No more than one application window can be active at any given time.

17. To close a window, you can double-click on its Control menu box.

18. Every document window contains at least one scroll bar.

19. To move the cursor to the end of a document, press the End key.

20. A dialog box cannot be moved around the screen.

21. The default value for an item within a dialog box must be changed each time you open that dialog box.

22. If a topic in on-line help can be located using the Search dialog box, then that topic will not appear on the Contents help screen.

23. In an on-line help screen, jumps are always indicated by solid underlines.

24. While using Help, you can access the previous topic by choosing the Back command button.

25. Identify the components A through G of the window shown in Figure 1.10 on the next page. Your answers should come from the following list:

Maximize button	Minimize button
Horizontal scroll bar	Vertical scroll bar
Title bar	Menu bar
Control menu box	

In Exercises 26 through 33, choose the correct answer.

26. In Windows, the *desktop* refers to:

    a. The area occupied by your computer, monitor, and mouse.
    b. The window on the screen that is currently active.
    c. The current application, together with its menus and documents.
    d. The entire screen.

FIGURE 1.10   The Window for Exercise 25

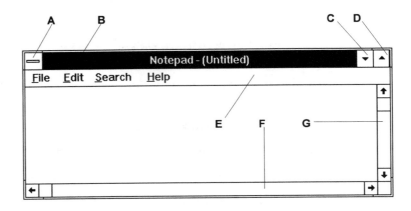

27. When you position the mouse pointer over an object on the screen, hold down the left button, and move the pointer to a new location, it is called:

    a. Clicking on the object.
    b. Double-clicking on the object.
    c. Dragging the object.
    d. None of the above.

28. If an item on a menu is dimmed (grayed), clicking on that item:

    a. Opens a dialog box.
    b. Opens another menu.
    c. Closes the menu.
    d. Does nothing at all.

29. From an application's Control menu, you cannot:

    a. Open the application window.
    b. Close the application window.
    c. Move the application window.
    d. Resize the application window.

30. Dialog boxes never contain:

    a. Command buttons.
    b. Option buttons.
    c. Shirt buttons.

d.   Text boxes.

31. You can access the Windows Help system by:

a.   Choosing Contents from the Help menu.
b.   Choosing Search for Help on from the Help menu.
c.   Pressing the F1 function key.
d.   Performing any of the above actions.

32. In Windows Help, the History command button:

a.   Provides a history of Windows' development.
b.   Displays a list of the Help topics you have accessed.
c.   Displays a list of applications you've run in the current session.
d.   Does none of the above.

33. To exit Windows, you can:

a.   Double-click on Program Manager's Control menu box.
b.   Choose Exit Windows from Program Manager's File menu.
c.   Press Alt+F4.
d.   Perform any of the above actions.

Hands-On   In Exercises 34 through 40, start up Windows (if it's not already running) and perform the indicated tasks. If you have trouble with a particular task, review the relevant material in the text.

34. a.   Within the Main window, select (highlight) the Clipboard Viewer by either clicking on it or using the Arrow keys to move the highlight cursor to it.
     b.   Open the Clipboard Viewer application window by double-clicking on it or by pressing the Enter key.
     c.   Maximize this window. Does it occupy the entire screen?
     d.   Close this window.
     e.   Reopen the Clipboard Viewer window. Did it open maximized (as it was when you closed it) or sized and positioned as it was when you opened it the first time?
     f.   Close the Clipboard Viewer window.

35. a.   Open Program Manager's Help window.
     b.   Bring up the topic called *Quitting Windows*. Give two ways of quitting Windows that are not mentioned in this Help screen.
     c.   Open the Glossary window. Does it seem to list only definitions pertaining to Program Manager?
     d.   View the definition of *choose*; then view that of *select*. Did you

realize that there was a difference in their use?

e. Use the Search dialog box to bring up information on quitting Program Manager. Is quitting Program Manager different than quitting Windows?

f. Use the Back button to return to the previous topic. What is it?

g. Close the Help window (returning to Program Manager).

36 a. Choose the Windows Tutorial item from the Help menu.

b. Run through the Mouse lesson as long as you can stand it. (To exit the tutorial and return to Program Manager, press the Escape key.)

Note: Most of the material in the "Windows Basics" lesson deals with the Program Manager application, which we will discuss in Chapter 2.

37. a. Open the Write application and ReadMe document by either double-clicking on the Read Me icon in the Main window, or by using the Arrow keys to highlight this icon and then pressing the Enter key.

b. Using the Arrow keys, move the *insertion point* (the blinking vertical bar in the upper-left corner of the document) so that it's positioned in front of the word SETUP.TXT.

c. Move the insertion point in front of the word "Note" by positioning the mouse cursor (an I-beam shape) at this location and clicking.

d. Scroll the window down one screen.

e. Move the insertion point to the end of the document. Can you do this with one keystroke combination?

f. Move the insertion point to the beginning of the last line. Can you do this with one keystroke?

g. Close this application window, returning to Program Manager.

38. a. Open the Write application and ReadMe document by either double-clicking on the Read Me icon in the Main window or by using the Arrow keys to highlight this icon and then pressing the Enter key.

b. Choose the Print item from the File menu.

c. In the Print dialog box:
   - select the Pages option;
   - leave To at 1 and change From to 2 (do not press Enter after typing these numbers);
   - set Copies to 2, Print Quality to medium;
   - choose the Cancel button.

d.   Close the Write application.

39. a.   Open the Accessories window by either double-clicking on its icon at the bottom of the screen or by choosing Accessories from Program Manager's <u>W</u>indow menu.

b.   Open the Clock application by either double-clicking on its icon or by using the Arrow keys to highlight its label and pressing the Enter key.

c.   Resize the Clock window. What happens when it becomes larger or smaller?

d.   Experiment with the options on the <u>S</u>ettings menu. (If the title and menu bars disappear, either double-click on the Clock window or press the Escape key to get them back.)

e.   Close the Clock application and the Accessories window.

40. a.   Open the Games window by either double-clicking on its icon at the bottom of the screen or by choosing Games from Program Manager's <u>W</u>indow menu.

b.   Open the Minesweeper application by either double-clicking on its icon or by using the Arrow keys to highlight its label and pressing the Enter key.

c.   With the aid of its Help system, learn to play Minesweeper.

d.   Close the Minesweeper application and the Games window.

Creative Writing

41. Explain, in one or two paragraphs, why *Windows* is an appropriate name for the operating environment you're studying in this text.

42. Explain, in one or two paragraphs, why Windows provides you with so much power to manipulate (move, resize, and so on) its on-screen windows.

43. What are some of the similarities and differences between a Windows menu and a restaurant menu.

44. If you were designing a dialog box, explain (in general terms) when you would use each of the following types of options: command buttons, option buttons, check boxes, text boxes, and list boxes.

45. Suppose it's your job to design a dialog box called Draw Circle. (When OK is chosen in this dialog box, a circle will be drawn on the screen.) The Draw Circle dialog box should contain options that allow the user to:

a.   Position the center of the circle a given distance (in inches) from the left and top screen borders.

    b.   Draw the circle with a given radius (in inches).

    c.   Fill the interior of the circle, if the user wishes, with any one of eight specified colors.

Either sketch a suitable dialog box or describe its components in detail.

46. Suppose you are working within an application and need help in printing the screen you have just created. Explain, in one or two paragraphs, how you would use the application's Help system to obtain this information.

Working
with
Applications

OVERVIEW Windows provides many improvements over plain old DOS when it comes to running your programs — your *applications software*. These include the ease with which you can manage and start applications, the convenience of running more than one application at a time and switching among them, and the ability to move information between one application and another. In this chapter, we will discuss these features of Windows. Specifically, you will learn:

1. To use the groups and program items in Program Manager.

2. The contents of the predefined groups supplied with Windows.

3. To manipulate group icons, group windows, and program item icons.

4. Various ways to start applications.

5. How to switch among the currently running applications.

6. How to transfer information between applications.

7. How to run a DOS application in a window.

8. How to transfer information to or from a DOS application.

9. How to quit an application.

2.1   An Introduction to Program Manager

Program Manager is the software that comprises the heart of the Windows environment. It starts automatically when you start Windows, displaying the start-up Windows screen, and is always running and available until you end your Windows session. Its function is of fundamental importance — to help you organize and start your applications in a user-friendly fashion. In the first two sections of this chapter, we will discuss how Program Manager accomplishes these goals.

Groups and Program Items

First, let's take a look at the components that make up a Program Manager window. A typical layout is shown in Figure 2.1.

FIGURE 2.1   A Typical Program Manager Window

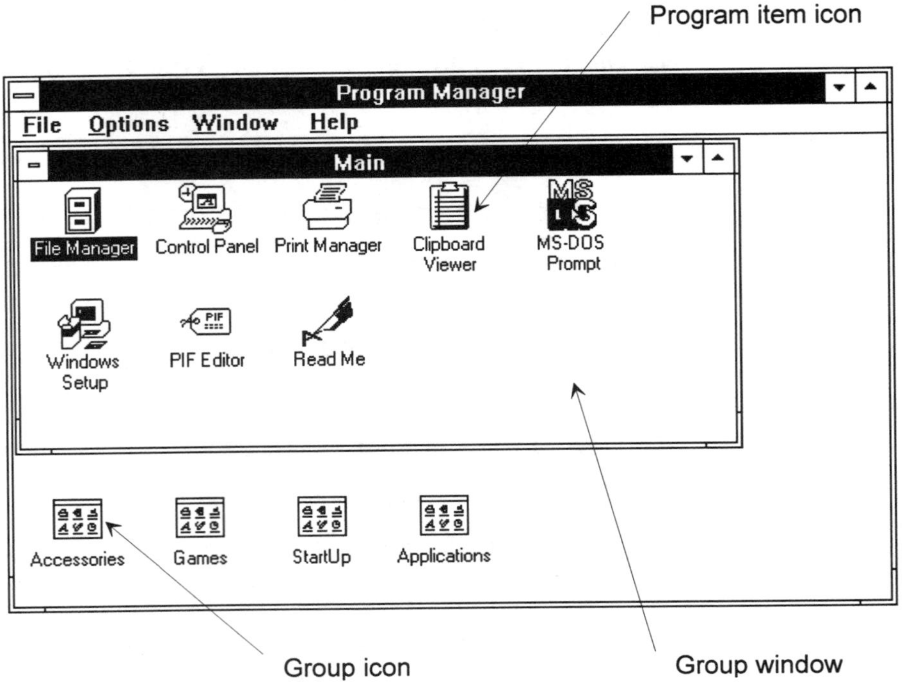

Program Manager organizes selected applications and files (collectively called **program items**) into **groups**. Program items are represented by **program item icons** which reside within **group windows**. For example, in Figure 2.1, the group window Main contains the program item icons labeled File Manager, Control Panel, Print Manager, and so on. All these icons represent applications except Read Me, which — as you may recall from Chapter 1 — represents the ReadMe document.

When a group window is closed or minimized, it becomes a **group icon**, displayed at the bottom of the Program Manager window. The group icons in Figure 2.1 are labeled Accessories, Games, StartUp, and Applications.

In any given Windows session, you may want to work with several specific applications, which may be contained within different groups. Thus, it is often useful to have a few group windows open, so that the program item icons can be easily accessed, and to close others to avoid clutter. Since a group window is a type of document window, it can be reduced to, or restored from, its icon by any of the methods given in Section 1.3.

To be more specific, the easiest way to open a group window is to double-click on its icon. You can also open a group window by clicking *once* on its icon, which displays its Control menu,

The Control
menu for a
group icon

and then choosing <u>R</u>estore or Ma<u>x</u>imize.

To *close* a group window, double-click on its Control menu box (the box containing the symbol ⊂⊃ to the left of the title bar) or click on its minimize button (the box containing the symbol ▾ just to the right of the title bar). For example, to close the Main window and open the Games window, you could double-click on the Control menu box of the Main window and then double-click on the Games icon.

**Keyboard
Alternatives**

You can use the keyboard to *open* a group window in one of the following ways.

- Press Ctrl+F6 or Ctrl+Tab repeatedly to cycle through the group icons and group windows. When the icon you want to restore to a window is selected (highlighted), either press Enter or choose Restore from its Control menu. (To open the Control menu using the keyboard, press Alt+Hyphen.)

- Pull down Program Manager's Window menu and choose the name of the group you want to open. For example, to open the Accessories group window, pull down the Window menu, press the Down Arrow key to move the highlight bar to the Accessories item, and press Enter.

To *close* a group window (reducing it to an icon), first *select it* — make it the active window. You can do this from the keyboard by repeatedly pressing Ctrl+F6 or Ctrl+Tab (which cycles through the group windows and icons) until the title bar of the window you want to close becomes highlighted. Then, either press the shortcut key Ctrl+F4 or open the Control menu (by pressing Alt+Hyphen) and choose Close.

Windows' Predefined (Built-in) Groups

When Windows is installed, it normally sets up the following *predefined* groups within Program Manager:

1. The **Main group** contains *utility programs* that help you to manage certain aspects of Windows and your computer system. These programs and their functions are:

    - File Manager provides you with a user-friendly means of manipulating (moving, copying, deleting, etc.) your disk files. You can also use it to start applications. We will cover File Manager in Chapters 3 and 4.

    - Control Panel supplies the power to customize the Windows environment to your liking (for example, by choosing colors). We will discuss this feature in Chapter 5.

    - Print Manager, Windows Setup, and PIF Editor provide control over certain aspects of using and setting up applications. They will be discussed in Chapters 4, 5, and 9, respectively.

- Clipboard Viewer is useful in transferring information between applications; it will be described in Section 2.4.

- MS-DOS Prompt, discussed in Section 2.3, provides a plain vanilla (actually, plain black-and-white) DOS interface. If you are comfortable using DOS, MS-DOS Prompt gives you a way of working within this environment without exiting Windows.

- Read Me represents a file, not an application. Recall from Chapter 1 that when you choose Read Me from the Main window, the Write word processor is started and the ReadMe document is opened within it.

2. The **Accessories group** contains several applications supplied by Windows. Although these programs are not as powerful as similar applications that can be purchased separately, they can be quite useful. We will discuss the Write word processor and Notepad text editor in Chapter 6, the Paintbrush graphics program in Chapter 7, and other accessories (Terminal, Cardfile, Recorder, Calendar, Calculator, Clock, and Character Map) in Chapter 8.

3. The **Games group** contains two games, Solitaire and Minesweeper, supplied by Windows. These games are not only fun to play but can also help a beginning user gain some familiarity with the Windows way of doing things.

4. The **StartUp group** serves a special purpose. If you want a particular application to start automatically when Windows starts, you can move or copy its icon to this group (as described in Section 2.3).

5. Depending on how your copy of Windows has been set up, the **Applications group** may or may not appear on your desktop. If it does, it probably contains icons for the applications Windows found on your hard disk during the setup process.

2.2 Changing the Layout of Program Manager

After you use Windows for a while, you will probably develop definite preferences for the way it should look and operate. Fortunately, the ease with which you can customize various aspects of Windows is one of its strong points. In particular, you can alter the layout of the Program Manager window in many ways. For example, you can open as many group windows as you like, arrange them in a particular way on the screen, and then position program item icons within these groups to suit your taste. As you will see, all this (and more) is easy to accomplish.

Manipulating Group Windows

The first step in creating your ideal Program Manager setup is to decide which program items you want to have instantly available and to open the corresponding group windows. For the sake of argument, and to provide an illustrative example, suppose that you primarily use the Write word processor and Paintbrush graphics program (in the Accessories group) and like to play the Solitaire card game (in the Games group). You also frequently use the File Manager and Print Manager utilities (in the Main group). So, you decide to open the Accessories, Games, and Main group windows.

The first problem you may encounter is that one of these windows covers a group icon that you want to restore. For example, the newly-opened Accessories window might cover and hide the Games icon. In this case, you could choose the Games group from Program Manager's Window menu to open the Games window, but it's easier to move and/or size the Accessories window so that it no longer covers the Games icon. (If you've forgotten how to perform the move or size operation, see Section 1.3.) After opening the Accessories, Games, and Main group windows, the Program Manager window will resemble the one pictured in Figure 2.2.

The Tile and Cascade commands

This layout is far from ideal. The Main window almost totally obscures the Accessories window and also partially covers the Games window. In particular, notice that the Solitaire icon in Games is hidden. To correct the situation, just move and size the three windows to your liking. Another solution is to use Program Manager's Tile and Cascade commands, both of which can be found on the Window pull-down menu.

■   Choosing the Tile command from the Window menu (or pressing the shortcut key Shift+F4) arranges the group windows side-by-side, so that none of the windows obscures any of the others (Figure 2.3). In the process, some windows may be reduced in size, requiring you to scroll to see all the icons within them.

FIGURE 2.2   Three Windows Open in Program Manager

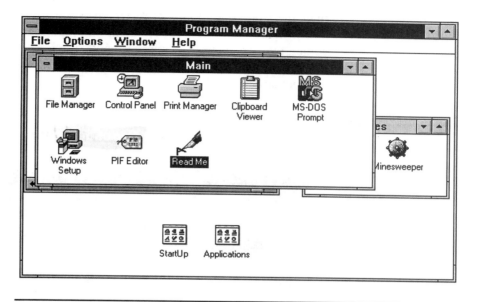

FIGURE 2.3   The Effect of the Tile Command

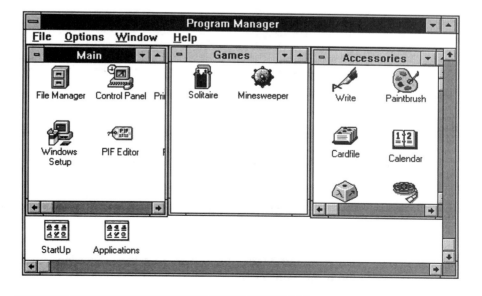

■ Choosing the Cascade command from the Window menu (or just pressing Shift+F5) overlaps the group windows so that little more than the title bars of the back windows can be seen (Figure 2.4). The window that was active when this command was issued becomes the one in front. To bring another window to the front, just select it by clicking anywhere on it or by using the keyboard as described earlier in this chapter.

FIGURE 2.4   The Effect of the Cascade Command

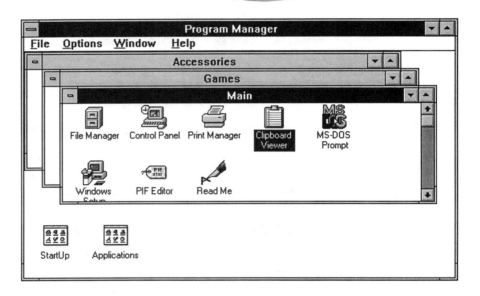

Manipulating Group and Program Item Icons

Once you have arranged the group windows to your liking, you may want to change the way the program item icons are arranged within a group or the way that group icons are arranged within Program Manager. For example, referring to Figure 2.3, you might want to rearrange the icons in the Main window so that the File Manager and Print Manager icons are both visible.

Windows gives you the power to position group icons anywhere within the Program Manager window and to move or copy program item icons to any position within a group window. Here's how to accomplish these actions using the mouse:

- To move a group icon, position the mouse pointer over it and drag it to a new location within the Program Manager window.

- To move a program item icon, position the mouse pointer over it and drag it to a new location within any group window. You can also drag a program item icon onto a group *icon*, which moves the program item to that group.

- To *copy* a program item icon (so that it appears in two places), hold down the Ctrl key as you drag it with the mouse to a new location within any group window or onto any group icon.

Keyboard Alternatives

To use the keyboard to move a *group icon* to a new location:

1. Select the group icon (using Ctrl+F6 or Ctrl+Tab).

2. Open its Control menu (by pressing Alt+Hyphen).

3. Choose the Move command from the Control menu.

4. Use the Arrow keys to move the icon.

5. Press the Enter key when it is positioned as you'd like.

To move a *program item icon* to a new position within a group window:

1. Select the group window within which the icon resides (by using Ctrl+F6 or Ctrl+Tab).

2. Use the Arrow keys to select the icon.

3. Choose Move from the Program Manager File menu (or just press F7).

4. In the To Group list of the resulting dialog box, select the name of the group to which you want to move the icon, by using the Up and Down Arrow keys, and press Enter.

If you want to *copy* a program item icon to another group, modify step 3 of the *move* procedure above as follows: choose Copy from the File menu or just press F8.

As an example, let's return to Figure 2.3 on page 45. To rearrange the icons in the Main window so that both File Manager and Print Manager are visible:

■ Maximize the Main window to provide some elbow room.

■ Now, arrange the icons (by moving them one at a time) into two vertical columns so that File Manager and Print Manager are at the top of the first column.

■ Finally, restore the Main window.

After these operations are performed, the Main group window should look something like this:

The Main group of Figure 2.3 after rearranging icons

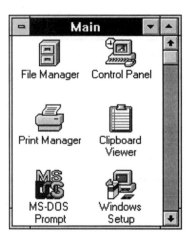

After moving icons around, they might not line up in rows and columns as evenly as you would like. Fortunately, Windows provides an Arrange Icons command to automatically arrange the icons in a neat, orderly way.

To arrange the *group* icons so they are evenly spaced across the bottom of the Program Manager window:

1. Select any group icon.

2. Choose Arrange Icons from the Window menu.

To arrange *program item* icons in an orderly fashion within a specified group window:

1. Select this group window.

2. Choose Arrange Icons from the Window menu.

Windows also has an Auto Arrange option that automatically rearranges program item icons in evenly spaced rows and columns whenever their window is resized or an icon in their group is moved or copied. Auto Arrange is in effect whenever a check mark (✓) appears next to its name on the Options menu. To turn the Auto Arrange feature on or off, choose it from the Options menu.

We will discuss procedures for *creating* and *deleting* program item and group icons in Chapter 4.

Saving Your Changes

You've now put a lot of work into getting Program Manager to look right. To ensure that it looks the same way the next time you start Windows, you have to *save the current settings*. You can do this in two ways:

- Open the Options menu. If there is a check mark (✓) next to the Save Settings on Exit item, indicating that this option is in effect, close this menu (by pressing Alt or by clicking anywhere else on the screen). If no check mark appears, choose this item to turn on the Save Settings option. Then, when you start Windows again, the Program Manager window will look the same way it did at the end of the previous session.

- To save the current layout without exiting Windows, just hold down the Shift key while choosing Exit Windows from the File menu. When you do this, you will *not* in fact exit Windows, but the current settings will be saved.

Hands-On

2.2

Start up Windows (if it's not already running) and try the following exercise. To create a printed copy of your work, see Appendix B.

1. Maximize the Program Manager window.
2. Open the Main, Accessories, and Games group windows; close the others.
3. Tile the windows; then cascade them. In which configuration are more program item icons visible?
4. Use Arrange Icons to rearrange the remaining *group* icons. How

many group icons are now visible on the screen?

5.   Reduce all three group windows to icons. Where did Windows position the last group window that was reduced to an icon?

2.3   Starting Applications

Windows supplies a variety of ways — some user-friendly and others not so user friendly — to *start* or *launch* an application; to load it into RAM and start it running. This section describes the various techniques and also discusses when one method might be more desirable than another.

Starting Applications from Program Manager

Program Manager can launch any application on your hard or floppy disks. If an application is represented by an icon, then there is a very easy way to start it running; just follow these steps:

The easy way   1.   Open the group window that contains the program item icon.

2.   *Choose* the program item icon by double-clicking on it (or selecting it with the Arrow keys and pressing Enter).

 If the group window in which you're interested is already open but covered by another window, select the desired window as described in Section 2.2. If the icon for the desired application is not visible, you can either scroll the window until the icon appears or maximize the window so that all icons in it are visible. (See Section 1.3 for more information about scrolling and maximizing a window.)

The Run   If the application you want to start is not represented by an icon, but
command   you know its directory and file name (its full *path name*), use the Run command on the File menu. (We will discuss files, directories, and paths in Section 3.1.) When you choose this command, the Run dialog box is displayed:

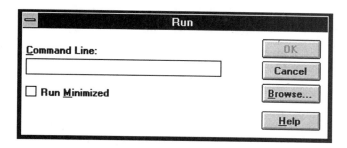

Now type the path name of the desired application and press the Enter key. (If the Run Minimized box is checked, the application will start and immediately be reduced to an icon.) For example, to start an application in the LOG directory on drive C named CABIN.EXE, choose the Run command from the File menu, type c:\log\cabin.exe and press the Enter key.

The Run command is often used to *install* new Windows applications from the manufacturer's distribution diskettes to your computer's hard disk. The procedure usually goes like this:

1.   Insert the first diskette into the A: drive.

2.   Choose the Run command from the File menu.

3.   Type a:setup and press the Enter key.

4.   Follow the on-screen instructions.

If the application you want to launch is not represented by an icon, and you don't know its directory and/or file name, you could use the Browse feature of the Run dialog box to find it or use File Manager to start the application. We will discuss both techniques in Chapter 4.

Using the StartUp Group

If you want an application to run automatically when you start Windows, simply move or copy its icon to the StartUp group. For example, if you want the date and time displayed whenever Windows is started, copy the Clock icon from the Accessories group to the StartUp group. Recall that the easiest way to do this is:

1.   Open the Accessories group window.

2.   Hold down the Ctrl key and drag the Clock icon into the StartUp

group window if it's open, or onto the StartUp group icon, if it's not.

3. Save the change by holding down the Shift key while choosing Exit Windows from the File menu.

If you have more than one icon in the StartUp group, the applications will start in the order they appear. For example, suppose your StartUp group contains the icons for Clock and Calculator, like this:

The StartUp
group with
Clock and
Calculator
icons

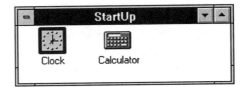

Then, when Windows starts, the Clock will be displayed and then the Calculator. Your screen will look something like the one in Figure 2.5. (Notice that only a small part of the Clock window shows behind the Calculator window.)

Using MS-DOS Prompt

MS-DOS Prompt

Notice that one of the icons in the Main group (see Figure 2.1) is entitled **MS-DOS Prompt**. When you choose this icon, a typical black-and-white DOS screen will be displayed and you will be confronted with the DOS prompt and its accompanying flashing cursor (Figure 2.6).

You can now enter almost any valid DOS command, including one to start a DOS application. For example, to start the program with file name DOSPROG.EXE on the A: drive, type a:dosprog and press the Enter key. After you are done using the DOS program, type exit and press the Enter key to return to Program Manager.

A DOS application is usually started from within Windows by double-clicking on its icon in a group window or by typing its file name in the Run dialog box (which is opened by choosing Run from the File menu). The real purpose of MS-DOS Prompt is to provide DOS aficionados with the ability to return to this environment to issue a command, without exiting Windows.

FIGURE 2.5   Windows Start-up with Clock and Calculator

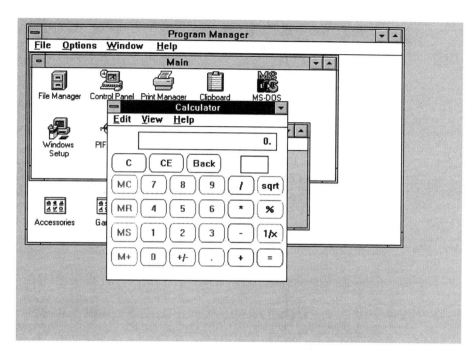

FIGURE 2.6   The MS-DOS Prompt Start-up Screen

■ Type EXIT and press ENTER to quit this MS-DOS prompt and
  return to Windows.
■ Press ALT+TAB to switch to Windows or another application.
■ Press ALT+ENTER to switch this MS-DOS Prompt between a
  window and full screen.

```
Microsoft(R) MS-DOS(R) Version 6
           (C)Copyright Microsoft Corp 1981-1993.

C:\WINDOWS>_
```

Start up Windows (if it's not already running) and try the following exercise. To create a printed copy of your work, see Appendix B.

1. Start the File Manager application by choosing its icon from the Main group. Does File Manager's window occupy the entire screen?
2. Quit File Manager by choosing E_x_it from its _F_ile menu.
3. Insert the Lab Projects diskette supplied with this textbook into its drive.
4. Start the DOSPROG application on this disk by using the Run command. (Type a:dosprog.exe in the text box.) Does this application occupy the entire screen?
5. Exit DOSPROG by following the on-screen instructions.
6. Start DOSPROG by using MS-DOS Prompt. (Type a:dosprog at the DOS prompt and press Enter.) Does this application look any different than when it was started before?
7. Exit DOSPROG and MS-DOS Prompt.
8. Remove the Lab Projects disk from its drive.

2.4 Working with Several Applications at Once

As you may recall, Windows allows you to have several applications running at the same time, each of which is instantly available. To see how this can be useful, suppose that you want to use the word processor, called Write, supplied as part of the Windows package. (We will discuss how to use Write in Chapter 6.) To do so, you start Windows and then launch Write. At this point, there are already two applications running under Windows: Program Manager and Write.

In the course of using the word processor, you realize that a picture will illustrate your point better than the proverbial thousand words. To create one, you start Paintbrush, the paint program supplied with Windows (and discussed in Chapter 7). There are now three applications running simultaneously. After completing the picture, you copy it into your word processing document and continue writing. Before you finish this Windows session, you might also start other applications, perhaps Print Manager, File Manager, and (to take a break) a computer game.

To make use of the kind of flexibility described in this scenario, you have to be able to quickly and easily switch among applications and to transfer information from one application to another. We will discuss these techniques in the remainder of this section.

Switching Among Applications

If you are working with one application and want to use another as well, your next move depends on whether or not the latter has already been started.

- If the other application is not currently running, switch to Program Manager (make it the *active* application) and start the desired program.

- If the other application is running, you can switch to it directly (making it the active one).

Switching to an application can be accomplished in any of the following ways:

1. If any part of the application's window is visible on the screen, click on it and it will become the active one.

2. If the application is running as an icon (if it has been minimized) and that icon is visible on the screen, double-click on it — its window will open and be the active one.

3. You can cycle through the applications currently running by holding down the Alt key and repeatedly pressing Tab. When you see the desired application's title appear in a small window on the screen, release the Alt key. That application's window will open and be the active one.

4. You can also cycle through the applications that are running by repeatedly pressing Alt+Esc until you see the desired application's window or highlighted icon (if it is running minimized). In the latter case, double-click on the icon or just press Enter and the application will open as the active one.

5. Display the Windows **Task List** by performing any of the following actions:

   - Double-click on the desktop (outside of all open windows).

   - Press Ctrl+Esc.

   - Open the application's Control menu (by clicking on the Control menu box or pressing Alt+Spacebar) and choose Switch To.

A typical Task List looks like this:

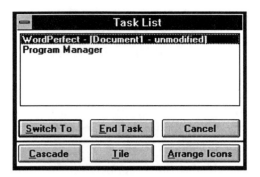

To switch to a particular application on the Task List, either double-click on its name, or select it using the Down Arrow key and press Enter. (As you might guess from its command buttons, Task List can also be used to cascade or tile application windows, to close an application, and to arrange minimized icons in an orderly fashion on the desktop.)

If you want to switch to an application whose window or minimized icon is visible on the screen, any of the five techniques just mentioned will work. However, the *easiest* way to switch is to click on the application's window or double-click on its icon. If the application is not visible, Alt+Tab switching, the third technique, is fastest, but Task List will also do the job. The fourth technique, Alt+Esc switching, is rarely used.

Transferring Information Between Applications

The process of transferring information — a block of text or a picture — from one application (the *source*) to another (the *target*) usually involves these steps:

1. In the source application, *select* or *mark* the information to be transferred. To select a block of text, either:

    - Position the mouse pointer at the beginning of the desired block of text and drag the insertion point to the end of the block.

    or

    - Position the insertion point at the beginning of the desired block of text, hold down the Shift key, and move the insertion point (using, for example, the Arrow keys) to the end of the block. Then, release the Shift key.

In either case, the selected text will now be highlighted. (We will describe how to select a picture when we discuss Paintbrush in Chapter 7.)

2. Then, *cut* or *copy* the selected information to the Windows **Clipboard**, a special area of internal memory set aside for this purpose. When information is **cut**, it is deleted from the source application and transferred to the Clipboard; when information is **copied**, it is also transferred to the Clipboard, but the source application remains unchanged. To perform the cut or copy operation, choose Cut or Copy, respectively, from the source application's Edit menu. (If no information has been selected, both these items will be dimmed.)

3. Now start, or switch to, the target application (unless the target and source are the same application).

4. Finally, **paste** (insert) the information on the Clipboard into the target application. To carry out this operation, position the cursor where you want to insert the information and choose Paste from the target application's Edit menu.

Pictorially, the transfer process looks like this:

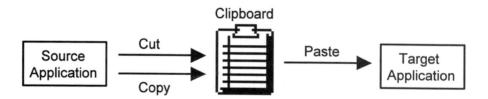

There are two important *exceptions* to the general "cut and paste" process:

- If you want to transfer information to or from a DOS (non-Windows) application, a different procedure is used. We will describe it in Section 2.5.

- If you want to copy the entire screen to the Clipboard, press the Print Screen key. If you want to copy the active window to the Clipboard, press Alt+Print Screen. In both cases, pasting into the target application is carried out in the same manner as described in step 4 above. (The procedures for copying a window or the entire screen may not work on all computer systems.)

When you cut or copy information to the Clipboard, it erases any information currently residing there. If you want to know what is presently on the Clipboard, you can open the Windows **Clipboard Viewer** application (Figure 2.8). To do so, switch to Program Manager and choose the Clipboard Viewer icon from the Main group. Clipboard Viewer also allows you to:

Clipboard Viewer

- Delete all the information on the Clipboard by choosing Delete from the Edit menu or by pressing the Delete key.

- Save the information on the Clipboard to disk by choosing the Save As command from the File menu.

- Copy the information in a previously saved clipboard file to the Clipboard by choosing Open from the File menu.

An Example

Now, let's take a look at a specific example of this process. Suppose you want to copy some information from the ReadMe document (used as an example in Chapter 1) to the Notepad (whose icon can be found in the Accessories group). First, choose the Read Me icon from the Main group, which starts the Windows Write word processor and also opens the ReadMe file as pictured in Figure 2.7.

FIGURE 2.7   The Beginning of the ReadMe File

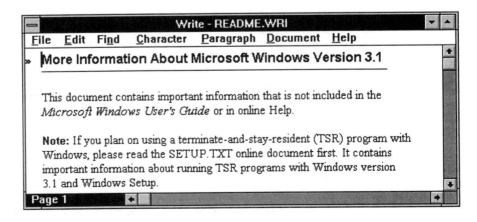

Suppose you want to copy the first sentence: "This document contains ..." To do so, select this block of text by either:

■ Positioning the mouse pointer just before the beginning of the sentence (just before the T) and dragging it to the end of the sentence (just after the period); then releasing the button.

or

■ Using the Arrow keys to position the insertion point at the beginning of the sentence (just before the T) and holding down the Shift key while using the Arrow keys to move the insertion point to the end of the sentence (just after the period); then releasing the Shift key.

In either case, the selected text will be highlighted.

Now copy the selected text to the Clipboard by choosing Copy from the Edit menu. If you want to verify that the proper information has been copied to the Clipboard, switch back to Program Manager and start Clipboard Viewer. Its window should look similar to the one in Figure 2.8. Then, close Clipboard Viewer by choosing Exit from its File menu or double-clicking on its Control menu box.

FIGURE 2.8   The Clipboard Viewer with the Copied Text

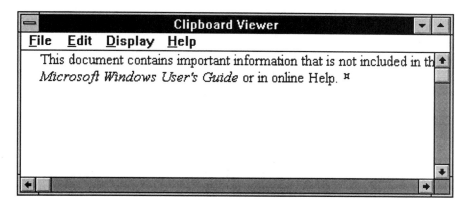

Finally, to paste the contents of the Clipboard into Notepad, open the Accessories group window and double-click the Notepad icon to start this application. Then, choose Paste from its Edit menu and the originally selected text will be transferred to the beginning of the Notepad document, as pictured in Figure 2.9 on the next page.

FIGURE 2.9   Notepad with the Copied Text

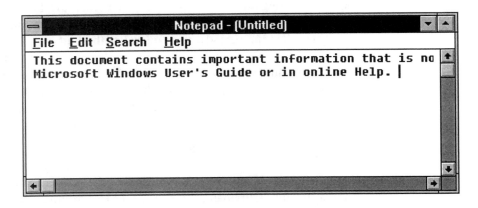

Start up Windows (if it's not already running) and try the following exercise. To create a printed copy of your work, see Appendix B.

Hands-On
2.4

1. Choose the Read Me icon and then the Clipboard Viewer icon from the Main group.
2. Switch to the ReadMe document. Were you able to do this without using the keyboard?
3. In the ReadMe document, select the text "More Information About Microsoft Windows".
4. Copy the selected text to the Clipboard. Does it still appear in the ReadMe document?
5. Switch to Clipboard Viewer. Does the selected text look exactly the same here as in the original document? If not, in what ways has it changed?
6. Launch Notepad from the Accessories group.
7. Paste the selected text into Notepad. Does the selected text look exactly the same here as in the original document? If not, in what ways has it changed?
8. Close the applications one-by-one by pressing Alt+F4 and answering "No" to any message that appears. Then, close the Accessories window.

2.5   Working with DOS Applications*

A **DOS application** (also called a **non-Windows application**) is one that runs under the DOS operating system but was not specifically written to run under Windows. Such applications can be started up and switched to in exactly the same way as Windows applications. Nevertheless, most DOS applications have a much different look and feel than their Windows counterparts.

Running a DOS Application in a Window

When a DOS program is launched from within Windows, it normally uses the entire screen and looks the same as it would had it been started from the DOS prompt. We say that the application is running in *full-screen mode*. On most computer systems, DOS applications can also run in *window mode* — within windows occupying part or all of the desktop.

Switching to window mode

If a DOS application is running full-screen, it can be placed in a window by pressing Alt+Enter. (To return to full-screen mode, press Alt+Enter again.) For example, if you start MS-DOS Prompt by choosing its icon from the Main group, it initially runs full-screen, as shown in Figure 2.6 on page 53. Pressing Alt+Enter runs it in a window, as shown below.

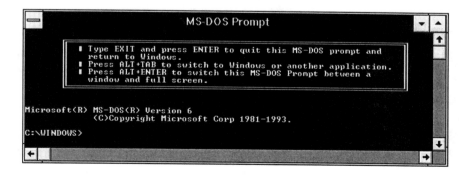

---

*You may skip this section if you do not expect to use Windows to run non-Windows applications.

Running a DOS application in a window has advantages and disadvantages over full-screen mode. On the plus side, you can size and move the window so that other applications are also visible on the desktop. It also allows you to transfer information to and from the Clipboard. On the other hand, when running a program in a window, especially a small one, you see less information at any given time and have to do more scrolling.

When a DOS application is placed in window mode, its window contains all the usual elements: title bar, Control menu box, minimize and maximize buttons, and so on. The Control menu, which can be opened by clicking on the Control menu box or pressing Alt+Spacebar, looks like this:

The Control menu for a DOS application running in a window

As you can see, the Control menu provides the usual sizing, moving, and switching options, together with a few new ones:

■   Choosing Edit allows you to mark (select) information in the window, and transfer information to and from the clipboard. We will discuss this shortly.

■   Choosing Settings opens a dialog box that provides some control over how the application operates.

■   The Fonts item allows you to change the size of the on-screen characters (the *font*) within the window. Choosing Fonts opens the Font Selection dialog box shown in Figure 2.10. The main component of this dialog box is the Font list box on the left that gives the available character sizes in *pixels*, the tiny dots of light from which the characters are formed.

For example, if you select (highlight) "6 × 8", the Selected Font box will show a sample of text in which each character is formed within a rectangular box that is 6 pixels wide and 8 pixels high. If this font doesn't look right, select another size from the list. When you find a font you like, double-click on this size or choose the OK button, and you will be returned to the application with all text displayed in the new size.

FIGURE 2.10   The Font Selection Dialog Box

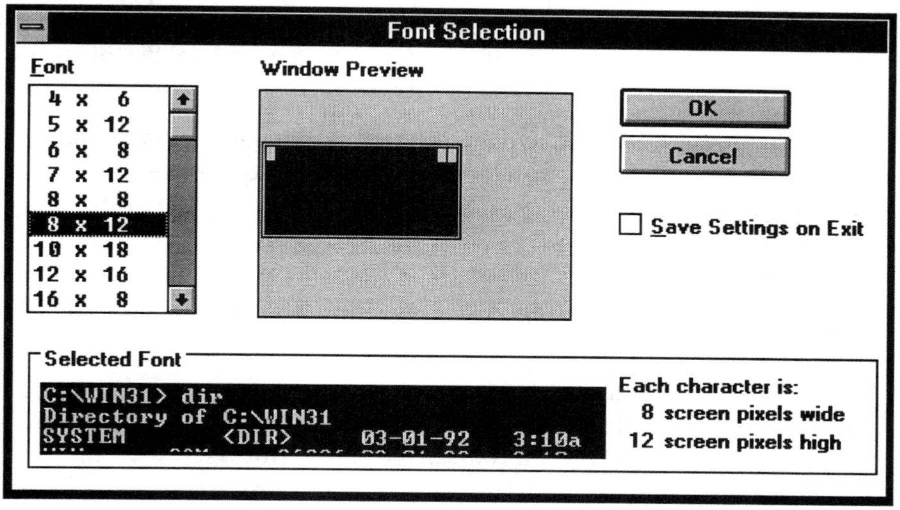

Transferring Information To and From the Clipboard

While running a DOS application under Windows, you can usually transfer on-screen information to and from the Clipboard. However, the procedures are more complicated than the ones for Windows applications, and won't work with all Windows setups.

- To copy an entire DOS screen to the Clipboard, press the Print Screen key.

- To paste information from the Clipboard to a DOS application:

    1. Position the cursor at the desired on-screen insertion point.

2. Open the application's Control menu (by clicking on its Control menu box or by pressing Alt+Spacebar).

3. Choose <u>E</u>dit from the Control menu and then <u>P</u>aste from the submenu that appears.

■ To copy selected information to the Clipboard from a DOS application, run it in a window (by pressing Alt+Enter if it's running full-screen) and:

1. Select the information to be copied. To do this, choose <u>E</u>dit from the Control menu and then Mar<u>k</u> from the submenu. (A flashing rectangular cursor will appear in the window.) Now, position the cursor at the beginning of the block to be selected and either drag it to the end of the block or hold down Shift and use the Arrow keys to move it to the end of the block.

2. Copy the selected information to the Clipboard. To do this, just press the *right* mouse button or the Enter key.

Hands-On

2.5

Start up Windows (if it's not already running) and try the following exercise. To create a printed copy of your work, see Appendix B.

1. Start Notepad from the Accessories group and MS-DOS Prompt from the Main group.
2. Run MS-DOS Prompt in a window by pressing Alt+Enter.
3. Copy the on-screen "box" (together with the text in it) from MS-DOS Prompt to the Clipboard. Has this information been deleted from MS-DOS Prompt?
4. Switch to Notepad (by pressing Alt+Tab) and paste the information on the Clipboard into Notepad. Does it look the same in Notepad as it did in MS-DOS Prompt? If not, how has it changed?
5. Quit Notepad by pressing Alt+F4 (answering "No" to the Save Changes message) and exit MS-DOS Prompt by typing exit and pressing Enter.

2.6 Quitting Applications

When you are done using an application, you should *quit* (or exit) it. Doing so frees some of the computer's internal memory and other Windows' resources and usually speeds response times in applications that are still running. In this section, we will describe how to quit an application.

Ways to quit Windows applications

All *Windows* applications — those written specifically to run under Windows — can be exited in one of the following ways. Take your pick.

- Choose Exit from the application's File menu.

- Choose Close from the application's Control menu.

- Double-click on the application's Control menu box.

- Open Task List, select the application to be exited, and choose the End Task button.

- Press Alt+F4.

If you have used the application to make changes to a document and did not subsequently save the document to disk, Windows will display a warning message:

The Save Changes warning message

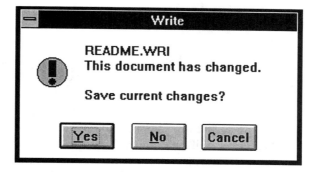

Choose Yes or No, as you wish, and the application will close. Choose Cancel (or press the Escape key) to return to the document.

Quitting DOS applications

Some DOS (non-Windows) applications have menu bars and, if so, can usually be quit by choosing Exit from their File menus. In general, however, there is not much conformity among DOS applications; they are notorious for performing common tasks in their own peculiar ways and exiting is no exception. You'll just have to learn the particular keystrokes or mouse clicks necessary to quit each DOS application you use.

In an emergency ...

There is one additional way to exit *any* application running under Windows, but it should only be used in an emergency; for example, if the application no longer responds to the keyboard or mouse. In this case, press Ctrl+Alt+Del (hold down the Ctrl and Alt keys and press the Delete key, then release all keys). The following message will be displayed:

```
This Windows application has stopped responding to the system.

*   Press ESC to cancel and return to Windows.
*   Press ENTER to close this application that is not responding.
    You will lose any unsaved information in this application.
*   Press CTRL+ALT+DEL again to restart your computer. You will
    lose any unsaved information in all applications.
```

First, try pressing the Escape key. If this doesn't cure the problem (it probably won't) and the above message disappears, press Ctrl+Alt+Del to display it again. This time, press Enter. The problem application should close and you will be returned to Windows, losing any unsaved changes in the application in the process.

Press Ctrl+Alt+Del when this message is displayed only as a last resort. This action will restart (*reboot*) your computer; all unsaved changes in all running programs will be lost and Windows and these programs will have to be restarted.

The "normal" way to exit Windows is to quit the open applications one at a time and then quit Windows itself as described in Chapter 1. (Remember that Windows must be exited from within Program Manager and it is not possible to quit Program Manager without exiting Windows.) If you want to end a Windows session quickly when several applications are still running, just switch to Program Manager and exit Windows. Windows will automatically close any open applications, displaying Save Changes warning messages when appropriate.

Chapter Summary

Key Terms

Accessories group [page 43]	Applications group [43]
Clipboard [57]	Clipboard Viewer [58]
Copy information [57]	Cut information [57]
DOS application [61]	Games group [43]
Group [41]	Group icon [41]
Group window [41]	Main group [42]

MS-DOS Prompt [52]   Non-Windows application [61]

Paste information [57]   Program item [41]

Program item icon [41]   Program Manager [40]

StartUp group [43]   Task List [55]

Topics **Predefined (Built-in) Groups**
Covered

Accessories	Windows-supplied programs
Applications	Other programs
Games	Windows-supplied computer games
Main	Windows system utilities
StartUp	Programs that start when Windows starts

Manipulating Group Icons

To select a group icon	Click on it; or press Ctrl+F6 or Ctrl+Tab until it is highlighted.
To open its Control menu	Click on the icon; or select it and press Alt+ Hyphen.
To move an icon	Drag it with the mouse; or choose Move from the Control menu, use the Arrow keys, and press Enter.
To arrange icons neatly	Select any group icon and choose Arrange Icons from the Window menu.

Manipulating Group Windows

To select a window	Click on any part of it; or press Ctrl+F6 or Ctrl+Tab until its title bar is highlighted.
To open a window	Double-click on its group icon; or select its group icon and choose Restore from its Control menu; or choose the group from the Window menu.
To close a window	Click on its minimize button; or double-click on its Control menu box; or press Ctrl+F4.
To tile windows	Choose Tile from the Window menu; or press Shift+F4.

To cascade windows	Choose Cascade from the Window menu; or press Shift+F5.

Manipulating Program Item Icons

To select an icon	Open its group window and click on the icon; or open its group window and use the Arrow keys to highlight the icon.
To move an icon	Drag it with the mouse; or select it, choose Move from the File menu, and choose To Group from the dialog box.
To copy an icon	Hold down Ctrl while dragging it with the mouse; or select it, choose Copy from the File menu, and choose To Group from the dialog box.
To arrange icons neatly	Select their group window and choose Arrange Icons from the Window menu.

Ways to Start (Launch) an Application

Choose its program item icon from the appropriate group window in Program Manager (by double-clicking on it or selecting it and pressing the Enter key).

Choose the Run command from Program Manager's File menu, type the application's full path name, and press Enter.

Move or copy its icon to the StartUp group; the application will start automatically whenever Windows starts.

Start MS-DOS Prompt (from the Main group window), type the application's full path name, and press Enter.

(Also see Chapter 4 for starting an application from File Manager.)

Ways to Switch to Another Application

Click on any part of its window.

Double-click on its icon (if it's running minimized).

Cycle through running applications using Alt+Tab or Alt+Esc until it appears.

Open Task List (by double-clicking on the desktop or pressing Ctrl+Esc), select the application from the list, and choose Switch To.

Transferring Information between Applications

To copy the entire screen or the active window to the Clipboard, press Print Screen or Alt+Print Screen, respectively.

To cut or copy selected information to the Clipboard, choose Cut or Copy, respectively, from the application's Edit menu.

To paste information on the Clipboard into an application, choose Paste from the application's Edit menu.

Working with a DOS Application

To run it in a window	When running it full-screen, press Alt+Enter.
To run it full-screen	When running it in a window, press Alt+Enter.
To open its Control menu	Click on its Control menu box or press Alt+Spacebar.
To copy information to the Clipboard	Run the application in a window, select the information, and press Enter or the right mouse button.
To paste information from the Clipboard	Run the application in a window, position the cursor at the desired point, choose Edit from the Control menu, and then choose Paste.

Ways to Quit a Windows Application

Choose Exit from its File menu.

Choose Close from its Control menu.

Double-click on its Control menu box.

Press Alt+F4.

Open Task List (press Ctrl+Esc or double-click on the desktop), select the application, and choose End Task.

Chapter Exercises

Short Answer

Complete each statement in Exercises 1 through 15.

1. Program item icons represent either _____ or _____.

2. To close a group window, you can double-click on its _____.

3. The _____ group contains the Windows system utilities.

4. The _____ command automatically arranges group windows in a non-overlapping manner.

5. To copy a program item icon, hold down the _____ key as you move the icon to the new location.

6. To arrange all the program item icons in the active group in an orderly way, choose the _____ command from the <u>W</u>indow menu.

7. To save the changes you have made to Program Manager's layout, you can hold down the _____ while choosing E<u>x</u>it Windows from the <u>F</u>ile menu.

8. To start an application represented by a program item icon, open its group window and _____ its icon.

9. If you want an application to start automatically whenever you start Windows, move or copy its icon to the _____ group.

10. To switch to a new application that is not visible on the screen, you can cycle through the applications that are running by pressing the _____ key combination.

11. When information is cut or copied from an application, it is transferred to the Windows _____.

12. To view the information that is currently on the Clipboard, start the _____ application from Program Manager's Main window.

13. A program that runs under DOS, but that was not written specifically to run under Windows is called a _____ application.

14. To run a DOS application in a window, press the _____ key combination.

15. If an application has stopped responding to the keyboard and mouse, press the _____ key combination.

Determine whether each of the statements in Exercises 16 through 28 is true or false.

16. Clicking once on a group icon opens the corresponding group window.

17. Group windows can be moved and resized.

18. To select a group window (to make it the active one), just click anywhere on it.

19. Program Manager's <u>W</u>indow menu lists only those applications that are currently running.

20. The Applications group contains all the programs that are supplied with the Windows package.

21. When the Cascade command is issued, windows are displayed on the screen in a non-overlapping manner.

22. A program item icon cannot appear in two different groups.

23. To start an application, it must be represented by a program item icon in Program Manager.

24. The Task List dialog box allows you to switch to any application that is currently running.

25. When information is copied from an application to the Clipboard, it is deleted from that application.

26. On most computers, pressing the Print Screen key will copy the entire screen to the Clipboard.

27. If a DOS application is running in a window, pressing Alt+Enter will return it to full-screen mode.

28. When you quit an application, it frees some of the computer's resources for use by the programs that are still running.

In Exercises 29 through 35, choose the correct answer.

29. The Clipboard Viewer icon is located in the:

   a. Main group.
   b. Accessories group.
   c. Games group.
   d. Applications group.

30. To copy a program item icon from one group to another:

   a. Drag it to the new group.
   b. Hold down the Ctrl key while dragging it to the new group.
   c. Hold down the Shift key while dragging it to the new group.
   d. Hold down the Alt key while dragging it to the new group.

31. Which of the following techniques cannot be used to start an application?

    a. Choose its icon from a Program Manager window.
    b. Type its path name in the Run dialog box and press Enter.
    c. Select its name from Task List and choose the <u>S</u>tart button.
    d. Type its path name at the DOS prompt and press Enter.

32. Which of the following techniques cannot be used to switch from the current application to a new one?

    a. Click on the new application's window.
    b. Click on the new application's minimized icon.
    c. Repeatedly press Alt+Tab until the new application's title is displayed.
    d. Repeatedly press Alt+Esc until the new application's window or minimized icon is displayed.

33. To transfer selected information to the Clipboard and simultaneously delete it from the current application:

    a. Choose Cu<u>t</u> from the application's <u>E</u>dit menu.
    b. Choose <u>C</u>opy from the application's <u>E</u>dit menu.
    c. Choose <u>P</u>aste from the application's <u>E</u>dit menu.
    d. Choose <u>D</u>elete from the application's <u>E</u>dit menu.

34. To display the Windows Task List:

    a. Press Alt+F4.
    b. Press Alt+Tab.
    c. Press Alt+Esc.
    d. Press Ctrl+Esc.

35. Which of the following techniques cannot be used to exit a Windows application?

    a. Double-click on its Control menu box.
    b. Press Alt+F4.
    c. Choose <u>Q</u>uit from its <u>E</u>dit menu.
    d. Choose <u>C</u>lose from its Control menu.

Hands-On In Exercises 36 through 40, start up Windows (if it's not already running) and perform the indicated tasks. To create a printed copy of your work, see Appendix B.

36. a. Maximize both Program Manager and the Main group.
    b. Arrange the icons in the Main window (by moving them one by one) in rows so that each row contains as many icons as possible.
    c. Choose the Arrange Icons command from the Window menu. Did any of the icons change position?
    d. Turn off the Auto Arrange option, if it's currently in effect.
    e. Restore the Main window. Did the icons maintain the same position relative to one another?
    f. Turn on Auto Arrange. Did this rearrange the icons in the Main group? Did any of the other icons change position?

37. a. Open the Accessories window and close all the others.
    b. Move the Clock icon to the StartUp group.
    c. Save this change by holding down the Shift key while choosing Exit Windows from Program Manager's File menu.
    d. Exit Windows.
    e. Restart Windows. Is Clock the active application?
    f. Move the Clock icon back to the Accessories group and save this change.
    g. Exit the Clock application.

38. a. Open the Accessories group.
    b. Start as many of the applications in this group as possible. Did Windows allow you to start them all? If not, what message was displayed?
    c. Cycle through all running applications. Do they appear in the order they were started? If not, what determines their order of appearance?
    d. Arrange the desktop so that all open applications are running in windows and each window is at least partly visible.
    e. Switch to Program Manager.
    f. Choose Exit from the File menu, but Cancel the resulting dialog box. Are any accessories still running?
    g. Quit all applications.

39. a. Start the Write application from the Accessories group.
    b. Type the sentence: "This is a test." (Don't worry if you make mistakes.)
    c. Select this sentence and *cut* it to the Clipboard. Does the sen-

tence still appear in the Write document?

d. Now type "Hello, world!", select it, and *copy* it to the Clipboard. Does this sentence still appear in the Write document?

e. Open the Clipboard Viewer. What text is on the Clipboard?

f. Switch back to Write and paste the information on the Clipboard into the Write document. What text is displayed now?

g. Quit Write and Clipboard Viewer. (Answer N̲o to any messages.)

40. a. Insert the Lab Projects diskette in its drive.

b. Start the DOSPROG application on this disk by choosing R̲un from Program Manager's F̲ile menu, typing a:dosprog.exe in the dialog box, and pressing Enter.

c. Press Alt+Enter to run DOSPROG in a window and maximize this window. Does it occupy the entire screen?

d. Open the Control menu, choose F̲onts, and change the font to the smallest size listed. Is it large enough to read the text on the screen?

e. Run DOSPROG full-screen (by pressing Alt+Enter). Did the font size change? Return to window mode.

f. Try to exit DOSPROG by double-clicking on its Control menu box, by opening its Control menu and choosing C̲lose, by pressing Alt+F4, and by opening Task List and choosing E̲nd Task. Which, if any, of these methods worked?

g. If none of the methods in part (f) worked, exit DOSPROG by following the on-screen instructions. Remove the Lab Projects disk from its drive.

Creative Writing

41. Open the Accessories window and maximize it so that you can see all the icons. Based only on their names and what you've read so far in the text, write a brief description of what you think is the function of each accessory.

42. Imagine that you have several applications running at the same time and that you need to switch among them from time to time. What are the advantages and disadvantages of

a. Running the active application in a maximized window?

b. Tiling the applications on the desktop?

c. Cascading the applications on the desktop?

43. Suppose that you frequently use the following programs: Write, Paintbrush, Clock, File Manager, and Solitaire. Also suppose that the

Applications group is empty. Give a step-by-step procedure to:

■ Move these five applications into the Applications group.

and

■ Arrange the layout of Program Manager so that the Applications group is the only window open within it when Windows starts.

44. DOS applications are those that have not been specifically written to run under Windows. Describe the ways in which these applications suffer (compared to Windows applications) as a result.

Managing Files and Directories

OVERVIEW Although Windows does its best to shield you from DOS, the computer's operating system, you still occasionally have to deal with some basic DOS structure, namely *files* and *directories*. You will frequently have to give names to files, and from time to time, copy, move, delete, and rename them. Directories, too, must sometimes be manipulated: created, changed, moved, or deleted. This chapter describes how you can direct Windows to perform these and other operations related to the maintenance of files, directories, and disks. Specifically, you will learn:

1. Basic information about files and directories.

2. To start and quit File Manager.

3. Some terminology concerning the File Manager window.

4. To open more than one directory window at a time.

5. To change the layout of a directory window and the kind of information it displays.

6. To change drives and directories and to select multiple files and directories.

7. To copy, move, rename, and delete files and directories and to create directories.

8. To format and copy floppy disks.

3.1   Files and Directories

Disks, especially hard disks, are capable of storing a lot of information — both data and programs. In order to manipulate this information, the computer's operating system (DOS), with your help, organizes it into files and directories. In this section, we will provide some useful information about these concepts.

What are Files and Directories?

Files   A **file** is a collection of information that has been created by a program and copied (or *saved*) to disk. A file may contain an application, in which case it's called a *program file*, or data created by an application, which is a *data file*. For example, if you create a report using your word processing software (itself a collection of files on your disk), you would normally save the report to disk before quitting the application. When you issue the "Save" command, DOS copies the data making up the report from internal memory (RAM) to a disk, and attaches a file name of your choosing to it, so that it can be accessed later on.

Directories   A typical hard disk can contain thousands of files. To keep track of all these files, it is necessary to organize them into **directories**, each of which is a collection of related files that you (or a programmer) have grouped together and given a name. For example, you might place all the letters you've written in one directory called Letters and all your reports in another directory called (you guessed it) Reports.

Sometimes it makes sense to place a related group of directories into a larger directory. In this case, the bigger directory is called the **parent directory** and each of the directories within it becomes a **subdirectory** of its parent. For example, you might have several directories for word processing data files: Letters, Reports, and so on. To better organize your disk, you could place all of these in a (parent) directory called, say, WP. A parent directory can contain files as well as directories. For example, you might place the word processing *program* files in the WP directory, as well.

The directories on a disk form a tree-like structure with the subdirectories branching out from their parents, which in turn may be subdirectories themselves. On each disk there is one directory, known as the **root directory**, that contains all the others. (The root directory can rightfully be called the "mother of all directories," at least for that particular disk.) Figure 3.1 shows a *directory tree* — a graphical way of representing the directory structure of a disk. It may take a little imagination to see this diagram as a "tree"; in particular, notice that the root is at the top.

FIGURE 3.1   Picture of a Typical Disk's Directory Structure

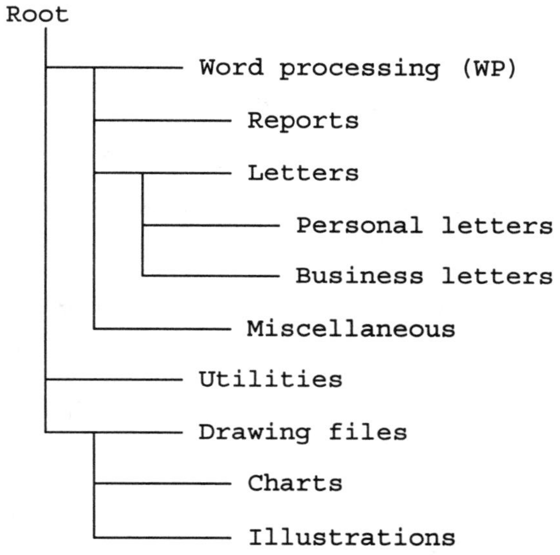

```
Root
   |
   |————————————— Word processing (WP)
   |    |———————————— Reports
   |    |———————————— Letters
   |    |    |———————————— Personal letters
   |    |    |———————————— Business letters
   |    |———————————— Miscellaneous
   |————————————— Utilities
   |————————————— Drawing files
        |———————————— Charts
        |———————————— Illustrations
```

Naming Files and Directories

Disk drive designations

Every disk drive, directory, and file on a computer must have a name. Disk drive designations, which are assigned by the operating system, consist of a single letter followed by a colon; for example, A: and B: are the usual names for a computer's floppy disk drives. (DOS does not distinguish between uppercase and lowercase letters, so A: is the same as a:.) The hard disk is usually designated as drive C:, even if there is only one floppy drive. Other letters (D:, E:, and so on) might be assigned to the system's hard disk, CD-ROM, and tape drives.

The names for both files and directories obey the following rules:

Rules for Naming Files and Directories

■ Each name may consist of two parts:

1. A required core *filename* consisting of one to eight characters.

2. An optional *extension* consisting of up to three characters.

If the extension is present, it must be separated from the filename by a period (.). For example, in the file JOE.LTR, JOE is the core filename and LTR is the extension.

■ The name must begin with a letter or digit (0, 1, 2, ..., 9).

■ Otherwise, the name may contain any characters *except*:

period (.)	comma (,)	colon (:)
semicolon (;)	quotation mark (")	brackets ([ ])
slash (/)	backslash (\)	equals sign (=)
vertical bar (¦)		

Moreover, *no spaces* are permitted in a name.

■ Lowercase letters are not distinguished from uppercase letters. (So, the names MyFile, myfile, and MyFiLe are considered identical.)

For example, the following are *valid* file or directory names:

    Ch1   Ch1.TXT   Ch-1.{   History.rpt   A   1(#$%).dat

However, the following names are *invalid*:

inventory.dat	(Core filename is too long)
Top Gun	(Spaces are not allowed)
File:1	(Illegal character — colon)
#2-batch.ltr	(Name must begin with letter or digit)

The root directory violates these conventions; its name consists of a single backslash, \. In general, directories are usually given names without extensions, but for files, the extension is often present and used to describe what kind of file it is. For example, you could use DAT for data files, RPT for reports, LTR for letters, and so on; also, EXE, COM, BAT, and PIF are common extensions for program files.

Path Names

When you start an application from within Program Manager, Windows automatically changes the directory to the one specified for that application (see Section 4.2). The specified directory becomes the **current** (or *default*) **directory**, the one in which you are working. The disk drive on which it is located is the **current** (or *default*) **drive**. If you want to refer to any file in the current directory, you need only give its file name. For example, if you save a file, naming it Sam.Ltr, it is automatically placed in the current directory.

If you want to refer to a file that is not in the current directory, you may have to give its full **path name**, a kind of road map that tells DOS how to find the file. The full path name for a file consists of the file's name, preceded by a *directory path* for the directory in which it's located.

A directory path begins with the current drive designation (for example, C:), followed by the names of the root directory (\) and all subdirectories (from larger to smaller) that contain the given directory, and ending with the name of the given directory itself. All subdirectory names must be followed by backslashes. For example, the path for the personal letters directory in the directory tree of Figure 3.1 might be:

C:\WP\Letters\Personal\

Continuing this example, the full path name for a file called Joe.Ltr in the Personal directory would then be:

C:\WP\Letters\Personal\Joe.Ltr

If this file is located on the current drive, then the drive designation may be omitted, so that the path name becomes:

\WP\Letters\Personal\Joe.Ltr

Often, floppy disks do not contain any directories except for the root directory. In such a case, the full path name of the file Joe.Ltr on the diskette in drive A: would be A:\Joe.Ltr. In this situation, it is permissible to leave out the backslash; A:Joe.Ltr would also work.

3.2 An Introduction to File Manager

Windows provides the **File Manager** program to help you organize and manipulate your files and directories. In this section, we will introduce this important utility; its capabilities will be described in more detail in the remainder of the chapter.

Starting File Manager

File Manager

To start File Manager, choose its icon (by, for example, double-clicking on it) from the Main group in Program Manager. When you do, a window similar to the one in Figure 3.2 will open. If your File Manager window looks substantially different than this one, read on; it will soon become clear why.

FIGURE 3.2 A File Manager Window

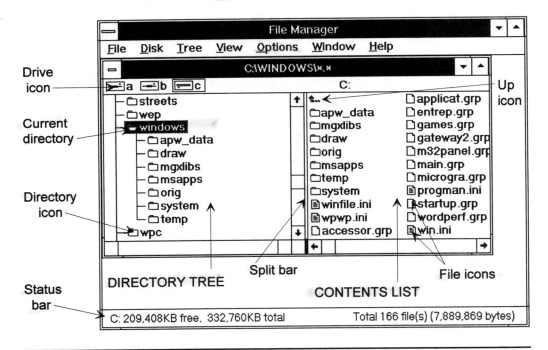

The File Manager window contains all the usual components (title bar, menu bar, etc.) plus a **status bar** at the bottom. The left side of the status bar displays the total number of kilobytes (KB) on the specified drive, as well as the number *free* (unused). The right side displays, for the directory on view, the number of files and the total number of bytes they contain. The status bar can be hidden (if it's currently displayed) or displayed (if it's currently hidden) by choosing Status Bar from the Options menu. A check mark next to this menu item indicates that this option is in effect.

The Directory Window

The document window contained within File Manager (Figure 3.2) is called a **directory window**. Under its title bar is a list of icons representing the disk drives present on your computer system, with the current drive (which is C: in Figure 3.2) enclosed in a rectangle. The remainder of the directory window is divided into two parts or *subwindows*: the **directory tree** on the left and the **contents list** on the right. (The double line separating the two is called the *split bar*.) To make either subwindow active, just click the mouse anywhere within it. When you do, one of the files or directories listed in that subwindow will become highlighted.

Keyboard Alternative

You can use the keyboard to cycle through the three parts of a directory window: drive icons, directory tree, and contents list. To do so, repeatedly press the Tab key or F6 function key. With each tap of the key, a drive icon, directory, or file will be highlighted, indicating which part is active.

The Directory Tree and Contents List Subwindows[*]

Directory Tree

The directory tree subwindow provides a graphical representation of the current disk's directory structure, listing directory names and showing the relationships among them. The directory tree helps you select the directory with which you want to work. It indicates the *current directory* — the one on view in the contents list subwindow ("windows" in Figure 3.2) — by highlighting it and preceding its name by an "open folder" icon, shown below on the left. All the other directory icons are identical; one is shown below on the right.

**Current
Directory Icon**

**Other
Directory Icon**

If you want a listing of the contents of another directory, you must

---

[*]In DOS, you can display the information in the directory tree subwindow by using the TREE command and the information in the contents list subwindow by using the DIR command.

change directories. To select a new directory on the current drive, either:

■ Click on its name or icon in the directory tree. If the new directory's name is not currently visible in the directory tree, you may have to scroll this subwindow; if it's still not visible, you will have to *expand* the directory tree as described in Section 3.3.

or

■ Move to the directory tree subwindow, if necessary, by pressing Tab or F6 once or twice. Then, use the Arrow keys to highlight the new directory.

If the new directory is on another drive, you must first *change drives* to view the directory tree for that drive. To do so, just click on that drive's icon or hold down the Ctrl key and press that drive's letter — for example, Ctrl+A changes to drive A:. (We will have much more to say about selecting drives and directories in Section 3.4.)

Contents List   The contents list subwindow displays the names of the files and directories within the current directory. It is used primarily to help you select files and directories to be copied, moved, renamed, or deleted. Each name in the contents list is preceded by an icon. (At the top of the list, there might also be an icon — the Up icon — without a name.) These icons represent directories or various types of files:

The *Up icon* represents a directory — the parent of the current directory.

This icon represents a subdirectory of the current directory.

This icon represents a *system file*, used by DOS to perform very basic operating system tasks.

This icon represents a *document file* — one that has been *associated* with an application. (See Section 4.3.)

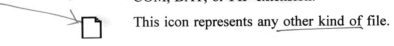

This icon represents a *program file* — it has an EXE, COM, BAT, or PIF extension.

This icon represents any other kind of file.

Opening Additional Directory Windows

As you will see later in this chapter, it is sometimes useful to have more than one directory window open (for example, when copying files from one drive to another). There are several ways to open a new directory window without closing the existing one. Each method produces a different effect:

1. To open a directory window for another disk drive, double-click on that drive's icon. (Remember that clicking *once* on the icon opens the new directory window, but closes the existing one.) To do this from the keyboard, press Tab until a drive icon is highlighted, use the Arrow keys to highlight the desired drive icon, and press Enter.

2. To open a new directory window that lists the contents of a specified directory, hold down the Shift key while double-clicking on that directory's icon. (From the keyboard, use the Arrow keys to highlight the desired directory and press Shift+Enter.)

3. To open a duplicate of the existing window, choose the New Window command from the Window menu.

Figure 3.3 shows two directory windows open within File Manager.

FIGURE 3.3   Two Directory Windows Open in File Manager

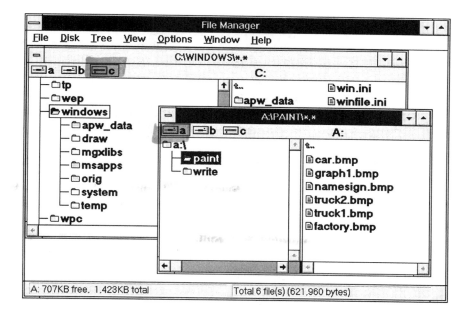

In Figure 3.3, notice that the title bar of each directory window gives the path of the files displayed, making it easy to keep track of several open windows. Since a directory window is a type of document window, it can be minimized, maximized, moved, and resized using the techniques described in Section 1.3.

As usual, only one window can be active at a time, and the active one is indicated by a highlighted title bar. To *switch* to another directory window (to make it the active one), do one of the following:

- Click on any part of it that is visible (or double-click on its icon, if it has been minimized).

- Choose its title from the Window menu.

- Press Ctrl+Tab or Ctrl+F6 to cycle through the open directory windows until the desired one becomes active.

To *close* a directory window, make it active and either double-click on its Control menu box, press Ctrl+F4, or open its Control menu (by clicking on it or by pressing Alt+Hyphen) and choose Close.

Quitting File Manager

You quit (or exit) File Manager in the same manner as any other application; the simplest ways are to double-click on its Control menu box, to press Alt+F4, or to choose Exit from its File menu. When you quit File Manager, any changes you made to its Options menu settings (such as whether or not the status bar is visible) are saved automatically — when you restart File Manager, these changes will remain in effect.

However, the general layout of File Manager (whether it is maximized, which directory windows are open, and so on) is not necessarily saved on exit. To save these kinds of changes, you can either:

- Turn on the Save Settings on Exit item on the Options menu. (A check mark next to this menu item indicates that it's in effect.)

or
- Hold down the Shift key while choosing Exit from the File menu. When you do this, the current layout is saved *without* exiting File Manager.

These procedures should look familiar; they're very similar to those discussed in Chapter 2 for saving Program Manager settings.

Looking Ahead ...

File Manager is used primarily to perform operations on files, directories, and disks. Performing these operations sometimes requires some preparatory work. You may have to first:

- Change the layout of a directory window and the way that information is displayed within its subwindows.

- Select single or multiple files and directories in the directory window.

You can then perform these operations:

- Move, copy, delete, or rename files and directories.

- Format (prepare for use) and copy floppy disks.

In the remainder of this chapter, we will describe how to use File Manager to accomplish these tasks. File Manager can also be used to start applications. We will discuss this topic in Section 4.3.

Hands-On 3.2

Start File Manager (if it's not already running) and try the following exercise. To create a printed copy of your work, see Appendix B.

1. Select (change to) the root directory of the current drive, at the top of the directory tree. Did the contents list change?
2. Insert the Lab Projects diskette in its drive and change to this drive (by clicking on its icon).
3. Minimize the diskette's directory window. Is the original directory window still open? Restore the diskette's window.
4. Open an additional directory window for the hard disk drive. Move or resize the two directory windows, if necessary, so that parts of both are visible.
5. Close the floppy drive window; then try to close the other directory window. Is this possible?
6. Quit File Manager.

3.3   Changing the Look of a Directory Window

File Manager allows you to view the list of files and directories in a directory window in many ways. In this section, we will discuss how this is done.

Some Basics

Increasing the viewing area

To display more information in the directory window, you can maximize File Manager and the directory window itself. You can also change the relative sizes of the directory tree and contents list subwindows in two different ways:

1. Position the mouse pointer over the split bar (Figure 3.2) so that it becomes a double-headed arrow. Then drag the bar left or right to increase the size of one subwindow and decrease the size of the other. (You can also do this by choosing Split from the View menu and using the Arrow keys to move the split bar.)

2. Open the View menu and choose:

    ■ Tree and Directory to view both subwindows.

    ■ Tree Only to view only the directory tree.

    ■ Directory Only to view only the contents list.

    A check mark on the View menu indicates which option is currently in effect.

Still another way of displaying more information (or conversely, of displaying less information that is more easily read) is to select Font from the Options menu. The Font dialog box will open:

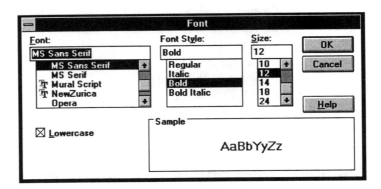

Now, experiment a little. In the <u>S</u>ize list box (click on it or press Alt+S), select a smaller number to view more information or a larger one for greater readability. Choose the OK button to see the effects of your choice on File Manager. (We will discuss fonts and the Font dialog box in much greater detail in Chapter 6.)

Manipulating the Directory Tree

On a large hard disk, there may be dozens of directories spread over many *levels*, each deeper level consisting of the immediate subdirectories of a parent directory. To make it easier to view parts of the directory tree, Windows allows you to expand and collapse directories. When you *expand* a directory, its subdirectories are listed; when you *collapse* a directory, its subdirectories are hidden.

Expandable
directories

We say that a directory is *expandable* if it contains subdirectories. You can indicate which directories listed on the directory tree are expandable by turning on the <u>I</u>ndicate Expandable Branches option on the <u>T</u>ree menu. With Indicate Expandable Branches turned on, a plus sign (+) or minus sign (-) appears within the icon of all expandable directories in the directory tree. (The minus sign indicates that the branch is already expanded; the plus sign that it is not.) For example, in the tree of Figure 3.4a, the following directories are expandable: announce, windows, draw, mgxlibs, and wpc_fig.

FIGURE 3.4   Examples of (Partial) Directory Trees

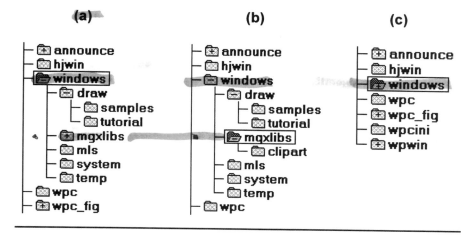

(a)   **(b)**   **(c)**

Expanding and collapsing directories

You can expand and collapse a directory tree using the other options on the Tree menu or (sometimes) with mouse clicks.

■ To display the immediate subdirectories of a given directory, assuming it's marked by a + sign, double-click on it. (Alternatively, you could select it and then press the Plus (+) key or choose Expand One Level from the Tree menu.) For example, in Figure 3.4a, if you expand the "mgxlibs" directory one level, the result is the tree of Figure 3.4b.

■ To collapse the entire chain of subdirectories extending from a given directory marked by a - sign, double-click on that directory. (Alternatively, you could select the given directory and press the Hyphen (-) key or choose Collapse Branch from the Tree menu.) For example, if you collapse the "windows" directory in Figure 3.4b, you get the tree of Figure 3.4c.

■ To display the entire chain of subdirectories of a given directory, assuming it's marked with a + sign, select that directory and either press the Asterisk (*) key or choose Expand Branch from the Tree menu. This operation has the opposite effect of Collapse Branch. For example, if you expand the entire "windows" directory branch of Figure 3.4c, you are returned to the tree of Figure 3.4b.

■ To display *all* directories in a directory tree, press Ctrl+Asterisk or choose Expand All from the Tree menu.

Displaying File Details in the Contents List Subwindow

In Figure 3.2 (on page 82), notice that only names and icons are displayed in the contents list. If you want, you can also display certain other information. To do so, open the View menu and choose either All File Details or Partial Details.

If you choose Partial Details, the following dialog box opens:

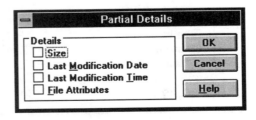

Selecting the appropriate check box (and then choosing OK) places the following information in the contents list on the same line as the file name:

- <u>S</u>ize — the file size in bytes.

- Last <u>M</u>odification Date — the date the file was last modified and saved to disk.

- Last Modification <u>T</u>ime — the time the file was last saved to disk.

File attributes
- <u>F</u>ile Attributes — an abbreviation indicating the type of file:

a	Archive	The file has been modified since last backed up.
h	Hidden	The file is not normally listed.
s	System	An operating system file; not normally listed.
r	Read-only	The file cannot be changed and saved to disk.

If you select all four check boxes, the contents list subwindow will display all the information as shown in Figure 3.5.

FIGURE 3.5   Contents List Displaying All File Details

qext.sys	5853	11/13/91	2:42:02am	a
resume	1707	2/24/93	5:53:40pm	a
share.exe	10912	4/9/91	5:00:00am	a
ste-ca.bat	26	3/13/93	4:13:30pm	a
vgatest.exe	60508	8/24/89	1:40:50pm	a
vsetup.exe	39137	8/24/89	1:39:42pm	a
wina20.386	9349	3/10/93	6:00:00am	r
wt.bat	24	5/18/90	4:21:30pm	a

Choosing <u>A</u>ll File Details from the <u>V</u>iew menu has the same effect as choosing <u>P</u>artial Details and then selecting all four check boxes. Choosing <u>N</u>ame from the <u>V</u>iew menu displays only the names of the files in the contents list; it hides the file details.

Restricting and Sorting the Contents of the Contents List[*]

By file type   Since a single directory may contain hundreds of files, the View menu provides various ways of organizing the contents list so that it can be more easily used. Choosing By File Type lets you display only selected types of files and/or directories in this subwindow. When you choose this item, the By File Type dialog box opens:

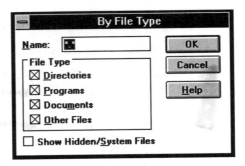

Now, select the check boxes of the file and/or directory types that you want displayed. For example, if you're interested in working with the data files you've created, you would clear the Directories and Programs check boxes and select Documents and Other Files.

Wildcards   Use the Name text box together with *wildcards* to further restrict the files to be displayed. **Wildcards** are symbols that represent one or more characters of any kind. As you will see, they are used frequently by Windows in situations (like this one) that involve specifying groups of files. There are two wildcards:

   *   represents any combination of any number of characters.

   ?   represents any single character.

For example, in the current directory:

.	represents all files, with or without an extension;
*.Ltr	represents all files with extension Ltr;
S*	represents all files with names starting with S and having no extension;
WP.???	represents all files with core filename WP and any three-character extension;

---

[*]This material provides the Windows equivalent of using the DOS DIR command with *wildcards* to restrict the types of files listed or with the /o *switch* to sort the list of files.

?D.*   represents all files beginning with any valid character followed by D and any extension.

After making your selections in the By File Type dialog box, choose the OK button and the contents list of the active directory window will reflect the changes.

Sorting the contents list

The Yiew menu also allows you to sort the contents list in one of several specified orders. You can choose:

- Sort by Name to display the files in alphabetical order by file name.

- Sort by Type to display the files in alphabetical order by extension.

- Sort by Size to display the files in order of increasing file size.

- Sort by Date to display the files by last modification date; most recently modified files are listed first.

The Sort by Date option is more useful than it might first appear. As you may know, it is desirable to "back up" files, just in case your hard disk becomes damaged. A common back up strategy is to copy all the data files you have modified or created during the current session to a floppy disk before quitting Windows. To do this quickly, at the end of your session start File Manager and select the directory in which you've been working. Now, choose Sort by Date from the Yiew menu and your new files will all appear at the top of the contents list. We will show you how to copy these files to a floppy disk in Section 3.5.

Hands-On 3.3

Start File Manager (if it's not already running) and try the following exercise. To create a printed copy of your work, see Appendix B.

1. Change to the WINDOWS directory.
2. Arrange the directory window so that only the contents list is visible (by selecting the appropriate option from the Yiew menu).
3. Choose All File Details from the Yiew menu and resize the directory window, if necessary, so that all details are visible. Which file or directory is at the top of the window?
4. Sort the contents list by date. Which file or directory is at the top of the contents list now?
5. List only those files with the extension TXT. How many are there?
6. Restore the directory window to the condition in which you found it.

3.4 Selecting Drives, Directories, and Files

As you know, the primary purpose of File Manager is to provide you with a user-friendly environment in which you can work with your files. The first step in the process, once you have started File Manager and arranged its layout to your liking, is to *select* the drives, directories, and files in which you are interested.

Selecting a Disk Drive[*]

The drives available to your computer are represented by icons at the top of every directory window. The current drive's icon is enclosed in a rectangle. To select another drive to be the current one — to *change drives* — perform one of the following actions:

- Click on its icon. (This is the easiest way.)

- Hold down the Ctrl key and press the letter representing the desired drive. For example, to select the A: drive, press Ctrl+A.

- Choose Select Drive from the Disk menu, select the desired drive in the resulting dialog box, and choose OK.

- Repeatedly press Tab or F6 to move to the drive icon list. Then, use the Arrow keys to highlight the desired drive, and press Spacebar.

If File Manager is running when you save a file within another application, information about that file will usually be updated automatically upon returning to File Manager. However, if the current drive is a floppy drive and you change disks, the contents of the original diskette will still be displayed in the directory window. To get a listing for the new disk, select that drive again (even if it is currently selected). As an alternative, you could choose Refresh from the Window menu, or just press the F5 function key.

---

[*]In DOS, we refer to this as *changing drives*; it is done by typing the drive designation (for example, A:) at the DOS prompt and pressing the Enter key.

Selecting a Single File or Directory

The simplest way to select a single file or directory from the directory tree or contents list is to click on it. Once selected, its name and icon become highlighted. As an alternative, select the appropriate subwindow (by pressing Tab once or twice) and use the Arrow keys to highlight it.

When you select a directory from the directory tree, it becomes the current directory and its contents are listed in the contents list. We say that you have *changed* directories. If, on the other hand, you select a directory from the contents list, the current directory remains unchanged. To change to a directory in this subwindow, either double-click on it or select it and press Enter. Double-clicking on the Up icon (or selecting it and pressing Enter) changes to the parent of the current directory.

Moving around in a subwindow

If necessary, you can scroll both the directory tree and contents list subwindows by using the appropriate scroll bar, or with the help of the Arrow keys. As the following table shows, other keys can be useful here, even if you have a mouse.

Key	Selects ...
Home	First entry in subwindow
End	Last entry in subwindow
Page Up/Page Down	First/last entry one screen up/down
A letter or number	Next entry beginning with that character

Selecting Multiple Files and Directories

To save time when performing operations on files and directories, it is often useful to work with several of them at once. Selecting multiple files or directories (multiple *items*) can only be done from the contents list subwindow, but it can be done in several ways:

- If there are only a few items to be selected, click on the first item; then hold down the Ctrl key while clicking on the others.

- If the items to be selected are in consecutive order, or *in sequence*

(Figure 3.6a), click on the first item, then hold down the Shift key and click on the last. Now, release Shift.

■ If there are many items to be selected and they're not in sequence (Figure 3.6b), you can combine the two techniques just described. If some of the items are in sequence, click on the first of these, hold down Shift and click on the last. Now, select other sequences by holding down Ctrl, clicking on the first item in it, pressing and holding down Shift (without releasing Ctrl), and clicking on the last item. You can now release both keys. If there are individual items to be added to those already selected, just hold down Ctrl while clicking on them.

FIGURE 3.6   Selecting Files

(a)   In sequence   **(b)   Not in sequence**

ssmarque.scr	thatch.bmp		ssmarque.scr	thatch.bmp
ssmyst.scr	winfile.exe		ssmyst.scr	winfile.exe
ssstars.scr	winfile.hlp		ssstars.scr	winfile.hlp
sysini.wri	winhelp.exe		sysini.wri	winhelp.exe
tada.wav	winhelp.hlp		tada.wav	winhelp.hlp
tartan.bmp	winini.wri		tartan.bmp	winini.wri
taskman.exe	winlogo.bmp		taskman.exe	winlogo.bmp
terminal.exe	winmine.exe		terminal.exe	winmine.exe
terminal.hlp	winmine.hlp		terminal.hlp	winmine.hlp

If some items have been selected and you want to select more, don't forget to hold down the Ctrl key while you click. Otherwise, the original items will be deselected, and you'll have to start all over again.

If you want to deselect specific items, hold down Ctrl and click on them again. Here, too, don't forget to hold down Ctrl. Otherwise, all items *except* the one you've clicked on will be deselected!

Keyboard Alternatives

To use the keyboard to select multiple items:

■ If the items are in sequence, use the Arrow keys to highlight the first item. Then, hold down the Shift key as you use the Arrow keys to move the highlight bar to the last item. Now release the Shift key.

■ If the items are not in sequence, use the Arrow keys to highlight the first item to be selected. Then, press Shift+F8. (The *selection cursor*, a blinking rectangle, appears around this item in the contents list.) Now, using the Arrow keys to move the selection cursor, press the Spacebar whenever you want to select an item. When you're done, press Shift+F8 again.

The Select Files Command

Sometimes the easiest way to select a large number of files or directories in the contents list is to use the Select Files command. To do so, choose Select Files from the File menu. The following dialog box will appear:

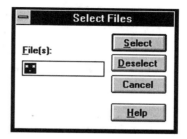

Now, you can select a single directory or file by typing its name in the File(s) text box or you can select multiple items by using wildcards. Then choose Select and Close. The file named, or all files that fit the specified wildcard pattern (see Section 3.3), are selected. Here are some examples:

.	selects all files and directories in the contents list;
*.Ltr	selects all items with an Ltr extension;
S?.*	selects all items beginning with S which have a core filename that is two characters long.

Searching for a File or Directory

With hundreds, or even thousands, of files on a disk, it's understandable if you should have trouble locating one of them. If you could pin it down to one or two directories, scanning their contents lists would probably find it, but this isn't always possible.

Fortunately, Windows supplies the Search command to help you find "lost" files or directories. If you know the name of the file, locating it with the help of this command will be easy. Even if you just remember *something* about the errant file's name — its extension or the characters it begins with — you might be able to find it. On the other hand, if you've completely forgotten what it's called, you may have to use other software, capable of searching for key words or phrases in a file, to locate the lost file.

To use the Search command:

1. Choose Search from the File menu. The following dialog box is displayed:

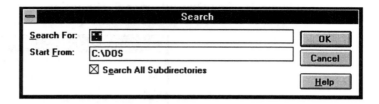

2. Type the name of the file or directory to be located in the Search For text box. If you're not sure of its name, use wildcards. For example, if you know that its extension is LTR, type *.LTR; if you know it begins with the letter S, type S*.*.

3. In the Start From text box, type the path name of the directory in which you believe the file is located. (The current directory appears there by default.) Windows is capable of searching *all* subdirectories of the specified one, so you don't have to be too precise. If you're really at a loss, type a backslash (\) here, denoting the root directory. Of course, the more precise you can be about the location of the lost file, the quicker the search will be.

4. If you do not want all subdirectories of the Start From directory searched, clear the Search All Subdirectories check box.

5. Choose the OK button to begin the search. Choose Cancel to cancel it.

After a while the Search Results window is displayed. For example, in searching the C:\DOS directory and all its subdirectories for *.TXT, we obtain the following results:

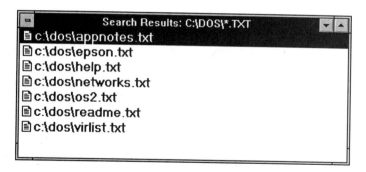

Files and directories listed in a Search Results window can be moved, copied, deleted, or renamed, as described in the next section. To close the Search Results window, double-click on its Control menu box or press Ctrl+F4.

Hands-On

3.4

Start File Manager (if it's not already running) and try the following exercise. To create a printed copy of your work, see Appendix B.

1. Change to the WINDOWS directory.
2. In the contents list, select the first ten files, skip a file, and then select the next five files.
3. Deselect the last file selected; then deselect all files except for the first.
4. Search (only) the WINDOWS directory for all files that have extension BMP. How many are there?
5. Now search the WINDOWS directory and all its subdirectories for files with extension BMP. How many are there? Is the first Search Results window still open?
6. Close all open Search Results windows.

3.5 Operations on Files and Directories

File Manager allows you to perform four basic operations on files and directories: copy, move, rename, and delete. In this section, we will describe how each of these tasks is accomplished.

Moving Files and Directories[*]

When you **move** a file, it is deleted from its original location and placed in a new location. When you *move a directory*, the directory and all its contents (files and subdirectories alike) are deleted from their original location and moved to the new one.

You can move a file or directory from one directory (the *source*) to another (the *destination*) in two basic ways:

1, By using the mouse to **drag-and-drop** it onto an icon representing the destination.

2. By choosing the Move operation from the File menu.

Although both techniques are relatively easy to carry out, most people prefer the first because it is more intuitive and can be done without using the keyboard.

Drag-and-Drop Moving   To move files or directories (*items*) using the drag-and-drop method sometimes takes a little preparation, but the actual operation is very simple. It involves the following steps:

1. Select the items to be moved, as described in Section 3.4.

2. Arrange the File Manager window so that both the source and destination are visible. (If multiple items have been selected, only one of them need be visible.) This may necessitate scrolling the directory tree containing the destination or opening a new directory window containing the destination. It also may be useful to resize or tile open directory windows.

3. Position the mouse pointer over any selected item, hold down the Shift key and drag the pointer to the destination. As you do, the item's icon will seem to move across the screen together with the mouse pointer (see Figure 3.7). Moreover, as the pointer approaches the destination, a rectangular box will appear around this directory to let you know that you're "on target." Now, release the mouse button and then the Shift key.

Confirmation
messages   This completes the heart of the drag-and-drop *move* procedure, but before you go on to other matters, you may have to deal with one or two

---

[*]To move files using DOS takes two steps: one uses the COPY or XCOPY command to copy the files to the new location; then, the DEL or ERASE command to delete them from the original location.

FIGURE 3.7   Moving a File from One Location to Another

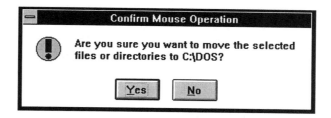

confirmation messages. The first of these messages may look like this:

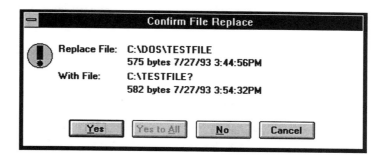

If this message accurately describes what you are trying to do, choose Yes. Otherwise, choose No and the operation will be cancelled. (If you don't see this confirmation message after a drag-and-drop operation, it has been turned off, as described later in this section.)

The second confirmation message (if there is one) will look like this:

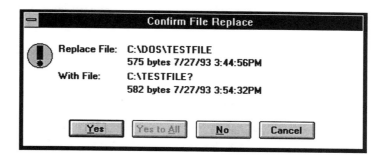

This message appears if a file at the destination has the same name as one of the files being moved. Choose Yes if you want the source file to replace the destination file in this directory, *deleting the destination file in the process*; choose No otherwise. Choose Yes to All if you want *all* source files with the same names as destination files to replace the latter. Choosing the Cancel button aborts the move operation.

When moving items between directories *on the same drive*, you do not have to hold down the Shift key while performing the drag-and-drop. However, if you fail to hold down the Shift key while dragging an item *between drives*, it will be *copied*, not moved, from source to destination (see "Copying Files and Directories" later in this section).

You can move a file by dragging-and-dropping it, while holding down Shift, onto a disk drive icon. The file will be moved to the current directory on that disk; if there is no current directory, it will be placed in the root directory. This is a convenient way of moving files to a floppy disk.

The Move Command   This alternative to drag-and-drop moving works well if you know the path name of the destination and don't want to go to the trouble of making its icon visible on the screen. To use this method:

1. Select the files to be moved.

2. Choose Move from the File menu or just press the F7 function key. The following dialog box will appear:

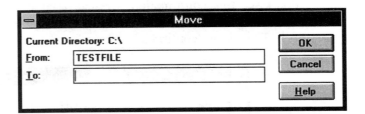

3. Type the destination directory's path in the To text box and choose OK (or press Enter). For example, to move TESTFILE to the DOS subdirectory of C:\, type either c:\dos or just dos (since the current directory is C:\), and press Enter.

As with the drag-and-drop method, you might now have to deal with the Confirm File Replace dialog box. The Confirm Mouse Operation message will not appear if you use this technique.

Copying Files and Directories*

When you **copy** a file (or directory) from one location to another, a duplicate of that file (or that directory and all its contents) is placed in the new location, but it is not deleted from the original. The procedures for copying an item are very similar to those for moving it which were discussed earlier in this section. Here, too, there are two basic techniques: using drag-and-drop or issuing the Copy command.

Drag-and-Drop Copying
The drag-and-drop method for copying items is almost identical to the corresponding method for moving them. To copy items from one location (the *source*) to another (the *destination*):

1. Select the items to be copied.

2. Arrange the File Manager window so that both the source and destination are visible. (If multiple items have been selected, only one of them need be visible.)

3. Position the mouse pointer over any selected item, hold down the Ctrl key (*not* the Shift key) and drag the pointer to the destination. As you do so, the item's icon will seem to move across the screen together with the mouse pointer. Now, release the mouse button and then the Ctrl key.

As with the move procedure, you may now be confronted with one or two confirmation messages before the process is complete. Deal with these in the same manner as described earlier.

When copying items between directories *on different drives*, you do not have to hold down the Ctrl key while performing the drag-and-drop. However, if you fail to hold down the Ctrl key while dragging an item from one location to another *on the same drive*, it will be moved, not

---

*Copying a file with DOS makes use of the COPY or XCOPY command; copying a directory requires the use of XCOPY.

copied, from source to destination

You can copy a file by dragging-and-dropping it (without holding down Ctrl) onto a disk drive icon. It will be copied to the current directory of that disk; if there is no current directory, it will be copied to the root directory. This is a convenient way of copying files to a floppy disk.

diff drive

The Copy Command   The alternative to drag-and-drop copying follows the same steps as its *move* counterpart; just choose the Copy command instead of the Move command from the File menu. To be more specific:

1. Select the files to be copied.

2. Choose Copy from the File menu or just press the F8 function key.

3. When the dialog box appears, type the path name of the destination directory in the To list box and choose OK (or press Enter).

If the Confirm File Replace dialog box appears, deal with it exactly as described earlier in the *move* procedure.

Deleting a File or Directory[*]

When you **delete** a file, its contents are erased from disk. When you delete a directory, the contents of all files contained within it and all its subdirectories are erased, in addition to the directories themselves. Consequently, if not used properly, the deletion operation can wipe out megabytes of data (and perhaps countless hours of work) in a matter of seconds. Needless to say, this is an operation that must be treated with respect.

The delete procedure is (perhaps, unfortunately) very easy to carry out. To delete items from a disk:

1. Select the items to be deleted.

2. Press the Del (Delete) key or choose Delete from the File menu, and the Delete dialog box will be displayed:

---

[*]This material provides the Windows equivalent of erasing files with the DOS DEL command and removing directories with the DOS RD command. Using DOS, you cannot remove a directory if it's not empty; Windows does not provide this particular protection against accidental deletion.

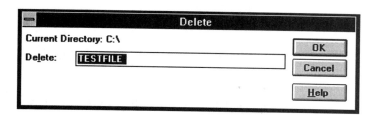

3. If you do not want to delete the files or directories listed in the text box, choose Cancel. Otherwise, choose OK.

4. If you choose OK in step 3, another dialog box might appear:

This is Windows' way of giving you a second chance to cancel the delete operation. Choose Cancel to abort the entire delete procedure or No to prevent deletion of the specified item. (If only one item has been selected, Cancel and No have the same effect.) Choose Yes to allow deletion of the item specified and choose Yes to All to allow deletion of all items.

Be very careful when deleting files and, especially, directories. After you've been using Windows for a while, you will probably develop a tendency to not read dialog boxes very carefully — after all, you've read them before and know what they say. This is a dangerous practice when deleting files. Force yourself to read the names and current directory of the items being deleted and make sure you really want to delete them.

If you do accidentally delete a file or directory, contact your instructor or lab coordinator immediately. DOS does not actually delete the *contents* of a file when that command is given, so it may be possible to recover the "lost" data. However, don't delay! DOS will eventually write new information over the original data, and it will be lost forever.

Renaming a File or Directory[*]

To **rename** (change the name of) a file or directory:

1. Select that file or directory.

2. Choose Rename from the File menu. The Rename dialog box will be displayed:

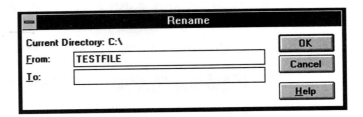

3. Type the new name for the file or directory in the To text box and choose OK (or press Enter).

If the name you choose is the same as one in the current directory, a message similar to the following one will be displayed:

Choose OK (or press Enter) to clear this message from the screen, and the rename operation will be cancelled. If you still want to give the selected file the name of an existing file, you will have to first rename or delete the existing file.

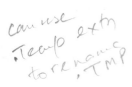

---

[*]Unlike DOS, Windows makes renaming a directory as easy as renaming a file. To rename a file in DOS, one uses the REN command; to rename a directory, one must "copy" it to the new name (using XCOPY) and then delete the original (using RD).

Creating a Directory*

All the operations we've discussed so far apply to both files and directories. The "creation" operation is an exception — directories may be created within File Manager, but files must be created within an application. To create a new directory:

eg wp, lotus, data .

1. Choose the Create Directory command from the File menu. The following dialog box will be displayed:

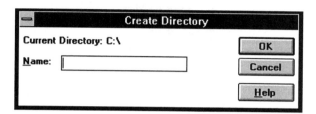

2. Type the path name for the new directory in the Name text box and press Enter or choose the OK button. For example, if you want to create a new directory called DOG within the C:\ directory, type c:\dog and press Enter. Or, since the directory you want to create is a subdirectory of the current one, all you need to type in the text box is dog.

If a directory already exists with the same path name you have just specified, the following message will be displayed:

Clear the message (which cancels the *create directory* operation) by choosing OK or pressing Enter.

---

*This material provides the Windows equivalent of the DOS MD command.

Turning Off Confirmation Messages

Windows tries to protect you from yourself. If you are about to do something which might be a big mistake (such as deleting a file), a message is normally displayed asking if you really mean it. To turn off some of these messages, choose Confirmation from the Options menu. The following dialog box will be displayed:

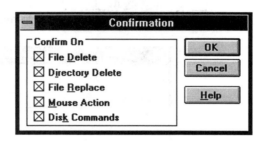

Selecting the check box:

- File Delete displays the Confirm File Delete dialog box (shown earlier in this section) when you attempt to delete a file.

- Directory Delete displays the Confirm Directory Delete dialog box when you attempt to delete a directory.

- File Replace displays the Confirm File Replace dialog box (shown earlier in this section) when you attempt to move or copy a file into a directory that already contains an item with that name.

- Mouse Action displays the Confirm Mouse Operation dialog box (shown earlier in this section) when you attempt to move or copy items using the drag-and-drop technique.

- Disk Commands displays a warning message before formatting or copying a floppy disk (see Section 3.6).

After you have selected or cleared the desired check boxes in the Confirmation dialog box, choose the OK button to put the changes into effect.

 You may find confirmation messages annoying and they may slow down your work slightly, but remember that they are there for your own good. Think twice (or count to ten) before turning off any of these messages.

Hands-On **3.5**

Start File Manager (if it's not already running) and try the following exercise. To create a printed copy of your work, see Appendix B.

1. Insert the Lab Projects diskette in its drive.
2. Copy the TESTFILE file from the root directory of this disk to the WINDOWS directory of your hard disk.
3. Rename this file (the one on the hard disk) TEST.FIL.
4. Create a subdirectory of WINDOWS called DOG.
5. Move TEST.FIL to the DOG subdirectory.
6. Delete TEST.FIL and DOG. Can this be done in one step by just deleting DOG?
7. Remove the Lab Projects disk from its drive.

3.6 Dealing with Diskettes

All of the procedures described in the previous section apply to files or directories on floppy disks (diskettes), as well as on hard disks. Two additional operations are useful with floppies: formatting and copying disks. In this section, we will discuss these procedures.

Formatting a Diskette*

Before information can be stored on a disk, the disk must be **formatted**. This process prepares the disk for use, dividing it into *sectors* and creating a *file allocation table* for it. Hard disks are usually formatted by the manufacturer or dealer; most floppy disks must be formatted by the user.

The format procedure erases all information on the disk! So, never format a disk unless you are sure that there is nothing stored on it, or (if there is information on the disk) that you no longer need its contents. Unless the disk is fresh out of the box, it's wise to check its contents. To do so, insert it in its drive, start File Manager, and select the appropriate drive icon. If the contents list indicates "No files found," then the disk is already formatted; if the message at the top of the next page is displayed, then the disk does not contain any useful information, but must be formatted.

---

*The operations discussed here are accomplished in DOS by using the FORMAT command.

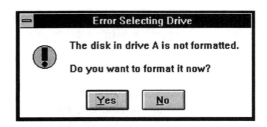

If you format a disk and then realize you've made a mistake — it did contain some information you need — immediately contact your instructor or lab coordinator. It *might* be possible to recover the desired files if you have not yet used the newly-formatted diskette.

To format a floppy disk:

1. Insert it in its drive.

2. Choose the Format Disk command from the Disk menu. The following dialog box will be displayed:

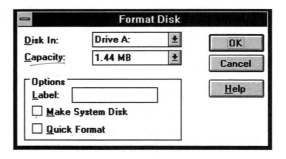

3. In the Disk In box, select the appropriate drive. (If your computer has one floppy drive, it is designated Drive A:; if there is more than one floppy drive, A: is usually on top or on the left.)

4. In the Capacity box:

   ■ Select 1.44 MB for *high density* 3½-inch disks; select 1.2 MB for *high density* 5¼-inch disks. (High density diskettes usually have an "HD" designation on the label.)

   ■ Select 720 K for *low density* 3½-inch disks; select 360 K for *low density* 5¼-inch disks. (Low density diskettes usually have a "DD" designation on the label.)

5. In the Options area of the Format Disk dialog box:

    ■ In the Label text box, you can type an electronic label (up to eleven characters long) for your disk. The label is optional, so you don't have to fill in this box. If there is a label, it appears in the directory window when the disk's contents are displayed.

    ■ Select the Make System Disk check box if you want to have the computer copy certain DOS system files to this diskette, making it a **system disk**. If a system, or *bootable*, diskette is in Drive A: when the machine is turned on, the computer will access the information on this diskette, instead of the hard disk, to start DOS. The disadvantage of creating a system disk is that it contains less room for data and programs than a non-system disk.

    ■ Select the Quick Format check box if you are formatting a diskette that has, at any time in the past, already been formatted. (You might want to reformat a disk to "wipe it clean" before using it to store new information.) Quick Format speeds up the format process considerably.

6. Choose the OK button. The Confirm Format Disk dialog box will normally be displayed:

Make sure that the disk you want to format is in the specified drive. If you have any doubt that this disk is free of useful information, now is the time to back out; in this case, choose No.

If you choose Yes in step 6, the formatting process begins and the Formatting Disk dialog box is displayed. After the process is complete, the Format Complete dialog box appears and you are asked whether or not you want to format another diskette. Choose Yes or No, as you wish.

You can label a disk or change an existing label after that disk has been formatted, if so desired. To do so, insert the diskette in its drive, select that drive in File Manager, and choose L̲abel Disk form the D̲isk menu. Then, type the new label in the resulting dialog box and choose OK.

Moreover, you can sometimes create a system (bootable) disk after it has been formatted. To do so, insert the diskette in its drive and choose M̲ake System Disk from File Manager's D̲isk menu. (If your computer has more than one drive, a dialog box will appear at this point asking you to specify the proper drive.) Some formatted diskettes cannot be made bootable without formatting them again. If this is the case, Windows will display a message to this effect.

Copying an Entire Diskette[*]

If your computer has two floppy disk drives, you can use the *copy* command described in the previous section to copy all files from one diskette to another. A complete description of this procedure is left as an exercise (see Exercise 43 at the end of this chapter).

Windows provides an easier way to copy the entire contents of one diskette to another *of the same size and capacity,* even if you have only one floppy drive on your system. Here's how it works:

1. Insert the diskette to be copied (the *source* disk) into its drive. If your computer has a second floppy drive *of the same type*, insert a diskette into it as well. The second diskette is the *destination* disk; it need not be formatted.

2. Choose C̲opy Disk from the D̲isk menu.

3. If your computer has two floppy disk drives, the following dialog box is displayed:

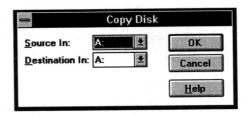

Select the source and destination drives. If the two drives are of

---

*One would do this in DOS by using the DISKCOPY command.

different types, the source and destination must be the same. (If your computer has one floppy disk drive, this dialog box will not appear.)

4. The Confirm Copy Disk dialog box is now displayed.

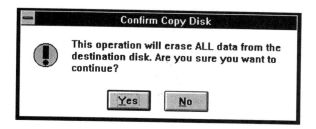

As you can see, the Copy Disk procedure erases all information on the destination diskette (formatting it, if necessary), so choose No to abort the procedure if you're not sure what's on this disk. Choose Yes to continue the process.

5. If you have two floppy drives of the same type, the copying is now done automatically. If you are copying from a drive onto itself, you must follow the on-screen instructions for changing disks before the process is complete.

Chapter Summary

Key Terms

Contents list [page 83]	Copy a file [103]
Current directory [80]	Current drive [80]
Delete a file [104]	Directory [78]
Directory tree [83]	Directory window [83]
Drag-and-drop [100]	File [78]
File Manager [81]	Format a disk [109]
Move a file [100]	Parent directory [78]
Path name [81]	Rename a file [106]
Root directory [78]	Status bar [82]
Subdirectory [78]	System disk [111]
Wildcard [92]	

Topics
Covered

Names for Files and Directories:

Have a required core filename of one to eight characters and an optional extension of up to three characters, separated from the core by a period.

Begin with a letter or digit.

Do not contain spaces or any of the following characters:

.   ,   :   ;   "   [   ]   /   \   =   ¦

Basic File Manager Operations

Starting File Manager	Choose the File Manager icon from the Main group.
Changing drives	Click on the drive icon; or hold down Ctrl while typing the drive letter.
Changing directories	In the directory tree, click on the directory or select it with the Arrow keys; in the contents list, double-click on the directory or select it and press Enter.
Opening an additional directory window	Double-click on the drive icon; or hold down Shift while double-clicking on the directory; or choose New Window from the Window menu.
Changing the font	Choose Font from the Options menu.
Searching for a file	Choose Search from the File menu.
Quitting File Manager	Double-click on the Control menu box; or press Alt+F4; or choose Exit from the File menu.

Changing the Information Displayed in a Directory Window

Displaying the directory tree and/or contents list	On the View menu, choose Tree and Directory, Tree Only, or Directory Only.
Expanding/collapsing a directory	Double-click on the directory; or choose a command from the Tree menu.
Displaying file details	Choose Partial Details or All File Details from the View menu; or choose Name from the View menu to hide details.
Sorting the contents list	Choose the appropriate sort option from the View menu.

Selecting Files and Directories in the Contents List

A single file	Click on it.
Files in sequence	Click on the first and hold down Shift while clicking on the last.
Additional files	Hold down Ctrl while clicking.
Selecting files by type	Choose Select Files from the File menu.

Operations on Files, Directories, and Diskettes

Move selected files or directories	Hold down Shift while dragging-and-dropping; or choose Move from the File menu; or press F7.
Copy selected files or directories	Hold down Ctrl while dragging-and-dropping; or choose Copy from the File menu; or press F8.
Delete selected files or directories	Press the Del key or select Delete from the File menu.
Rename selected files or directories	Choose Rename from the File menu.
Create a directory	Choose Create Directory from the File menu.
Format disk/copy disk/ label disk/make system disk	Choose the appropriate command from the Disk menu.

Chapter Exercises

Short Answer Complete each statement in Exercises 1 through 13.

1. If one directory is contained within another, the first is called a _____ of the second.

2. File names may contain a maximum of _____ characters (not counting the period that separates the core from the extension).

3. The full path name for a file is C:\Windows\Draw\Map.Dwg. The file's name is _____ and it is stored in the _____ directory.

4. To open a directory window for drive A: without closing the existing one for drive C:, _____ on the drive A: icon.

5. To view both directory tree and contents list (if one is not currently displayed) choose _____ from the <u>V</u>iew menu.

6. The commands to expand or collapse a directory are on File Manager's _____ menu.

7. The commands to display or hide file details are on File Manager's _____ menu.

8. The commands to sort the contents list are on File Manager's _____ menu.

9. To select (from the contents list) several files that are not in sequence, hold down the _____ key while you click on them.

10. To search a directory for all files with the extension BMP, use the wildcard pattern _____ .

11. To move a file from one drive to another, while dragging the file to its destination, hold down the _____ key.

12. To rename a file, choose the Re<u>n</u>ame command from File Manager's _____ menu.

13. Before you can store information on a disk, that disk must be _____ .

Determine whether each of the statements in Exercises 14 through 25 is true or false.

14. All other directories on a disk are subdirectories of the root directory.

15. The name of a directory is not allowed to have an extension.

16. JOHN DOE is a valid file name.

17. When the C:\ directory is selected, the contents list displays the names of all files on the C: drive.

18. The wildcard pattern ?.? represents all files in the current directory.

19. When you sort the contents list by date, the oldest files appear at the top of the list.

20. To select (from the contents list) several files that are in sequence, click on the first, hold down the Shift key, and click on the last.

21. After several files (in the contents list) have been selected, to deselect one of them, click on it while holding down the Shift key.

22. To search a disk for a given file, choose Searc<u>h</u> from the <u>F</u>ile menu.

23. To copy a file on drive C: to the root directory of the disk in drive A:, just drag it onto the icon for drive A:.

24. To format a 3½-inch diskette labelled MF2HD, select a capacity of 1.44 MB in the Format Disk dialog box.

25. It is not possible to use the Copy Disk command to copy the contents of a 3½-inch diskette onto a 5¼-inch diskette.

In Exercises 26 through 35, choose the correct answer.

26. To change to the A: drive without opening a new directory window:

    a. Click on the A: drive icon.
    b. Double-click on the A: drive icon.
    c. Select the A: drive icon and press the Spacebar.
    d. Perform any of the above actions.

27. To arrange the directory window so that only the contents list is displayed:

    a. Choose Tr<u>e</u>e Only from the <u>V</u>iew menu.
    b. Choose Directory <u>O</u>nly from the <u>V</u>iew menu.
    c. Choose <u>C</u>ontents List Only from the <u>V</u>iew menu.
    d. Double-click anywhere on the contents list.

28. To expand an entire branch, select the directory to be expanded and:

    a. Click on it.
    b. Double-click on it.
    c. Choose Expand <u>B</u>ranch from the <u>T</u>ree menu.
    d. Perform any of the above actions.

29. To arrange the contents list in alphabetical order by extension:

    a. Sort it by Name.
    b. Sort it by Size.
    c. Sort it by Type.
    d. Sort it by Date.

30. The wildcard pattern *.? represents all files with:

    a. Any core filename and any extension.
    b. Any core filename and any one-character extension.
    c. Any one-character core filename and any extension.
    d. None of the above is correct.

31. After selecting several files, to deselect one of them:

    a. Click on it.
    b. Double-click on it.
    c. Hold down Ctrl while clicking on it.
    d. Hold down Shift while clicking on it.

32. To copy a file from the A: drive to the current directory on the C: drive:

    a. Drag its file name onto the C: drive icon.
    b. Hold down Shift while dragging its file name onto the C: drive icon.
    c. Select the file and choose <u>M</u>ove from the <u>F</u>ile menu.
    d. Perform any of the above actions.

33. When you delete a directory in Windows:

    a. It cannot be the current directory.
    b. All files in it are deleted when the directory is deleted.
    c. All files in it must be deleted before the directory is deleted.
    d. All its subdirectories must be deleted before the directory is deleted.

34. A 3½-inch disk labeled "MF2HD" holds:

    a. 320 KB of information.
    b. 720 KB of information.
    c. 1.2 MB of information.
    d. 1.44 MB of information.

35. To quit (exit) File Manager:

    a. Press Shift+F4.
    b. Double-click on its Control menu box.
    c. Choose <u>Q</u>uit from its Control menu.
    d. Perform any of the above actions.

Hands-On In Exercises 36 through 40, start up Windows and File Manager, if necessary, and maximize the File Manager window. To create a printed copy of your work, see Appendix B.

36. a. Change to the root directory on drive C: (C:\) and close any other open directory windows.

    b. Insert the Lab Projects diskette into its drive and open a directory window for it without closing the existing one (by double-clicking on the appropriate drive icon). What is the title of the new directory window?

c. Maximize the C:\ window.

d. Switch to the floppy drive window. What keystrokes or mouse actions did you use to accomplish this?

e. Display the directory tree for the C:\ window and the contents list for the floppy drive window side-by-side on the screen (by using the <u>V</u>iew menu and then moving and resizing the two directory windows). How does Windows make it clear that this contents list does not "belong to" this directory tree?

f. Close the floppy drive window, remove the diskette from its drive, and return the C:\ window to its original form.

g. Try to close the C:\ directory window. Which, if any, techniques work?

37. a. Change to the root directory on drive C: (C:\) and display its directory tree if it's currently hidden.

b. Collapse the entire branch for this directory so that C:\ is the only directory listed.

c. Now, expand one level. How many subdirectories of C:\ are listed?

d. Using the Indicate Expandable Branches command, determine how many of the subdirectories of step (c) are expandable.

e. Display the entire directory tree for the C: drive. Can you do this in one step? How many directories are there on drive C:?

38. a. Change to the WINDOWS directory (probably on drive C:).

b. Arrange the directory window so that the contents list, but not the directory tree, is displayed.

c. In the contents list, display only the icon, name, and size of each file. In what order are the files listed?

d. Sort the files by file size. Are the smallest or the largest files at the top of the list?

e. Select the five largest files together with all files with extension TXT. How many files are selected?

f. By using the By File <u>T</u>ype command, restrict the contents list to those files with extension TXT. Are they still highlighted?

g. Search the WINDOWS directory and all its subdirectories for files with the extension TXT. Are the same files listed in the Search Results window and in the contents list of part (f)?

h. Return the directory window to its original form.

39. a. Insert the Lab Projects diskette in its drive and change to this drive. (We will assume it's A:; if it's not, replace all references to "A:" in this exercise with "B:".)

    b. Arrange the directory window so that both directory tree and contents list are displayed.

    c. Create two subdirectories of A:\; name them Subdir-1 and Subdir-2. Do they show up on the directory tree immediately or do you have to update the directory window first?

    d. Copy all files in A:\ to A:\Subdir-1.

    e. In the Subdir-1 directory, rename TESTFILE as MYFILE. Does TESTFILE still show up in the contents list for this directory?

    f. In Subdir-1, delete all files except MYFILE.

    g. Move MYFILE to Subdir-2. How many files are there now in Subdir-1 and Subdir-2?

    h. Delete the Subdir-1 and Subdir-2 directories.

    i. Change to the C: drive and remove the Lab Projects disk from its drive.

40. (This exercise requires an unformatted floppy disk.)

    a. Insert an unformatted diskette in its drive.

    b. Check that the diskette is unformatted by changing to that drive. If a message informing you that the disk is not formatted appears, answer No to the question: "Do you want to format it now?"

    c. If the diskette contains any files, do not continue this exercise! Otherwise, format this diskette, with the Make System Disk check box deselected.

    d. After the diskette is formatted, label it with your name. (If there are too many characters in your name, label it with a nickname.)

    e. Try to make this diskette a system disk. Did Windows display any messages?

    f. Open a directory window for this disk. How many files appear in the contents list? Where does your name appear?

    g. Remove the newly-formatted diskette from its drive.

Creative Writing

41. After you have done a few of the *Hands-On* exercises for this chapter, you may notice that they frequently make use of the root directory and WINDOWS directory on the hard disk, and one of the floppy drives. Give a step-by-step procedure to create a File Manager window in which these three directory windows are open and at

least partly visible on the screen.

42. Suppose you were teaching a class about computers. Write a one-page handout for this class containing general information about floppy disks. Include a description of the various types, how to care for diskettes, and how to insert one into a floppy drive. (There is information about floppy disks in this chapter and in the Introduction.)

43. Suppose that a computer has two floppy disk drives of different types. Give a step-by-step procedure for copying all the files on the diskette in drive A: onto the diskettte in drive B:.

44. The Confirmation dialog box, opened by choosing Confirmation from the Options menu, gives you the opportunity to turn five confirmation messages on or off. Explain in one or two paragraphs the advantages and disadvantages of turning confirmation messages off. Rank these five messages on the basis of "most dangerous to turn off" and briefly justify your rankings.

45. Suppose that you were using a computer to write this textbook. In addition to Windows, you are using a word processor to write the text and a drawing program to create graphics (such as diagrams and "screen shots"). The text for each chapter and each individual graphic is stored in a separate file. (Notice that the text has nine chapters, appendixes, and miscellaneous other material in it.) All the program and data files are to be located on the C: drive. Draw a directory tree for drive C:, naming each directory appropriately, that organizes all this information in a logical manner.

More On Applications and Files

OVERVIEW   Applications and files, the subject matter of the two previous chapters, are closely linked together. Every application consists of a collection of program files and each document produced by an application is stored in a data file. In this chapter, we will build upon the material introduced in Chapters 2 and 3 to discuss additional topics dealing with setting up, starting, and running applications under Windows. You will learn how:

1. To create groups in Program Manager.

2. To create and edit program items.

3. To delete program items and groups.

4. To start applications from File Manager.

5. To associate files with applications.

6. To open, switch among, save, print, and close documents.

7. To use Print Manager to control your print jobs.

4.1 Creating and Deleting Groups and Program Items

In Chapter 2, we discussed how to *manipulate* group and program item icons — how to move, copy, and rearrange them on the desktop. Here, we will describe how to create and delete these icons.

Creating Program Groups

As you know, Windows automatically creates four or five program groups (Main, Accessories, StartUp, Games, and sometimes Applications) during the initial set up process. Moreover, most Windows applications generate their own groups (and place program item icons within them) when they are installed. Windows also gives *you* the power to create "custom" groups whenever you want.

Creating a program group is an easy process and can add to the convenience of using Windows. Suppose, for example, that you frequently use the File Manager utility, the Write, Paintbrush, and Calendar accessories, and the Solitaire game. Instead of keeping three group windows (Main, Accessories, and Games) open on the desktop so that you can easily start these programs, you could create a new group and move the icons for these applications into it. Then, you'd normally only need to keep one group window open, and your frequently used programs would be instantly accessible.

Procedure for creating a group

Here's how to create a new program group:

1. In Program Manager, choose <u>N</u>ew from the <u>F</u>ile menu. The New Program Object dialog box will be displayed:

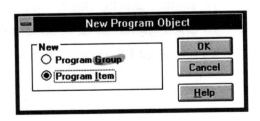

2. Select the Program Group option and choose OK, which will display the Program Group Properties dialog box:

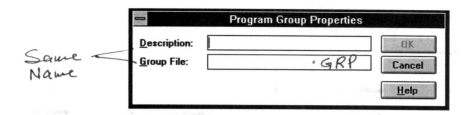

Same Name

3. In the Description box, type a *title* for the new group. This title will appear under the group icon and in the title bar of the group window. The title may contain up to 30 characters of any kind, including spaces. Of course, a meaningful name, like "Word Processing" is more useful than, say, "1KRF121". Also, keep in mind that brevity is the soul of wit.

4. You can leave the Group File box blank; Windows will assign a name, with a GRP extension, to the file that stores information about this group. However, if you want, you can assign a file name here instead.

5. Choose OK and the process is complete. The new group will appear in Program Manager with its window open.

Creating Program Items

You do not normally have to create program item icons for Windows applications; this is usually done automatically when the program is installed. Moreover, when Windows is initially set up, it can generate program items for some DOS (non-Windows) applications. However, you will probably have an occasional need to create your own program items; perhaps for a newly-installed DOS application or for a frequently used *document* that you'd like to open together with the application that produced it.

Program items can be created in several ways:

- By dragging a file name from File Manager onto a group in Program Manager. We will discuss this technique in this section.

- By choosing New from Program Manager's File menu. We will describe this procedure in Section 4.2.

- By using Windows Setup. We will not discuss this technique; if you're curious about it, see the Windows *User's Guide*.

Procedure for <u>creating a</u> program <u>item</u>

The easiest way to create program items for applications and certain documents is to drag their file names from File Manager and drop them on the desired program group in Program Manager. More specifically, follow these steps:

1. Start File Manager by choosing its icon in the Main group.

▢ - program icon

2. Select the appropriate drive and directory; then select the desired program or document file <u>from the contents list</u>. (A **document file** is a data file that has been *associated* with an application; we will discuss this topic in Section 4.3.) With this technique, only those items with a *program* or *document* icon can generate a program item.

▤ - document icon

3. Arrange the desktop so that the desired item in File Manager and the target group (either its icon or its window) in Program Manager are both visible on the screen. This <u>may</u> necessitate <u>restoring</u>, moving, and/or resizing the windows involved.

4. Drag the program or document file onto the group icon or window.

Windows automatically selects an icon and a label for the new program item. You can change these and other characteristics of the program item, if you want to. We will describe how to *edit* program item properties in Section 4.2.

Deleting Program Items and Groups

If you no longer have any use for a program item or group, there's no reason its icon should continue to take up room on your desktop. To delete either type of icon:

1. Select the icon (by, for example, clicking on it).

2. Press the Del key or choose Delete from the File menu. A dialog box similar to the following one will appear:

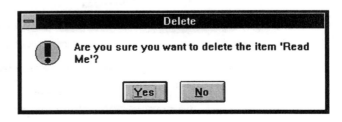

3. Choose <u>Y</u>es to delete the group or program item; <u>N</u>o to abort the deletion operation.

When a group is deleted, all program items in it are deleted as well. Note, however, that when program items (or groups containing program items) are deleted, the corresponding application or data files are *not* erased. It is therefore relatively easy to recreate the group and/or program items, should the need arise.

Hands-On

4.1

Start up Windows (if it's not already running) and perform the indicated tasks. To create a printed copy of your work, see Appendix B.

1. Insert the Lab Projects diskette into its drive.
2. Create a new group in Program Manager called Temp Group. After it's created, does it appear as an icon or a window?
3. Start File Manager and open a directory window for the root directory of the Lab Projects diskette.
4. For the DOSPROG.EXE application on the diskette, create a program item and place it in the Temp Group group. Describe the icon for the new program item. What is its label?
5. Delete the program item you just created. Has DOSPROG.EXE been deleted from the diskette?
6. Delete the Temp Group group. How could you have accomplished steps 5 and 6 at the same time?
7. Click on the C: drive icon, exit File Manager and remove the diskette from its drive.

4.2 More On Creating Program Items

In this section, we will continue our discussion of program items. We will describe another procedure for creating them and also discuss how to edit the properties of existing items.

Creating Program Items Using the New Command

This technique for creating program items takes longer than the drag-and-drop procedure described in the previous section, but it gives you more control over the process. It also allows you to create a program item for an application or *any* data file, not just a document file. Here's the way it works:

1. In Program Manager, select the icon of the group in which you want to place the new program item, or make this group window active.

2. Choose New from the File menu. The New Program Object dialog box will be displayed:

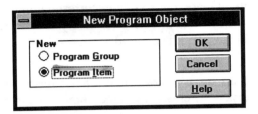

3. Select the Program Item option and choose OK. The Program Item Properties dialog box, shown in Figure 4.1, will appear.

FIGURE 4.1   The Program Item Properties Dialog Box

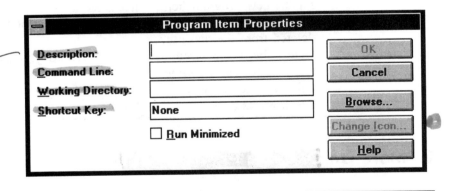

4. In the Description box, type a name that will be used to label the program item's icon. This label may contain up to 30 characters, including spaces. Make it meaningful, but keep it relatively short.

5. In the Command Line box:

   - If you're creating a program item for an application, type its full path name (see Section 3.1). For example, if the program file's name is DRAW.EXE and it is located in the WINDOWS directory on the C: drive, type: c:\windows\draw.exe

■ If you are creating a program item for a document, type the full path name of the application that created this document, followed by a space, followed by the full path name of the document's file. For example, if the MAP.DRW document has been created by the DRAW.EXE application (see the example in the previous paragraph) and is located in the GRAPHICS subdirectory of C:\WINDOWS, then type:

```
c:\windows\draw.exe   c:\windows\graphics\map.drw
```

6. In the Working Directory box, type the path name of the directory that you want to be the current (or *default*) directory when the application starts. The default directory is the one in which you normally store the application's data files. If you leave this box blank, the Working Directory is taken to be the Command Line directory.

7. The Shortcut Key is optional; it provides a quick way of switching to this application when it is running, but not active. The valid keys for this purpose are: Ctrl+Alt+*character*, Ctrl+Shift+*character*, and Ctrl+Alt+Shift+*character*. Here, *character* is usually taken to be a letter or digit, creating shortcut keys such as Ctrl+Alt+W and Ctrl+Shift+2. To set up a shortcut key for a program item, just press the corresponding keystrokes; do not type out the words Ctrl, Alt, or Shift. (Note that if your application is inactive and you press its shortcut key, the switch takes place even if that key has a function in the active application.)

8. Select the Run Minimized check box if you want the application to be reduced to an icon immediately after it's started. This is not as crazy as it sounds. For example, it is common practice to select Run Minimized for some applications placed in the StartUp group. This way, they are quickly available in every Windows session, but do not waste resources or clutter up the desktop as open windows.

9. Choose the OK button, and the newly-created program item's icon will appear in the group specified in step 1.

In filling in the Command Line of the Program Item Properties dialog box, you must type the correct name for the application or document file in question; there is no room for error here. If you're not exactly sure what the file is called or where it's located, choose the Browse button to display the Browse dialog box:

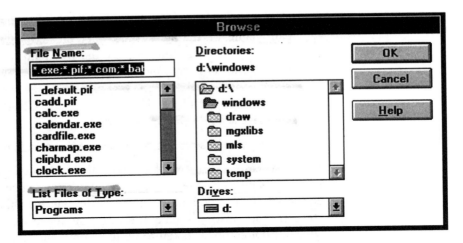

By default, Browse displays all program files in the current directory, but you can display files on other drives and in other directories by selecting them from the Drives and Directories list boxes. Moreover, within any directory, you can change the kinds of files displayed in two ways:

a. In the List Files of Type box, select All Files (instead of Programs) to display all files in the current directory.

b. In the File Name text box, use wildcards (see Section 3.3) to restrict the kinds of files displayed. For example, typing *.TXT lists only those files in the current directory with extension TXT.

Editing a Program Item

After a program item has been created for an application or a document, it's sometimes useful to change (or *edit*) its properties. You might, for example, want to change the working directory or install a different icon.

To edit a program item:

1. Select it (by, for example, clicking on its icon).

2. Choose Properties from the File menu or press the shortcut key Alt+ Enter. The Program Item Properties dialog box (shown in Figure 4.1 on page 128) will be displayed with the information about the selected item filled in.

3. Change any of the displayed information (Description, Command Line, and so on) as you wish.

4. If you want to change the program item icon, choose the Change Icon button. One of two dialog boxes will be displayed:

   a. The Change Icon dialog box might appear, with some of the available icons displayed and the current icon highlighted. A typical Change Icon dialog box looks like this:

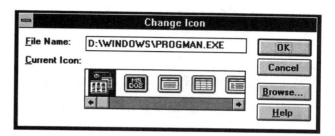

Scroll the Current Icon window to view the available icons. If you see an icon you like, select it and choose OK, and you will be returned to the Program Item Properties dialog box. If you don't see one you like, you can view additional icons by choosing the Browse button and then choosing a file from the list displayed. (In particular, the file MORICONS.DLL contains a lot of interesting icons.)

   b. A dialog box might be displayed informing you that "There are no icons available for the specified file." Close this dialog box by choosing OK and the Change Icon dialog box will appear with the icons available for Program Manager displayed. Now, proceed as in step (a) above.

5. To put your changes into effect, choose OK in the Program Item Properties dialog box. To leave the program item's properties as they were prior to your changes, choose Cancel.

At times, you may want to create a new program item that differs only slightly from an existing one. For example, let's say that your word processing directory has several subdirectories; one for letters, one for reports, and so on. In this situation, it would be convenient to have a program item corresponding to each subdirectory, so that choosing an icon not only starts the word processor, but also changes to the appropriate subdirectory. These program items would differ only in their Description and Working Directory.

To quickly create a new program item that has similar properties to an existing one:

1. In Program Manager, *copy* the existing icon (as described in Section 2.2) to the same group, so that now there are two of them with identical properties.

2. Select the new icon and edit its properties, as desired.

Hands-On 4.2

Start up Windows (if it's not already running) and perform the indicated tasks. To create a printed copy of your work, see Appendix B.

1. Use the <u>N</u>ew command on Program Manager's <u>F</u>ile menu to create a program item in the Main group with the following properties:
   - Its description is Setup Text.
   - Its file name is SETUP.TXT and it is located in the WIN-DOWS directory. (Leave the working directory box blank.)
   - It has the shortcut key Ctrl+Alt+Shift+S.
   Describe the icon Windows selected for this program item.
2. Choose the new icon from the Main group. What application was started?
3. Start File Manager and then use the shortcut key to switch to the Setup document. Did this key work?
4. Switch to Program Manager, open the Program Item Properties dialog box for Setup Text, and change its icon to one of your choice from the MORICONS.DLL list. Describe the icon you chose.
5. Delete the Setup Text program item.
6. Exit all running applications.

4.3 Starting Applications from File Manager

In Chapter 2, we presented several methods for starting (or *launching*) an application from Program Manager. In this section, we will describe how to use File Manager for this purpose.

Starting an Application from the Directory Window

If an application or document is represented by an icon in a Program Manager group, then the easiest way to launch it is to *choose* that icon (by double-clicking on it or selecting it with the Arrow keys and pressing Enter). However, if an application or document is not represented by an icon, using File Manager might be the easiest way to start it.

To launch an application from File Manager:

1. In the directory window, locate the application's *program file* (or) a *document file* associated with the application.

- program icon

- A program file usually has an EXE, COM, BAT, or PIF extension and is represented in the contents list by a *program icon* (pictured at the left).

- document icon

- A document file associated with an application is represented in the contents list by a *document icon* (also pictured at the left).

2. Double-click on the file name (or select it and press the Enter key). The application will start and, if a document file was chosen, that document will be opened, as well.

As you can see, this technique provides a nice way of launching an application and opening a document file within it. If you want to do this with a data file that is *not* a document file, you have several alternatives:

- Start the application and open the data file from within the application itself (see Section 4.4). This is the most common way of proceeding.

- In File Manager, use the mouse to drag the data file onto the program file icon for the application.

- Use the Run command on the File menu of either Program Manager or File Manager. This is probably the clumsiest of these three techniques, but it has its uses. We will describe it next.

The Run Command

The Run command allows you to start an application and, if you want, to open a data file at the same time, by specifying the file name(s). Run appears on the File menu of both Program Manager and File Manager. We briefly discussed Program Manager's Run command in Section 2.3. The File Manager version works almost the same way; to use it:

1. Choose Run from File Manager's File menu. The following dialog box will be displayed:

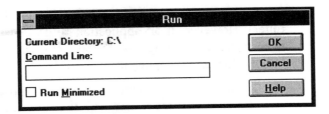

(The Program Manager version of the Run dialog box contains a Browse button which works like the one in the Program Item Properties dialog box shown in Figure 4.1. In File Manager, Browse is not necessary; it's easy enough to scan directories and files using File Manager itself.)

2. The current directory is displayed at the top of the dialog box and, if a file was selected prior to issuing the Run command, that file name is highlighted in the Command Line text box. If you do not want to use the highlighted file name, type the name of the desired program or document file. If this file is not in the current directory, you might have to give its full path name.

3. If you want to open a data file at the same time as an application:

    ■ If it's a document file, type this file's name in step 2.

    ■ To open any other kind of data file, type a space after the application's name and then type the name of the data file. If the data file is in a different directory from the program file, you might have to give its full path name.

    For example, to start the NOTEPAD.EXE application, located in the C:\WINDOWS directory, and to open the SETUP.TXT data file in the same directory, you could type

    c:\windows\notepad.exe setup.txt

    but since SETUP.TXT is a document file, it's sufficient to type

    c:\windows\setup.txt

    (or just setup.txt if C:\WINDOWS is the current directory).

4. Select the Run Minimized check box if you want the application to be reduced to an icon after it is started.

5. Choose OK to start the application (and open the data file, if any).

Associating Data Files with Applications

Some applications automatically attach a specific extension to data files they create (unless you specify otherwise). For example, the Write word processor adds the extension WRI to files saved without an extension. Extensions are also often chosen by the user (when saving files) to indicate the type of file just created; perhaps LTR for a letter or RPT for a report. In this way, certain extensions tend to correspond naturally to certain applications.

📄 - document
icon

For this reason, Windows provides a way for you to formally **associate** a given extension with a specific application. Then, any file with this extension is said to be *associated* with the specified application and is represented by a document file icon in the File Manager directory window. Associating a file with an application has the following benefits:

- You can create a program item icon in Program Manager for this file. When this icon is chosen, the corresponding application is started and the document is automatically opened within it.

- When you choose the file in File Manager (by double-clicking on it or selecting it and pressing Enter), the corresponding application is started and the file is automatically opened within it.

- When you type the file name in a Run dialog box and choose Enter, the corresponding application is started and the file is automatically opened within it.

- You can print the file from File Manager without first opening the corresponding application.

Procedure for
associating
an extension
with an
application

To associate a given extension with an application:

1. Choose Associate from File Manager's File menu. The following dialog box will be displayed:

own non std extn

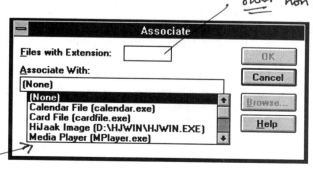

Select any

2. If a file was selected prior to issuing the Associate command, its extension will appear in the Files with Extension box. If you want to associate another extension with an application (or if an extension is not displayed), type the desired extension in this text box.

3 Select the application to be associated with the specified extension from the Associate With list box or type the program file name in the text box. If need be, use the Browse button to open the Browse dialog box, which allows you to scan (and select from) the available applications.

4. Choose OK and the process is complete.

If you decide later on that you want to change the application associated with a given extension, just go through the process again: choose Associate from the File menu and select another application for this extension in the resulting dialog box. The new association takes precedence over the old one. You can also easily *end* an association — remove the connection between an extension and an application — by selecting "(None)" from the Associate With list box.

Hands-On

4.3

Start up Windows and File Manager, if necessary, and perform the indicated tasks. To create a printed copy of your work, see Appendix B.

1. Select the WINDOWS directory.
2. Start the Calendar application by choosing CALENDAR.EXE from the directory window. What date and time is displayed within this application? Exit Calendar.
3. Double-click on the SETUP.TXT document file. What application is started? Exit this application.
4. Open the Setup document within the Write application by dragging SETUP.TXT onto WRITE.EXE. Then, exit Write.
5. Use the Run command to start Write and open the Setup document within it. Is the result exactly the same as that of step 4? Exit Write.
6. Open the Associate dialog box. Determine which application is associated with the HLP extension. Cancel this dialog box.
7. Exit File Manager.

4.4 Working With Documents

As far as Windows is concerned, a **document** is any data file created by an application. Thus, documents can contain text, graphics (pictures), spreadsheets, or even a meaningless collection of symbols. Nevertheless, there are certain basic tasks that need to be carried out on nearly all documents: they must be created, opened, edited, saved, printed, and closed. The way that a document is created or edited varies considerably from application to application, but most Windows-based applications follow very similar procedures for opening, saving, printing, or closing a document. In this section, we will discuss these common tasks, as well as the process for switching among documents.

Opening a Document

When you **open** a document, it is copied from disk into RAM and (at least part of it) is displayed in a **document window** within the application's window. To open a document in Windows accessories and in most Windows-based applications:

1. Choose Open from the File menu. A dialog box similar to the one in Figure 4.2 will be displayed.

FIGURE 4.2   The Open Dialog Box

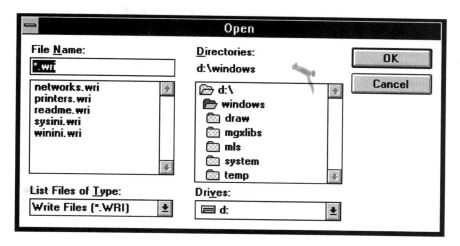

2. The File Name list box displays all files in the current directory satisfying the wildcard pattern shown in its text box (see Section 3.3 for information on wildcards). For example, in Figure 4.2, all files in the WINDOWS directory with extension WRI are displayed. You can change the files that are listed in several ways:

   - To change the current drive, select the one you want from the Drives drop-down list box by clicking on it (or by selecting it and pressing the Enter key).

   - To change directories, choose the desired one in the Directories box by *double*-clicking on it (or selecting it and pressing Enter).

   - To list all files in the current directory of a certain type, select the appropriate item from the List Files of Type box. As an alternative, use a wildcard pattern in the File Name text box. For example, type *.* to display all files in the current directory.

3. In the File Name list box, double-click on the document's name (or select it and choose OK). Alternatively, you can type the desired file name in the text box and press Enter (or choose OK). The selected data file will then open in the active application.

Saving a Document

When you **save** a document, it is copied from its temporary location in RAM to a more permanent place on disk. The save operation, with your help, provides a name for the document, as well. Most Windows-based applications provide two versions of the save operation:

- The Save command saves the document under its current file name. The version of the document stored on disk under this name is *over-written* (erased); the just-saved document, including all changes that you have made since the last save, replaces the former version.

- The Save As command lets you select a file name for the document being saved, and then saves the document under that name. You would use the Save As command if your document has not yet been saved to disk (and consequently has no name) or if the document has a name but you want to create another copy of it.

Issuing the
Save As
command

To issue the Save As command, follow these steps:

1. Choose Save As from the File menu. A dialog box similar to the one in Figure 4.3 will be displayed. (As you can see, it's almost

identical to the Open dialog box shown in Figure 4.2.)

FIGURE 4.3   The Save As Dialog Box

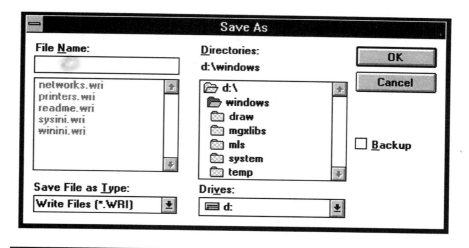

2. Accept the name (if any) that appears in the File Name text box or type a valid file name here (see Section 3.1).

3. If you want to save the document in a directory other than the current one, type a full path name in the File Name box or change the drive and/or directory by selecting from the Drives and Directories list boxes.

4. If you do not want to overwrite the existing version of the document, select the Backup check box. The old version will be saved with the extension BKP. For example, if its former name was TITLE.WRI, its new name will be TITLE.BKP.

5. Choose the OK button

6. If the file name you chose is the same as an existing one in the current directory, a warning message (like the one at the top of the next page) will be displayed. Choose Yes to save the file, overwriting the previous version of the document; choose No to return to the Save As dialog box.

**Issuing
the Save
command**

To issue the Save command, just choose <u>S</u>ave from the <u>F</u>ile menu.

- If the document has a name, it is saved under that name, automatically replacing the last-saved version.

- If the document does not yet have a name, the Save As dialog box (see Figure 4.3) will be displayed. Follow the Save As procedure that was just described to save the document.

When working on a document, it is generally wise to use the Save (or Save As) command frequently (perhaps every half hour or so) even if the document is not yet complete. Then, should disaster strike in the form of a power outage, a glitch in the system, or a mistake on your part, you won't have to recreate too much work. The last version of your document that was saved to disk is probably safe; you'll only have to redo the changes that were made since then.

Switching Among Documents

Some Windows applications allow more than one document to be open at the same time. In this case, each document occupies its own window within the application window. However, only one of these can be the **active document window**, the document which is affected by the commands you issue. The active window is indicated by a highlighted title bar.

**Opening
additional
document
windows**

If an application allows multiple document windows, to open a new document window without closing any existing ones, do either of the following:

- Choose <u>N</u>ew from the <u>F</u>ile menu to open an empty window.

or

■ Choose <u>O</u>pen from the <u>F</u>ile menu to create a new window and open the selected document in it.

When a new window is opened, it becomes the active one.

A typical Windows-based application <u>allows</u> from <u>two to nine</u> docu<u>ments to be open at the same time</u>. However, the only applications supplied by Windows itself that permit more than one open document window are Program Manager and File Manager. (The group windows of Program Manager and the directory windows of File Manager are types of document windows.)

Switching among open document windows

An application that allows multiple open document windows usually provides several ways to switch among them — to make another window active. Here are some typical techniques to switch to a new document window (all of which work with Program Manager and File Manager):

1. Click anywhere within that window. If it's not currently visible on the screen, you can resize, move, or minimize other document windows to make it visible. You can also use the <u>T</u>ile or <u>C</u>ascade commands on the application's <u>W</u>indow menu to achieve the same end.

2. Open the application's <u>W</u>indow menu and choose the document to which you want to switch.

3. Open the document's Control menu by clicking on its Control menu box or by pressing Alt+Hyphen. Then, choose Ne<u>x</u>t to switch to a new document.

4. Press Ctrl+F6 or Ctrl+Tab to cycle among the open document windows.

Printing a Document

When you **print** a document, you send a copy of it to your printer. There are two basic ways to print a document: using the application's Print command and using File Manager.

Using the Print Command   If your application is running, the easiest way to print a document is to use its Print command. To do so:

1. Choose the <u>P</u>rint command from the <u>F</u>ile menu. When you do, the Print dialog box will be displayed. The form this dialog box takes varies somewhat from application to application; Figure 4.4 shows the one for Windows Write.

FIGURE 4.4 A Typical Print Dialog Box

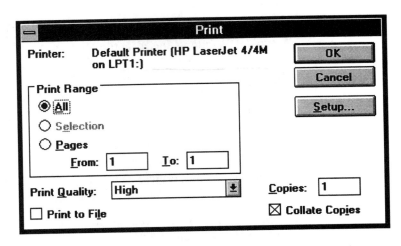

2. Make your selections using the option buttons, text and check boxes, and drop-down list box. (We will discuss these options in detail in Chapter 6.) The Setup command button displays the Printer Setup dialog box, which provides additional printer-dependent options.

3. Make sure that the printer is ready to receive information from your computer.

4. Choose the OK button.

Using File Manager   It may be possible to print a document from within File Manager if that document is associated with an application (see Section 4.3). Recall that in this case, it is represented by a *document icon* like the one pictured at the left. To print a document from File Manager, its application need not be running, but of course, you must start or switch to File Manager. Then, do either of the following:

- Start Print Manager from the Main group and reduce it to an icon that is visible, together with File Manager, on the desktop. Now, drag the document file from File Manager onto the Print Manager icon.

or
- In the File Manager directory window, select the document file to be printed and choose Print from the File menu. This displays a dialog

📄 - document icon

box similar to the following one:

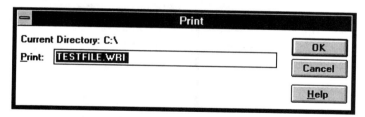

Now, choose OK.

In either case, the application's Print dialog box may be displayed, allowing you to select various options before the document is printed.

Closing a Document

When you **close** a document, it is removed from RAM and its window closes on the screen. When you exit an application, all documents are closed automatically. The technique for closing a document while an application is still running depends on whether or not that application allows multiple open documents.

If an application only allows one document to be open at a time, this document is closed automatically when you:

- Choose the <u>N</u>ew command from the <u>F</u>ile menu. This action closes the current document and opens an empty (untitled) one.

- Choose the <u>O</u>pen command from the <u>F</u>ile menu. As the selected document is opened, the existing one is automatically closed.

If an application allows more than one document to be open, to close one of them:

1. Switch to the document to be closed, which makes it the active one.

2. Choose <u>C</u>lose from the <u>F</u>ile menu (or, in some applications, press Ctrl+F4). As an alternative, double-click on the document's Control menu box, or open its Control menu (by clicking on its Control menu box or pressing Alt+Hyphen) and choose <u>C</u>lose.

If you have made changes to a document since the last save (or have never saved the document) and you try to close it, a warning message similar to the following one will be displayed:

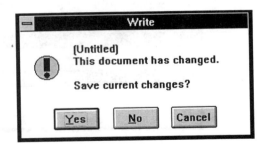

Choosing <u>Y</u>es saves the document (or displays the Save As dialog box if the document has never been saved), choosing <u>N</u>o closes the document without saving the new version, and choosing Cancel returns you to the document without saving it.

Hands-On

4.4

Start up Windows (if it's not already running) and perform the indicated tasks. To create a printed copy of your work, see Appendix B.

1. Insert the Lab Projects diskette in its drive.
2. Start the Write application from the Accessories group.
3. Type your name and save this document on the floppy disk as MyName.Wri.
4. Close this document without exiting Write. How did you accomplish this?
5. Open the MyName.Wri document. Then, save it as MyName-2.Wri on the floppy disk. What command did you use?
6. Exit Write. Which, if any, dialog box appeared after you issued the exit command? Remove the diskette from its drive.

4.5   Print Manager: Controlling the Printing Process

After you issue the Print command from within an application, a Windows utility program called **Print Manager** usually takes over the printing process. In this section, we will describe the ways in which you can use Print Manager to control the printing of your documents.

An Overview of Printing in Windows

Printing with DOS

To understand the usefulness of Print Manager, it's instructive to see how a DOS (non-Windows) application prints a document. When the Print command is issued in a DOS application, another program, called a *printer driver*, starts up to handle the job. The printer driver translates the contents of the data file (its text, fonts, graphics, etc.) into codes that your type of printer can understand, thus enabling it to correctly print the document. Almost every DOS application comes with dozens, sometimes hundreds, of printer drivers to accommodate the large variety of printers on the market.

With most DOS applications, from the time the print job begins until it is complete, your computer is tied up — it is unavailable to perform other tasks. With these applications, if you want to print a series of documents, you must wait until each is finished before starting the next. Nor do you have any way of *controlling* a print job (say, temporarily halting it) once it has begun.

Printing with Windows

Printing while using Windows is simpler for both the software developer and the user. Windows *does* make use of printer drivers to translate a data file into the printer's "language," but these drivers are supplied by Windows and can be used by all Windows-based applications. For this reason, Windows application programmers do not have to develop their own drivers and users need only set up their printer *once* to work with all Windows applications.

Moreover, Windows — through Print Manager — can print documents in the *background,* while the computer is being used for other purposes. Print Manager also gives you the power to put a series of documents in a *print queue,* which prints them one after the other without your intervention. On the other hand, if you *do* want to intervene — for example, to pause the printing process or change the order in which the documents are printed — you can do that, too.

Starting Print Manager

You do not have to launch Print Manager to use it; it starts automatically, reducing itself to an icon, whenever the Print command is issued from within an application. For this reason, you could use Windows for a long time without even realizing that Print Manager exists! During the printing process, you can switch to Print Manager just like any other application (by, for example, double-clicking on its minimized icon or pressing Alt+Tab until its name appears on the screen).

Print Manager

On occasion, though, you may want to start Print Manager "manually." To do so, choose the Print Manager icon from the Main group — double-click on its icon or select it using the Arrow keys and press Enter.

The Print Manager Window

To illustrate how you can use Print Manager to control your print jobs, suppose you want to print a sequence of documents from within the Write application (in the Accessories group). To do so, you successively open each document and choose the Print command from the File menu. If you now switch to Print Manager, its wndow will resemble the one in Figure 4.5.

FIGURE 4.5   The Print Manager Window

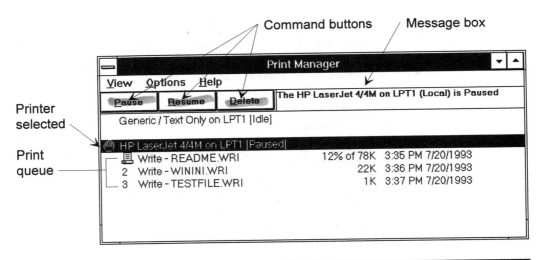

At the top of the Print Manager window are the usual components: Control menu box, title bar, menu bar, and so on. Below the menu bar are three command buttons, and to their right, a *message box*. (The message displayed in Figure 4.5 is: "The HP Laserjet 4/4M on LPT1 (Local) is Paused".)

The main part of the Print Manager window displays the installed printers, and for each, a **print queue** — a list of documents to be printed. The print queue for the Generic/Text Only printer in Figure 4.5 is empty; the one for the HP Laserjet contains three entries, or *print jobs*. The *active print job*, the document currently printing, is preceded by an icon; the others are preceded by a number that indicates the order in which they will be printed.

Each print job specifies: the name of the application, the name of the document, and (optionally) its file size, and the time and date it was sent to Print Manager. The percentage figure next to the active job's file size ("12% of 78K" in Figure 4.5) is the fraction of that document that has already been printed. The file size or time/date information can be hidden by opening the <u>V</u>iew menu and choosing the <u>P</u>rint File Size or <u>T</u>ime/Date Sent items, respectively. (To turn one of these items back on, choose it again; when the item is in effect, it is preceded by a check mark on the menu.)

Features of Print Manager

You can use the Print Manager menus and command buttons to accomplish a number of tasks. All the commands described here apply to the selected printer or print job; the one that is highlighted. To select another printer or print job, click on its name or use the Arrow keys to highlight it.

Pause/
resume

1. You can *pause* (temporarily stop) the selected printer by choosing the <u>P</u>ause button. The word *Paused* will appear next to the printer's name (in Figure 4.5, the Laserjet printer is paused). To *resume* the printing process, choose the <u>R</u>esume button.

Delete

2. You can *delete* (cancel) a print job by selecting it, choosing the <u>D</u>elete button, and then choosing OK when the confirmation message appears. Once deleted, the print job will be removed from the queue.

Print order

3. Print Manager can *change the order* of the print jobs in the queue. You might want to do this if there is one long document and several small ones to be printed. Moving the small jobs to the top of the queue lets you look at their printouts while the long one is printing.

To move a print job in the queue, select it and use the mouse to drag it to its new position. (Or, using the keyboard, select the print job to be moved, hold down the Ctrl key while using the Up or Down Arrow key to move the job to its new position, and then release both keys.)

Print speed   4. Print Manager can change the speed with which documents are printed. To select a print speed, open the Options menu and choose Low Priority, Medium Priority, or High Priority. As the priority is increased, Windows devotes more processor time to the background printing process (and less time to other tasks).

    If you don't need to use the computer while documents are printing, choose High Priority. Otherwise, Medium Priority is usually a reasonable compromise. (A check mark on the Options menu indicates the priority level that is in effect.)

Message display   5. During the printing process, Print Manager occasionally displays a message concerning a printer or print job. Some of these messages are displayed only if you want them to be. To determine the way Print Manager informs you of a situation that needs your attention, open the Options menu and choose:

- Alert Always displays the message in a dialog box which opens in the active application. If you choose this option, you will always see Print Manager messages.

- Flash if Inactive blinks the active application's title bar if Print Manager is not the active application when a message is generated. Switch to Print Manager to see the message.

- Ignore if Inactive does just that. If Print Manager is not the active application when certain messages are generated, no indication whatsoever is given.

A check mark on the menu indicates the option that is in effect.

The Printer Setup Dialog Boxes

From time to time, you may want to change the default printer (the one to be used unless you specify otherwise) or certain printer parameters, such as the quality of the print or the size of the paper used. You can make these adjustments from within most Windows applications or, as shown here, by using Print Manager.

To begin the process, choose Printer Setup from the Options menu. A dialog box similar to the following one will be displayed.

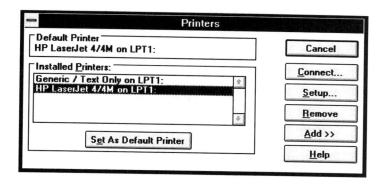

Changing the default printer

From this dialog box, you can easily change the default printer. Just follow these steps:

1. In the Installed Printers list box, select the one that you want to be the default printer.

2. Choose the Set As Default Printer command button.

Changing printer parameters

To change printing parameters for the selected printer, choose the Setup command button. This opens the Setup dialog box. The look of this dialog box varies quite a bit from printer to printer; Figure 4.6 (on the next page) shows the one for an HP Laserjet.

Although the Setup dialog box for your printer may look quite different, there are a few items in the dialog box of Figure 4.6 that are worth pointing out:

- In the Orientation area, you're given the choice of Portrait or Landscape. *Portrait* means that the printing will take place parallel to the short side of the paper; the page you're now reading is in portrait orientation. *Landscape* means that the printing takes place parallel to the long side of the paper; like a certificate or diploma.

- The Copies text box allows you to specify the number of copies to be printed.

- The Cartridges/SIMMs list box and Fonts command button allow you to install additional fonts (type styles) to be used with your printer.

- The Options button opens a dialog box with additional options specific to your printer.

FIGURE 4.6   A Typical Printer Setup Dialog Box

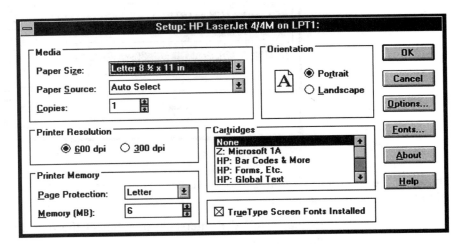

Deactivating Print Manager

Windows allows you to *deactivate* (turn off) Print Manager. When this is done, print jobs are sent directly to the printer; they are no longer printed in the background. When Print Manager is deactivated, you lose the use of your computer from the time the Print command is issued until the job is complete. You also lose the ability to queue print jobs or use any of the other Print Manager features described earlier.

To deactivate (or *disable*) Print Manager:

1. Choose the Control Panel icon from the Main group.

2. Choose the Printers icon from the Control Panel window. The Printers dialog box will be displayed. This dialog box is almost identical to the Printers dialog box accessed from Print Manager (on the previous page); the only difference is that this one contains a Use Print Manager check box in the lower left corner.

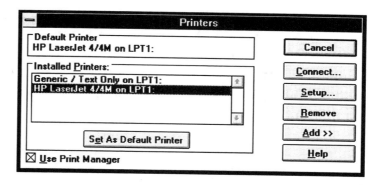

3. Deselect (clear) the Use Print Manager check box.

4. Choose the Close button.

To activate (turn on) Print Manager, use the same procedure but select the Use Print Manager check box in step 3.

For most of this section, we have been singing the praises of Print Manager, so why would one want to deactivate it? The answer is simple. In some applications, documents print faster, sometimes considerably faster, when Print Manager is turned off. So, if you have a large document that must be printed quickly (and you don't mind losing the use of your computer while it prints), deactivate Print Manager before issuing the Print command.

Quitting Print Manager

Print Manager automatically closes down when printing is complete. If you want to quit Print Manager "manually," choose Exit from the View menu. If any print jobs remain in the queue, the following dialog box will be displayed:

If you choose OK, then all remaining jobs are cancelled. So, if there are documents yet to be printed, and you want to get Print Manager out of the way, minimize it; don't exit it!

Start up Windows (if it's not already running) and perform the indicated tasks. To create a printed copy of your work, see Appendix B.

1. Start Print Manager. What printers are listed in its window?
2. Select the printer that you want to use and choose the <u>P</u>ause button. What message is displayed?
3. Start the Write application from the Accessories group.
4. <u>O</u>pen and <u>P</u>rint the WININI.WRI document, then the PRINTERS .WRI documents (both in the WINDOWS directory).
5. Switch to Print Manager and change the order in the print queue so that PRINTERS.WRI is first.
6. Delete the second print job.
7. Send the PRINTERS.WRI document to the printer by choosing the <u>R</u>esume button.
8. Immediately, exit Print Manager. What message is displayed? (Answer "OK" to this message.)

Chapter Summary

Key Terms

Active document [page 140]   Associate [135]

Close a document [143]   Document [137]

Document file [126]   Document window [137]

Open a document [137]   Print a document [141]

Print Manager [144]   Print queue [146]

Save a document [138]

Topics Covered

Program Items and Groups

To create a group   Choose <u>N</u>ew from Program Manager's <u>F</u>ile menu and Program <u>G</u>roup from the dialog box.

To create a program item   Choose <u>N</u>ew from Program Manager's <u>F</u>ile menu and Program Item from the dialog box.

To edit a program item	Choose Properties from Program Manager's File menu; or press Alt+Enter.
To delete a program item or group	Select the program item or group and either press the Del key or choose Delete from Program Manager's File menu.

Starting Applications from File Manager

From a program or document file	Double-click on the file name; or select the file name and press Enter.
From a data file	Drag the data file name onto the program file name.
From the Run command	Choose Run from the File menu, type the file name in the dialog box, and choose OK.
To associate a file with an application	Choose Associate from File Manager's File menu, type the desired extension and application in the dialog box, and choose OK.

Working with Documents

To open a document	Choose Open from the application's File menu.
To save a document	Choose Save or Save As from the application's File menu.
To switch to a document	Click on its window; or choose it from the application's Window menu; or repeatedly press Ctrl+F6 or Ctrl+Tab; or choose Next from the application's Control menu.
To print a document	Choose Print from the application's File menu; or drag the document file from File Manager onto the Print Manager minimized icon; or choose Print from File Manager's File menu.
To close a document	Exiting the application closes all documents. If the application allows multiple open documents, choose Close from its File menu, double-click on its Control menu box, or press Ctrl+F4. If the application does not allow multiple open documents, choose New or Open from its File menu.

Features of Print Manager

To pause or resume a print job	Choose the Pause or Resume button.
To delete a print job	Select the job and choose the Delete button.
To change the order of the print queue	Drag the print job to its new location; or select the job, hold down Ctrl, and use the Up or Down Arrow key to move the job to its new location.
To change the print speed	Choose Low Priority, Medium Priority, or High Priority from the Options menu.
To change the display of messages	Choose Alert Always, Flash if Inactive, or Ignore if Inactive from the Options menu.
To set up the printer	Choose Printer Setup from the Options menu.

Chapter Exercises

Short Answer

Complete each statement in Exercises 1 through 12.

1. To create a program group, begin by choosing _____ from Program Manager's File menu.

2. Program items can only be created for program files and _____ files, a special type of data file.

3. To have an application automatically reduce itself to an icon when it's started, select the _____ check box in the Program Item Properties dialog box.

4. Selecting a Shortcut Key in the Program Item Properties dialog box provides a quick way to _____ this application.

5. A document file is one that has been _____ with an application.

6. To start an application from the File Manager directory window, you can _____ on its program file name.

7. The Open, Save, and Print commands appear on an application's _____ menu.

8. To create an empty document window (to *clear* the window), choose the _____ command from the application's File menu.

9. To name a newly-created document, choose _____ or _____ from the application's Eile menu.

10. To print a document file using File Manager, you can drag its file name onto the _____ icon.

11. To temporarily halt a print job, choose the _____ button in Print Manager.

12. To print a document as quickly as possible, _____ Print Manager before issuing the Print command.

In Exercises 13 through 24, determine whether each statement is true or false.

13. When creating a program group, Windows automatically assigns a title for the group icon and window.

14. When a group is deleted, all program items in that group are also deleted.

15. When you choose the Change Icon button in the Program Item Properties dialog box, all available icons are displayed.

16. When creating a program item, you must specify a working directory.

17. To start an application from within Windows, it must have a program item icon in Program Manager.

18. A document file is represented by the icon: ☐

19. If the file JOE.LTR is associated with a certain application, then so is every file with extension LTR.

20. If you create a document, but never save it, and exit the application, then you will not be able to open that document.

21. Before you can print a document, you must start Print Manager.

22. When two documents are open, you can switch from one to the other by choosing the New command from the application's Eile menu.

23. Once the Print command has been issued, the only way to stop the printing process is to turn off the printer.

24. Every Windows document must be printed with the aid of Print Manager; it cannot be turned off.

In Exercises 25 through 32, choose the correct answer.

25. When you create a program item by dragging a file name from File Manager onto a group in Program Manager, Windows automatically:

     a. Assigns a shortcut key to it.
     b. Chooses an icon for it.
     c. Creates a new directory for it.
     d. Does all of the above.

26. When editing a program item, you can change:

     a. Its icon.
     b. Its shortcut key.
     c. The working directory.
     d. All of the above.

27. The Working Directory in the Program Item Properties dialog box is the one:

     a. In which the application's program file is located.
     b. In which the application's icon is located.
     c. To which Windows will switch when the application is exited.
     d. To which Windows will switch when the application is started.

28. You can start an application from File Manager by double-clicking on:

     a. A system file icon.
     b. The Up icon.
     c. A document file icon.
     d. The current directory icon.

29. If you type: c:\windows\write.exe a:resume.94 on the command line of the Run dialog box, you are asking Windows to:

     a. Start the WRITE.EXE application from the C:\WINDOWS directory.
     b. Open the data file RESUME.94 on the disk in the A: drive.
     c. Do neither (a) nor (b).
     d. Do both (a) and (b).

30. To save a document that is "untitled":

     a. You can use the Open command.
     b. You can use the New command.
     c. You can use the Save command.
     d. None of the above commands will accomplish this goal.

31. The Write application does not allow multiple documents to be open at the same time. To close a document in Write:

    a. You can use the New command.
    b. You can use the Save command.
    c. You can use the Print command.
    d. None of the above commands will accomplish this goal.

32. To print a document from a Windows application:

    a. You must start Print Manager and reduce it to an icon.
    b. You must start Print Manager and select the printer.
    c. You must start Print Manager and select the document to be printed.
    d. You need not do any of the above.

Hands-On   In Exercises 33 through 38, start up Windows (if it's not already running) and perform the indicated tasks. To create a printed copy of your work, see Appendix B.

33. a. Insert the Lab Projects diskette in its drive.
    b. Start File Manager and change to the drive that contains this diskette.
    c. Create a new group in Program Manager; call it Diskette Programs. Does it appear as an icon or as an open window on the desktop?
    d. Using the drag-and-drop method, create a program item in the Diskette Programs group for the DOSPROG.EXE program on the Lab Projects disk. Describe its icon. What is it labeled?
    e. Delete the Diskette Programs group. Was the DOSPROG program item deleted as well?
    f. Exit File Manager. Remove the diskette from its drive.

34. a. Open the Accessories group. Copy the Clock icon (by holding down Ctrl while dragging the icon) to the Main group.
    b. Open the Program Item Properties dialog box for this newly-created icon. What is its command line? Is there a shortcut key?
    c. Change its label to Clock-2 and give it the shortcut key Ctrl+ Alt+Shift+C. Did Windows allow these changes?
    d. Start Clock-2 and then the original Clock. What differences (if any) are there in the two open windows?
    e. Use the shortcut key to switch to Clock-2. Did this key work?
    f. Delete the Clock-2 program item. Is Clock-2 still running?
    g. Exit Clock and Clock-2, if necessary.

35. a. Start File Manager and change to the WINDOWS directory.
    b. Double-click on the file ACCESSOR.GRP. What happened?
    c. Double-click on CARS.BMP. Why did this action launch an application but double-clicking on ACCESSOR.GRP did not? Exit the application you just started.
    d. Start the NOTEPAD.EXE application and open the SETUP .TXT document (at the same time) by using the Run command. What command line did you use? Give another command line that also works. Exit Notepad.
    e. Start the WRITE.EXE application and the SETUP.TXT document at the same time by
       ■ using the Run command.
       ■ using drag-and-drop.
       Do the two windows look exactly the same?
    f. Exit Write and File Manager.

36. a. Start File Manager and change to the WINDOWS directory.
    b. Open the Associate dialog box and determine the applications associated with the following extensions: INI, BMP, and HLP.
    c. Associate the extension LTR with the Write application. Is the extension WRI still associated with Write?
    d. Insert the Lab Projects diskette in its drive and change to this drive. Is the file JOE.LTR represented by a document icon?
    e. Remove the association of LTR with Write. Refresh the directory window by pressing F5. Is JOE.LTR still represented by a document icon? Remove the diskette from its drive.
    f. Try to associate the "null" extension (no characters) with Write. Is this possible? If so, remove this association.
    g. Exit File Manager.

37. a. Insert the Lab Projects diskette in its drive and start the Write application.
    b. Open the document MEMO.WRI on the diskette.
    c. Save it under the name of MEMO2 to the Lab Projects disk. What name now appears on the title bar, MEMO or MEMO2?
    d. Print MEMO (or MEMO2).
    e. Close the open document without exiting Write. What command or mouse clicks did you use?
    f. Exit Write and remove the diskette from its drive.

38. a. Start File Manager and then Print Manager. What printers are listed in the Print Manager window?
    b. Open the Printers dialog box by choosing <u>P</u>rinter Setup from

the Options menu. Are the same printers listed here? What is the name of the default printer? Close the dialog box.

c. Choose the Pause button and then switch to File Manager.

d. Use File Manager to "print" SETUP.TXT, in the WINDOWS directory.

e. Switch to Print Manager. Describe the print queue. What message is displayed in the message box?

f. Hide the "file size" information. Does the "percentage" figure disappear, too?

g. Set the "print speed" to High Priority and the "message display" to Alert Always. Is there any change in the Print Manager window?

h. Delete the print jobs, return the options to their former settings, and exit Print Manager. Does Windows display any message?

i. Exit File Manager.

Creative Writing

39. Briefly describe all the ways that an application can be launched (started). Indicate which ones you prefer the most and the least, and explain why.

40. Compare the process of printing a document in a DOS application and in a Windows application (with Print Manager activated).

41. Describe the ways in which a document window is similar to, and the ways in which it is different from, an application window. Include in your discussion, the appearance of the windows and the kinds of operations that can be performed on them.

42. In the broad sense of the word, a group is a Windows *document*; when it is opened, it is displayed in a document window. In what ways is a group similar to, and in what ways is it different from, a document made up of text and graphics. Include in your discussion, the operations that can be performed on each, such as creating, saving, etc., and the way they are accomplished.

Customizing Windows: Control Panel

OVERVIEW People use computers in different ways and for different reasons. With this in mind, Windows provides users with the power to tailor it to their liking. When this capability is used properly, the result is a more pleasant and productive environment. You have already seen many examples of this customizing process in the first four chapters: sizing and moving windows, changing the layout of Program Manager, modifying the way File Manager presents information, and so on. This chapter is devoted exclusively to the topic of customizing the look and feel of the Windows environment, mostly through the use of the Control Panel utility. You will learn:

1. To change the Windows screen colors.

2. To decorate the desktop with a repeating pattern or wallpaper.

3. To adjust the text cursor blink rate.

4. To control icon and window spacing.

5. To make adjustments to hardware, such as keyboard speed and mouse settings.

6. To add or remove fonts from Windows.

7. To change the system date and time.

8. About other ways to customize Windows.

5.1 An Introduction to Control Panel

Control Panel

Control Panel is a utility program whose sole purpose is to help you customize the Windows environment — its colors, fonts, keyboard operation, etc. — so that it looks and feels the way you want. When you choose the Control Panel icon from the Main group (by double-clicking on it), a window similar to the one in Figure 5.1 will open. (Depending on how the system is configured, your Control Panel window may contain a selection of options that is different from the one pictured here.)

FIGURE 5.1   The Control Panel Window

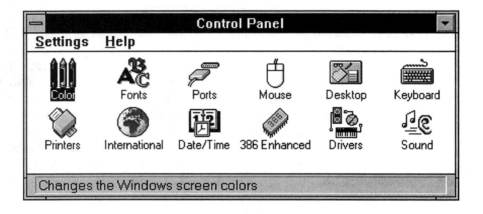

Control Panel Options

The following table describes all the Control Panel options supplied by Windows.

Name	Function
Color	Changes the Windows screen colors.
Fonts	Adds and removes fonts and sets TrueType options.
Ports	Specifies communications settings for serial ports.
Mouse	Changes settings for the mouse.

Desktop	Changes the look of your desktop.
Keyboard	Specifies the keyboard repeat rate and delay.
Printers	Installs and removes printers and sets printing options.
International	Specifies international settings.
Date/Time	Changes the date and time of your computer's clock.
Drivers	Installs, removes, and configures drivers.
Sound	Assigns sounds to system events.
386 Enhanced	Changes the 386 Enhanced mode settings (if you are using a computer equipped with a 386, 486, or Pentium processor).
Network	Controls the way you access a network (if your computer is connected to one).
MIDI Mapper	Selects, changes, or creates setups for a Musical Instrument Digital Interface (if your computer is equipped with one).

Choosing an option

To choose one of the available Control Panel options, perform any of the following actions:

- Double-click on the icon for that option.

- Use the Arrow keys to highlight the icon and press the Enter key.

- Choose the desired item from the Settings menu.

Quitting Control Panel

You can exit Control Panel in the same ways that you exit most other Windows applications. Any of the following actions will work:

- Double-click on the Control menu box.

- Press Alt+F4.

- Choose Exit from the Settings menu.

- Open the Control menu (by clicking on the Control menu box or pressing Alt+Spacebar) and choose Close.

- Open Task List (by pressing Ctrl+Esc), highlight Control Panel, and choose the End Task button.

5.2   Changing Screen Colors

Many people have strong preferences for certain colors and/or color combinations. If you're one of these people, you'll be happy to know that Windows provides a great deal of flexibility in choosing a desktop **color scheme** — the colors used for the various screen elements. There are three basic levels of control:

1. You can choose a predefined (built-in) color scheme.

2. You can create a *custom* color scheme (one of your own choosing) from predefined colors.

3. You can create a custom color scheme using custom colors in addition to the predefined ones.

Predefined Color Schemes

Windows comes with a wide variety of built-in color schemes. To select one of these:

Color

1. Open the Control Panel window (by choosing its icon from the Main group) and choose the Color icon. The dialog box shown in Figure 5.2 will be displayed.

2. Open the Color Schemes drop-down list (by clicking on it; or by pressing Alt+S, then Alt+Down Arrow). A list of the available color schemes will be displayed. These include both predefined schemes and custom schemes that have been previously saved.

3. Select a color scheme from the list. The *sample screen* in the dialog box (see Figure 5.2) will display the colors of the various *screen elements* (desktop, window background, window text, and so on).

4. Choose the OK button. The Color dialog box will close and the screen will reflect the new color scheme. (If you'd rather stay with the color scheme you had been using, choose Cancel.)

TIP

If you want to see which of the predefined schemes you like best, do *not* open the Color Schemes drop-down list. Just press the Up or Down Arrow keys and Windows will cycle through the available schemes, displaying the name of the current one in the text box and its colors in

FIGURE 5.2 The Color Dialog Box

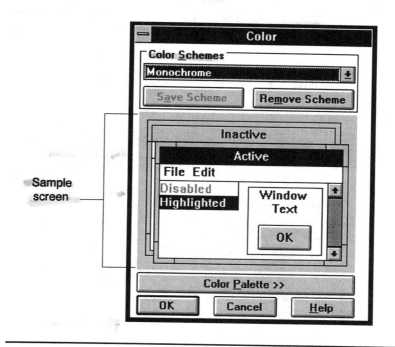

the sample screen. If you find a color scheme you like, press the Enter key or click on OK to put it into effect. (This is one of those times that the keyboard is more efficient than the mouse!)

Creating a Custom Color Scheme

If you're not entirely happy with any of the available color schemes, you can create one of your own design — a *custom* color scheme. To do so, you simply select a predefined scheme and then change the color of whichever screen elements you wish. More specifically:

1. Choose the Color icon from the Control Panel window to open the Color dialog box (shown in Figure 5.2).

2. In the Color Schemes box, select a scheme that resembles the one you would like to create. For example, if you are going to use shades of gray, you might select Monochrome.

3. Choose the Color Palette button, which expands the Color dialog
   box so that it looks like the one in Figure 5.3. The Screen Element
   drop-down box lists the elements that can be individually colored;
   the Basic Colors palette displays the available (built-in) colors.

FIGURE 5.3   The Expanded Color Dialog Box

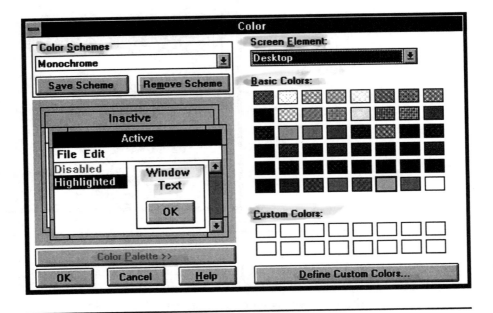

4. Select any of the twenty-one screen elements that can be modified
   by either:

   ■ Selecting that element in the Screen Element list box.

   or

   ■ Clicking on that element in the sample screen area. For exam-
     ple: to select the Active Title Bar, click on the bar; or, to select
     the Active Title Bar Text, click on the word "Active." The
     Screen Element box will display the name of the element, con-
     firming your choice. To select certain elements, you may have
     to click more than once. For example, clicking repeatedly on
     "Highlighted" cycles between the highlight bar and the high-
     lighted text.

5. Choose a color for the selected screen element by clicking on the appropriate box in the Basic Colors area. (Alternatively, you can press Alt+B and use the Arrow keys to enclose the box in a dotted rectangle.)

6. Repeat steps 4 and 5 until the sample screen looks the way you want.

7. Save the color scheme, if so desired, by choosing the Save Scheme button and typing a name for the scheme in the text box. (The name may contain up to 32 characters, including spaces; for example, "The Color Purple" is a valid name.) This scheme will then be added to the list of available schemes in the Color Schemes box.

   If you don't save your scheme (but choose OK in step 8), it will still be used in this and all future Windows sessions until another color scheme is selected. After that, however, the only way to retrieve the scheme is to recreate it step-by-step.

8. Choose the OK button. The Color dialog box will close and the new color scheme will go into effect.

After you've used Windows for a while, you will probably develop a preference for just a few color schemes. You may find it easier to switch among them if you remove the others from the Color Schemes list. To delete a scheme from the list:

1. Select the scheme you want to remove from the Color Schemes list.

2. Choose the Remove Scheme button.

3. Confirm the deletion by choosing Yes in the resulting dialog box.

4. Choose the OK button.

Creating Custom Colors

The Basic Colors palette supplies up to forty-eight different colors. If you want, you can create additional (custom) colors to use in a color scheme. To create a custom color, from the expanded Color dialog box (Figure 5.3), choose the Define Custom Colors button. The Custom Color Selector dialog box, shown in Figure 5.4, will open.

FIGURE 5.4 The Custom Color Selector Dialog Box

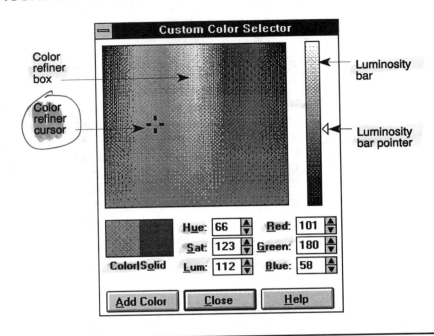

Using this dialog box to create a custom color is a three-step process. You must:

1. Specify the color you want.

2. Accept the color you have specified or the closest solid color.

3. Assign the color to a Custom Colors box.

When you have completed this process for each custom color you want to create, the new colors can be used, together with the predefined ones, to construct a custom color scheme. We will now describe each of the three steps in detail.

Specifying a Custom Color To describe a color in the Custom Color Selector, you either:

■ Specify the *hue*, *saturation*, and *luminosity* of the color. **Hue** is the position of the color in the spectrum; for example, blue is a hue. (Try saying *that* fast ten times!) **Saturation** is the purity of a given hue, from gray to the pure color; for example, altering the saturation of blue gives various shades of blue-gray. **Luminosity** is the bright-ness of a color; varying the luminosity of blue creates light blues, medium blues, and dark blues.

or

- Specify the *RGB-makeup* of the color — the amount of red (R), green (G), and blue (B) in the color. For example, a medium blue is obtained by using no red, no green, and the maximum amount of blue; to get lighter blues, add increasing *equal* amounts of red and green. (When the amount of red and green is the same as that of blue, you'll have white!)

If this sounds confusing, don't worry; as you'll see, Windows makes it easy to specify a custom color. As you describe the new color, it is displayed on the left side of the Color/Solid box (see Figure 5.4). By examining this box as you vary the makeup of your custom color, you can see what it looks like before you add it to the palette.

There are **three ways to use** the Custom Color Selector to specify a color:

The easy way to specify a color

1. Locate an approximation to the color you want in the color refiner box and click on this point. You can then adjust the color by:

   - Dragging the color refiner cursor (see Figure 5.4) to nearby locations.

   - Dragging the luminosity bar pointer (see Figure 5.4) up and down slightly.

   Remember: In each case, keep your eye on the left side of the Color/Solid box to view the color you're specifying.

2. Type values from 0 to 255 in the Red, Green, and Blue boxes (or click on the arrow buttons in these boxes until the desired value is reached). Here, 0 means the color is not present; 255 represents a maximum amount.

3. Type values from 0 to 255 in the Hue, Sat, and Lum boxes (or click on the arrow buttons in these boxes until the desired value is obtained). Here, increasing a value increases the strength of the corresponding property.

If you try each of the three ways of specifying a color, it soon becomes clear that the first method, using the color refiner box and luminosity bar, is by far the easiest. In using this technique, you are actually specifying a color's hue (by moving horizontally across the box), its saturation (by moving vertically), and luminosity (by moving the pointer on the luminosity bar). Notice that the color spectrum is clearest across the top of the color refiner box and gets muddier as you move down. The very bottom of the color refiner box is a uniform shade of gray.

Specifying the RGB-makeup of the color (method 2) is useful if you want to obtain certain special colors. For example, varying equal amounts of red, green, and blue produces all shades of gray. You may find it instructive (and possibly even fun) to try to guess the effect of typing certain RGB numbers and then checking your "answer" by looking at the left side of the Color/Solid box.

2 **Choosing Solid or Nonsolid Colors** The number of colors that can be displayed on the screen depends on your system's video adapter and the mode in which it is operating. The colors that it can produce are called **solid colors**. A screen element that is assigned a solid color seems, even under close examination, to be uniformly painted with that color.

To increase the variety of available colors, Windows can also simulate colors by using a pattern of differently colored pixels (dots). These colors are referred to as **nonsolid colors**. If you look at them closely, you can see the pattern on the screen. Although nonsolid colors allow you to design more interesting color schemes, they do have a couple of drawbacks: nonsolid colors slow down your system every time the screen is updated and some people find them distracting.

When you specify a color using the Custom Color Selector as described above, it is displayed on the left side of the Color/Solid box. (This color may be solid, but chances are it's not.) At the same time, the closest solid color is displayed on the right side of this box. If you do not want to use a nonsolid color in your custom scheme, you can specify the displayed solid color instead, by either:

- Double-clicking on the right side of the Color/Solid box.

or

- Pressing Alt+O.

3 **Adding a Custom Color to the Palette** After you have specified a custom color and decided whether to accept it or use the closest solid color instead, you have to add it to the palette of available custom colors. These are displayed in the Custom Colors boxes in the lower right of the expanded Color dialog box (Figure 5.3). To add a custom color:

1. Select a Custom Colors box by clicking on it (or by pressing Alt+C and using the Arrow keys to select it).

2. Choose the <u>A</u>dd Color button and the color you have specified will appear in the selected box.

Since there are sixteen <u>C</u>ustom Colors boxes, you can <u>create up to</u> <u>sixteen custom colors</u>. If you want <u>to erase a color</u>, just <u>select its box and</u> <u>add a new color to</u> it. If you want to <u>return the box to its original state</u>, add the color white to that box (in the Custom Color Selector, set <u>R</u>ed, <u>G</u>reen, and <u>B</u>lue, all to 255).

Hands-On

5.2

Start up Windows and Control Panel (if necessary) and perform the indicated tasks. To create a printed copy of your work, see Appendix B.

1. Open the Color dialog box. What is the name of the current color scheme?
2. Open the Color <u>S</u>chemes drop-down list box. Select each scheme and notice its effect on the sample screen. How many schemes are there? Which do you like the best?
3. Expand the Color dialog box by choosing the Color <u>P</u>alette button. Are there forty-eight *different* <u>B</u>asic Colors? How many <u>C</u>ustom Colors are defined?
4. Create a new color scheme with just two colors — black and white. Save it under your name and choose the OK button. Does any color other than black and white appear on the screen?
5. Open the expanded Color dialog box again. In the list of Color <u>S</u>chemes, remove the one you just created and then select the original scheme.
6. Create a custom color with:
    - Hue, saturation, and luminosity at maximum levels.
    - Red, green, and blue at minimum levels.

   In each case, describe the resulting color.
7. Close all dialog boxes.

5.3   Changing the Look of the Desktop

Changing colors, as described in the previous section, can make a dramatic difference in the appearance of the screen. You can create less dramatic changes by using Control Panel's Desktop option. By using Desktop, you can:

1. Decorate the desktop; cover it with a repeating pattern or picture (*wallpaper*) that is visible on the part of the desktop that isn't covered by any window.

2. Have the computer display an animated image — a *screen saver* — when your system has been idle for a specified period of time.

3. Change the rate at which the text cursor blinks.

4. Turn off the Alt+Tab application switching feature.

5. Change the spacing of icons and the way they're aligned.

6. Change the width of all window borders.

Desktop

To start the Desktop utility, choose its icon from the Control Panel window. The Desktop dialog box, shown in Figure 5.5, will be displayed.

FIGURE 5.5   The Desktop Dialog Box

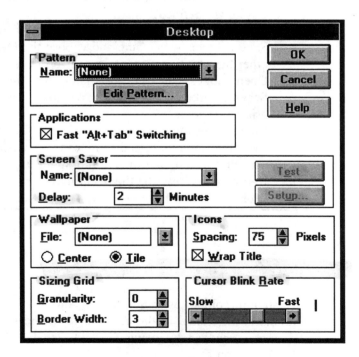

Choosing a Desktop Pattern

When application windows don't completely cover the screen, you can see the Windows desktop peeking out from "under" them. Normally, the desktop is the color specified in the current color scheme. However, if you want, you can place a repeating **desktop pattern** over this color. Windows has several built-in desktop patterns from which you can choose or you can create your own. (You can also decorate the desktop with *wallpaper* — a graphic image — as described later in this section.)

Selecting a Predefined Pattern   To use one of the Windows-supplied desktop patterns:

1. In the Control Panel window, choose the Desktop icon. The Desktop dialog box (Figure 5.5) appears.

2. In the Pattern section of this dialog box, the Name box gives the name of the current pattern. Open this drop-down list box to display the names of the available patterns.

3. Select the pattern you want to use from the list. The color of the pattern is that of the "Window Text" screen element specified in the Color dialog box (see Section 5.1).

4. Choose the OK button. The Desktop dialog box will close and the selected pattern will immediately go into effect.

To see the selected pattern in all its glory, reduce all applications, including Program Manager, to icons. (You also might have to remove the current Wallpaper, as described shortly.)

If you want to view a desktop pattern before closing the Desktop dialog box, choose the Edit Pattern button. A dialog box similar to the one shown in Figure 5.6 (on the next page) will open. A close up of the selected pattern is displayed in the Edit box and its effect on the whole screen can be seen in the Sample box.

The dialog box of Figure 5.6 also provides a quick way to view the available patterns one-by-one. With the Name box selected, use the Up and Down Arrow keys to cycle through the pattern names. As each name is highlighted, the corresponding pattern appears in the Edit and Sample boxes.

After you have viewed the desktop patterns, choose the Cancel button to return to the Desktop dialog box.

FIGURE 5.6   The Desktop - Edit Pattern Dialog Box

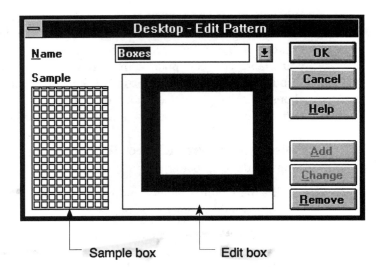

Sample box   Edit box

Creating Your Own Pattern   If your system has a mouse, you can create additional desktop patterns. To do so:

1. From the Desktop window (Figure 5.5), choose the Edit Pattern button. The Desktop - Edit Pattern dialog box (Figure 5.6) is displayed and the current desktop pattern appears as a collection of colored squares in the Edit box. (If you want to start from scratch, select "(None)" from the Name list in the Desktop window before choosing Edit Pattern.)

    For example, if the current pattern is Boxes, the Desktop - Edit Pattern dialog box will look exactly like the one in Figure 5.6. (The Boxes pattern is a collection of twenty-four squares.)

2. In the Name text box, type a name for your pattern. You may use up to twenty-two characters, including spaces.

3. To delete a square from the pattern, click on that square in the Edit box; to add a square to the pattern, click on its desired location. The Sample box will show the effect on the screen. For example, in the Boxes pattern, if you delete the squares in the four corners and add a square in the center, the resulting Sample and Edit boxes are:

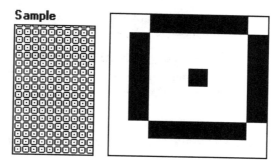

5. Choose the <u>A</u>dd button; then the OK button. You will be returned to the Desktop window. (To put the new pattern into effect, choose the OK button in the Desktop window.)

The Desktop - Edit Pattern dialog box also makes it easy to edit (<u>C</u>hange) and delete (<u>R</u>emove) existing patterns. (We ask you to supply the details of these procedures in Exercise 43 at the end of this chapter.)

Choosing Wallpaper

Instead of using a solid color or patterned Desktop, you can decorate it with a **bitmap image** — a picture formed from the screen pixels. This kind of decoration is called **wallpaper**. (Yes, using wallpaper to decorate a desktop does sound a little strange.) Choosing wallpaper is easy:

1. Open the Desktop dialog box (Figure 5.5) by choosing the Desktop icon from the Control Panel window.

2. In the Wallpaper section of the window, open the <u>F</u>ile drop-down list.

3. Select a wallpaper from the list. (Select "(None)" to remove the current wallpaper from the desktop.)

4. Choose either the <u>C</u>enter or <u>T</u>ile option button.

   - Choosing <u>C</u>enter positions the bitmap in the center of the screen. If it does not cover the entire screen, the solid or patterned desktop will be visible around it.

   - Choosing <u>T</u>ile repeats the bitmap as many times as necessary to cover the entire screen. With small graphics, including most of those supplied with Windows, you will probably want to choose the <u>T</u>ile option.

Figure 5.7 shows the effect of the Center and Tile options for the "arches" wallpaper.

5. Choose the OK button. The selected wallpaper will go into effect. If you want to view it at its best, reduce all applications, including Program Manager, to icons.

FIGURE 5.7   Centering versus Tiling a Wallpaper

Centered Wallpaper   **Tiled Wallpaper**

Choosing a Screen Saver

When a **screen saver** is in effect and neither the mouse nor the keyboard is used for a specified period of time, the screen will go blank or an animated graphic will be displayed. This deters others from viewing your work while you are away from your desk; it also might prevent damage to the screen from an unchanging image being "burned" in. Using the Desktop utility, you can choose from among several Windows-supplied screen savers (or choose not to use a screen saver). Desktop also allows you to customize a screen saver and set the *delay time* — how long your system must be inactive before the screen saver appears.

To choose a screen saver:

1. Open the Desktop dialog box (Figure 5.5) by choosing its icon from the Control Panel window.

2. In the Screen Saver section of the Desktop window, open the Name drop-down list.

3. Select a screen saver from the list, or select "(None)" if you don't want to use a screen saver.

4. To see the effect of the screen saver without closing the Desktop window, choose the T<u>e</u>st button. The selected screen saver will be activated for a few seconds.

5. To set the delay time (in minutes), type a number in the <u>D</u>elay box (or use the arrow buttons in this box).

6. Choose the OK button.

If you select a screen saver, it will be activated after the specified delay time, as long as a Windows application is active. (Screen savers do not work with DOS applications.) To have the active application reappear on the screen, press any key, or move or click the mouse.

You can customize a screen saver by choosing the Set<u>u</u>p button in the Screen Saver section of Desktop. The dialog box that then appears depends on the screen saver that is currently selected. For example, if you select Flying Windows and choose Set<u>u</u>p, the dialog box looks like this:

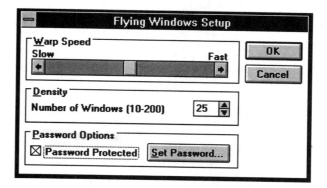

As you can see, with this screen saver, you can adjust the speed of the flying windows as well as the number that appear on the screen.

This dialog box also allows you to choose or remove a **password** for the screen saver by selecting or deselecting the Password Protected check box. If password protection is in effect when the screen saver appears, you cannot return to the active application until you type the password. This prevents others from viewing your work while you are away from your desk.

Other Desktop Options

From within the Desktop dialog box (Figure 5.5), you can also change the desktop in other ways.

Disabling Alt+Tab Switching   Recall that it is easy to switch among running applications by repeatedly pressing the Alt+Tab key combination. However, if Alt+Tab is used for a special purpose within an application, this may cause unexpected problems. In this case, you might want to *disable* (turn off) the Alt+Tab switching feature. To do so, deselect the Fast "Alt+Tab" Switching check box.

Setting the Cursor Blink Rate   The *text cursor* (or *insertion point*) is used in text boxes and text applications (such as word processors) to indicate where characters will appear on the screen when you type them at the keyboard. It is represented by a blinking vertical bar. To change the rate at which the text cursor blinks:

1. Open the Desktop dialog box (Figure 5.5) by choosing its icon from the Control Panel window.

2. In the Cursor Blink Rate section of the window, drag the scroll box to the right, or click the right arrow button, to increase the blink rate; drag the scroll box to the left, or click the left arrow button, to decrease it. (To use the keyboard, press Alt+R; then press the Right Arrow key to increase the blink rate or the Left Arrow key to decrease it.)

3. Choose the OK button.

Changing the Spacing between Icons   Windows usually places a reasonable amount of space between program item icons or application icons. In certain situations, however, icon titles may overlap, like this:

Clipboard Viewer MS-DOS Prompt

To correct this problem, in the Icons section of the Desktop window (Figure 5.5), try either or both of the following:

- Type a larger number in the Spacing text box. (Typically, there are about 75 pixels per inch on the screen, but this figure depends on the size of the monitor and which video mode is active.)

- Select the Wrap Title check box if it has been deselected. This allows Windows to spread multi-word icon titles over two lines on the screen.

Now, choose the OK button and check the effect of your changes on the icons in question.

Changing the Sizing Grid and Border Width   The Sizing Grid section of the Desktop window (Figure 5.5) allows you to make two additional adjustments to the desktop:

- Changing the Granularity to a number greater than 0 sets the *sizing grid*, making it easier for you to align application windows or mini-mized application icons in a neat, orderly way. (This feature does not apply to program item icons or document windows, such as Main.) To see how it works, set Granularity to 5, choose OK, and move the Control Panel window around the screen. Then, compare what happens when you set Granularity to 10 and do the same thing.

- Decreasing the window Border Width (given in pixels) increases your total work space slightly; increasing the Border Width makes it easier to move and resize windows. Most users leave this parameter at its default setting (3 pixels).

Both features go into effect when you choose the OK button.

Hands-On

5.3

Start up Windows and Control Panel (if necessary) and perform the indicated tasks. To create a printed copy of your work, see Appendix B.

1. Reduce Control Panel, Program Manager, and any other running applications to icons. Which solid color, pattern, and/or wallpaper appears on the desktop?
2. Restore the Control Panel icon and open the Desktop dialog box. Make a note of the current desktop pattern, wallpaper, and screen saver.
3. Set the wallpaper to "None". What color is the desktop now?
4. Select the "Diamonds" desktop pattern and create a new pattern from it (using the Desktop - Edit Pattern dialog box) in the shape of a plus sign that is 5 squares high and 5 squares wide.
5. Type your name in the text box and choose the OK button without

choosing <u>A</u>dd. Which, if any, pattern appears on the desktop?

6. Choose OK in the Desktop window. Which, if any, pattern appears on the desktop now?

7. Open Desktop again and select and T<u>e</u>st each screen saver. Which do you like the best?

8. Select the screen saver, desktop pattern, and wallpaper that was in effect when you started this exercise and choose the OK button from the Desktop dialog box. Restore the Program Manager window.

5.4   Using Control Panel to Tinker with Hardware

During the installation process, Windows configures itself to work with your system's hardware (its monitor, mouse, etc.). At times, however, you might want to modify the way existing devices operate or perhaps add a new one. This is usually done with Control Panel; it has options that allow you to:

1. Adjust the "speed" of the keyboard.

2. Adjust the way the mouse operates.

3. Control the sounds coming from your speaker.

4. Set up printers, communications ports, and device drivers.

In this section, we will discuss these features.

Changing the Keyboard Repeat Rate

Most keys on the keyboard have a *repeat feature*: when you press such a key and hold it down, the character or action corresponding to it is repeated until the key is released. For example, if you press the B key and hold it down for a couple of seconds, a sequence of Bs will appear on the screen.

The number of times a key repeats in a given period of time depends on two factors:

■ The *repeat delay* — how long it takes before a key starts repeating after it is pressed.

■ The *repeat rate* — how fast the key repeats after the delay time has elapsed.

To change these parameters:

Keyboard

1. Choose the Keyboard icon from the Control Panel window. The following dialog box will be displayed:

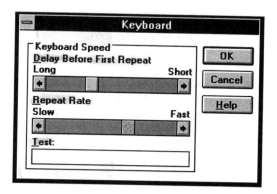

2. To *increase* the repeat delay, drag the Delay Before First Repeat scroll box to the left (or click the left arrow button); to *decrease* the delay, drag this scroll box to the right (or click the right arrow button). You can use the keyboard to increase or decrease the repeat delay by pressing Alt+D and then using the Left or Right Arrow keys.

3. To increase or decrease the repeat rate, drag the Repeat Rate scroll box in the appropriate direction or click the appropriate arrow button. You can use the keyboard to change the repeat rate by pressing Alt+R and using the Arrow keys.

4. To see the effect of your changes without closing the Keyboard dialog box, click on the Test box (or press Alt+T). Then, observe what happens when you press and hold down a character key such as B.

5. Choose the OK button to put your changes into effect; choose the Cancel button if you want to leave things the way they were when you opened the dialog box.

Both the repeat delay and the repeat rate contribute to the perceived speed with which keys repeat. If you want to increase this speed, first decrease the delay time and use the Test box to make sure that when you type *different* keys slowly, they do *not* repeat. If you want more speed, now increase the repeat rate. You may have to experiment a little, adjusting both delay and rate repeatedly and viewing the effect each time in the Test box, before you're happy with the result.

Changing the Feel of the Mouse

Windows understands that different people have different preferences for the way that the mouse "feels" when you move or click it. The feel of the mouse affects the ease with which you can select menu items, choose icons, move windows, and perform many other tasks. Windows allows you to:

- Change the mouse *tracking speed* — the speed with which its pointer moves across the screen when you move the mouse on the desk top.

- Change the *double-click speed* — the amount of time that must elapse before Windows interprets a double-click as two separate clicks.

- *Swap* the left and right buttons. By default, the left mouse button is the *primary button* — clicking it initiates the vast majority of mouse actions in Windows programs. If you want, you can "swap buttons" so that the right button becomes the primary one. Swapping buttons may be desirable if you want to use the mouse with your left hand.

- Leave *mouse trails* — a sequence of pointer icons that follows the path of the mouse across the screen. This feature may be desirable on some portable computers; it makes the mouse pointer easier to see.

To change the mouse settings:

Mouse

1. Choose the Mouse icon from the Control Panel window. The Mouse dialog box will be displayed. (Depending on the type of mouse you are using, you may see a dialog box that looks quite different from this one.)

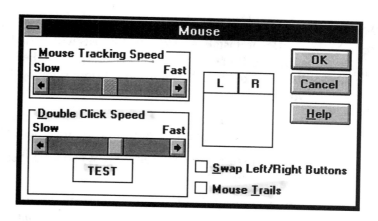

2. Set the tracking speed by dragging the Mouse Tracking Speed scroll box in the appropriate direction or by clicking on the appropriate arrow button.

3. Change the **double-click speed** by performing a similar operation in the Double Click Speed area of the dialog box. The faster you set the double-click speed, the quicker you'll have to follow the first click by the second when you want to double-click. To see if you're clicking quickly enough, double-click in the TEST box. It will blink or change color if Windows recognizes your action as a double-click.

4. If you want to swap mouse buttons, select the Swap Left/Right Buttons check box. The swap takes place immediately; even before you close the Mouse dialog box!

5. If you want to leave mouse pointer trails, select the Mouse Trails check box. (This feature may not be available on your system, in which case it will be dimmed.)

6. Choose the OK button. If you've swapped buttons, you have to click the right button on OK!

Adding or Adjusting Other Hardware

If you want to connect a new piece of hardware (such as a printer or a CD-ROM drive) to your system, you have to set it up to work with Windows. In some cases, you use Control Panel to do this; in others, you use Windows Setup. We will describe the Control Panel cases here and discuss Setup in Section 5.6.

Printers

Printers There are several ways to change the settings on a existing printer or install a new one for use with Windows. Control Panel provides the Printers option for this purpose. When you choose its icon from the Control Panel window, the Printers dialog box opens, which allows you to:

- Add a printer to, or remove a printer from, the Windows environment by choosing the Add or Remove buttons, respectively.

- Change a printer's settings by choosing Setup, and select an output port for it by choosing Connect.

- Select a *default printer*; the one to be used unless you specify otherwise. Choose the Set as Default Printer button to do this.

- Enable or disable Print Manager by selecting or deselecting the Use Print Manager check box. (See Section 4.5 for more information on this.)

Sound Every computer comes equipped with a small speaker located within the system unit and the ability to emit simple sounds from it. Most applications use this sound capability to issue a "beep" under certain circumstances. Other applications, such as video games, transmit more complicated sounds through the speaker.

However, to produce sophisticated sound, such as speech or music, a computer really needs to be equipped with better speakers and the circuitry (a *sound board*) to drive them. This equipment is sometimes sold with the computer, but can also be purchased later on, if the need arises.

Using the Windows Sound utility:

- You can enable (turn on) or disable (turn off) all system sounds. This is useful in those situations when you don't want your computer making undue noise.

- If a sound board is installed in your computer, you can assign different sounds to certain *system events* (such as starting or exiting Windows) or to replace the default "beep."

Sound

To start Sound, choose its icon from the Control Panel window. The Sound dialog box will open. If a sound board is not installed in your computer, you can only use this dialog box to enable or disable system sounds, by selecting or deselecting the Enable System Sounds check box. Choosing the OK button puts the change into effect.

If your computer *does* have a sound board, you can select events from the Events list and assign them (one at a time) to sounds selected from the Files list. The names of the files that contain the sounds all have the extension WAV and are usually descriptive, such as "chimes .wav". You can test the selected sound by choosing the Test button (or double-clicking the selected event or file name), which will "play" the WAV file. When you have finished assigning sounds to events, choose the OK button.

Ports If you want to connect a device, such as a modem, to one of your computer's serial ports, you have to *configure* that port (set its parameters) so that the device will work properly. For example, you may have to set the *baud rate* (the rate at which it transfers signals) and the number of *data bits* (the basic packet of information). The proper settings can be found in the device's operating manual.

To configure a serial port, choose the Ports icon from the Control Panel window. Then, select the desired port (they are labelled COM1, COM2, etc.), choose the Settings button, and type in the required information in the resulting dialog box.

Ports

Drivers Each peripheral device connected to your computer requires a program called a **device driver** to communicate with the system. Windows supplies drivers for many brands of mice, monitors, keyboards, sound cards, and so on. Drivers are also supplied (on disk) by the manufacturer of the hardware and with some software programs, as well. In addition to physically connecting a peripheral to your system (and, if it's a serial device, configuring the port), you have to install its driver.

To install a device driver:

1. Choose the Drivers icon from the Control Panel window. The Drivers dialog box, listing the drivers already installed, will be displayed.

Drivers

2. Choose the Add button. A list of additional drivers appears.

3. Select the driver you want to add and choose the OK button.

4. A dialog box may appear asking you to insert the disk that contai the driver. Insert this diskette into its drive and choose th ton.

5. Still another dialog box may appear, a settings for the new driver. Make the o the OK button to complete the process.

The new driver will be available the next time)

Hands-On 5.4

Start up Windows and Control Panel (if necessary) and perform the indicated tasks. To create a printed copy of your work, see Appendix B.

1. Choose the Keyboard icon. Describe the current settings for the delay and repeat rate (in terms of "long" and "short" or "fast" and "slow").
2. Set the delay as short as possible and type *different* keys slowly in the Test box. Do you find that any of the characters have repeated?
3. Cancel the Keyboard dialog box.
4. Choose the Mouse icon. Does your Mouse dialog box provide fewer, the same, or more options than the one shown on page 183?
5. Describe the current settings for the tracking speed and double-click speed (in terms of "fast" and "slow").
6. Cancel the Mouse dialog box.
7. By examining the Sound dialog box, determine whether or not your computer contains a sound board. Cancel this dialog box.
8. How many serial ports are listed in the Ports dialog box? Cancel this dialog box.

5.5   Other Control Panel Options

So far in this chapter, we have discussed those features of Control Panel that affect the screen colors, the look of the desktop, and the way certain hardware works with Windows. In this section, we will describe the remaining Control Panel options.

Managing Fonts

What is a font?

A **font** is a collection of characters — letters, numerals, and other symbols — of a given design, size, and style. Examples of fonts are "12-point Times New Roman" and "10-point Arial bold"; they look like this:

12-point Times New Roman   **10-point Arial bold**

The size of a font is given by its height, measured in points — a *point* is 1/72 of an inch. (Thus, 12-point type is roughly 1/6-inch high.) Fonts are also distinguished by their *style*; for example: regular, **bold**, and *italic*. Windows employs fonts for two basic purposes: *screen fonts* are used to display characters on the screen and *printer fonts*, not surprisingly, are used with printers.

Some fonts are available only in certain discrete sizes, such as 8-point, 10-point, etc. Others, called **scalable fonts**, can be scaled to any size. Times New Roman and Arial are examples of a kind of scalable font called **TrueType**, which is included with Windows 3.1. (TrueType fonts are also available from many other sources. So are scalable fonts of other kinds, notably the *PostScript* typefaces developed by Adobe Corporation.)

We will have more to say about fonts in general when we discuss word processing in Chapter 6. Here, we will concentrate on how you can use Control Panel to add (install) and remove fonts, and to set certain options for them. To perform these tasks:

Fonts

1. Choose the Fonts icon from the Control Panel window. The Fonts dialog box will be displayed:

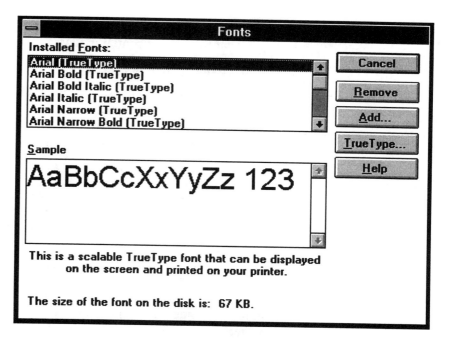

The Installed Fonts list contains all screen and printer fonts currently available for use with your Windows applications. Scalable fonts are listed by name only; for non-scalable fonts, the available sizes are also shown.

2. Add or remove fonts or set TrueType options, as described below.

3. Choose the Close button.

Adding Fonts   If you want to install fonts:

1. In the Fonts dialog box, choose the Add button. The Add Fonts dialog box will be displayed.

2. Select the drive and directory in which the file containing the fonts is located from the Drives and Directories lists.

3. Select the fonts you want to add from the List of Fonts box, or choose the Select All button if you want to add all the listed fonts.

4. Choose the OK button. The Fonts dialog box will reappear.

Removing Fonts   Removing fonts from Windows frees some RAM for use by applications and deleting the font files from disk frees some disk space. To perform these tasks:

1. In the Installed Fonts list of the Fonts dialog box, select the fonts that you want to remove from Windows.

2. Choose the Remove button. A Remove Fonts dialog box will appear.

3. To confirm the removal, choose Yes for each font, or Yes to All if you're sure you want to remove all selected fonts. If you also want to delete the fonts from disk, select the Delete Font File From Disk check box. When this operation is complete, the Fonts dialog box will reappear.

Selecting TrueType Options   Windows provides users with the option of turning off TrueType fonts (if you aren't using them in your applications) or showing only TrueType fonts (if you use them exclusively). To turn either option on or off:

1. In the Fonts dialog box, choose the TrueType button. The TrueType dialog box will be displayed.

2. If you're *not* using TrueType fonts, deselect the Enable TrueType Fonts check box. This will free some RAM. (This option goes into effect the next time you start Windows.)

3. If you *only* use TrueType fonts, select the Show Only TrueType Fonts in Applications check box. This will keep other types of fonts from appearing in an application's Fonts dialog box.

4. Choose the OK button. (If you've enabled or disabled TrueType fonts, a dialog box is displayed asking you if you want to restart Windows to put the change into effect immediately.)

Setting the System Date and Time

Your computer contains an internal clock, powered by a battery, that keeps track of the date and time for your computer system. These settings are used by File Manager, the Windows accessories Clock and Calendar, and numerous other applications for various purposes.

The internal clock normally keeps fairly accurate time, but it may need to be adjusted every once in a while. In particular, at the beginning and end of Daylight Saving Time, you will have to move it ahead or back an hour. To change the system date and time:

Date/Time

1. Choose the Date/Time icon from the Control Panel window. The following dialog box will be displayed:

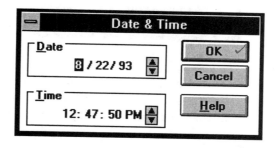

2. To change the date, in the Date box, select the month, day, or year part of the date and type the new value (or click the arrow buttons to move to the new value).

3. To change the time, in the Time box, select the hours, minutes, seconds, or AM/PM part of the time and type the new value (or click the arrow buttons to move to the new value).

4. Choose the OK button.

Changing International Settings

International

Windows software is used in just about every country in the world and must allow for different languages, currencies, and date formats. These factors can be changed by choosing the International icon from the Control Panel window, which opens the following dialog box:

```
┌─────────────────────────────────────────────────────────────┐
│  ▬                        International                       │
├─────────────────────────────────────────────────────────────┤
│  Country:          │United States          │▲▼│   ┌────────┐ │
│                                                   │   OK   │ │
│  Language:         │English (American)     │▲▼│   └────────┘ │
│                                                   ┌────────┐ │
│  Keyboard Layout:  │US                     │▲▼│   │ Cancel │ │
│                                                   └────────┘ │
│  Measurement:      │English                │▲▼│   ┌────────┐ │
│                                                   │  Help  │ │
│  List Separator:   │,│                            └────────┘ │
│  ┌Date Format─────────────────────┐ ┌Currency Format───────┐ │
│  │                  ┌──────────┐   │ │   $1.22  ┌─────────┐ │ │
│  │    8/22/93       │ Change...│   │ │          │Change...│ │ │
│  │  Sunday, August 22, 1993     │  │ │  ($1.22) └─────────┘ │ │
│  └──────────────────────────────┘  └──────────────────────┘ │
│  ┌Time Format─────────────────────┐ ┌Number Format─────────┐ │
│  │                  ┌──────────┐   │ │          ┌─────────┐ │ │
│  │   12:50:03 PM    │ Change...│   │ │ 1,234.22 │Change...│ │ │
│  │                  └──────────┘   │ │          └─────────┘ │ │
│  └──────────────────────────────┘  └──────────────────────┘ │
└─────────────────────────────────────────────────────────────┘
```

The only values in this dialog box that you are likely to want to change are those for date and time format. By default, in File Manager, Clock, Calendar, and other applications, Windows displays:

■ A *short date* format of Month/Day/Year (M/D/Y); for example, 1/2/94 for January 2, 1994. A D/M/Y format, on the other hand, would display this date as 2/1/94.

■ A *long date* format that consists of the day of the week followed by Month, Day, and Year (M/D/Y). For example, Sunday, January 2, 1994.

■ A *time* format that uses a 12-hour clock together with AM or PM instead of a 24-hour clock. For example, 8:23 PM instead of 20:23.

To change the date or time format, choose the Change button in the Date Format or Time Format box, respectively. In either case, a dialog box will appear allowing you to select the desired format. For example, if you want to change the time format from a 12-hour clock to a 24-hour clock:

1. Choose the Change button in the Time Format box. The following dialog box will be displayed:

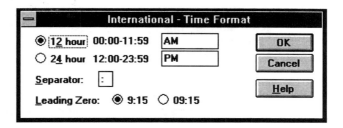

2. Choose the 2<u>4</u> hour option button.

3. In displaying the time, we normally use a colon to separate hours from minutes and minutes from seconds. If you want, you can use any other character by selecting the <u>S</u>eparator box and typing that character. For example, if you type a hyphen (-), time will be displayed like this: 7-54-22.

4. You can choose to use leading zeroes in the time format by selecting the 09:15 option button. The time will then be displayed using two digits each for hours, minutes, and seconds; for example, 07:54:22.

5. Choose the OK button. The International dialog box will reappear.

Optional Control Panel Features

There are three Control Panel features which, depending on the configuration of your system, may or may not be available. They are:

386 Enhanced

1. If Windows is running in 386 Enhanced mode (which requires at least two megabytes of RAM and a 386, 486, or Pentium processor), the 386 Enhanced icon will appear in the Control Panel window. If you choose this icon, you will be given options that affect the features available when Windows runs in this mode. These options are discussed in Section 9.2.

Network

2. If your computer is connected to a network and it has been set up to work with Windows, the Network icon will appear in the Control Panel window. If you choose this icon, you will be given options that affect the way that you communicate with the network; for example, sign on/sign off and password selection procedures.

MIDI Mapper

3. If a Musical Instrument Digital Interface (MIDI) has been installed to provide sophisticated sound capabilities for your system, usually through the use of a synthesizer, the MIDI Mapper icon will appear

in the Control Panel window. If you choose this icon, you will be given numerous options to ensure that your computer works correctly with the sound hardware connected to it.

Hands-On 5.5

Start up Windows and Control Panel (if necessary) and perform the indicated tasks. To create a printed copy of your work, see Appendix B.

1. Choose the Fonts icon to open the Fonts dialog box. How many fonts are listed? Do any TrueType fonts appear in the list? Are any other fonts listed?
2. Open the TrueType dialog box. Change the status of the <u>S</u>how Only TrueType Fonts in Applications check box (for example, if it is not checked, select it) and choose OK. Do any non-TrueType fonts appear in the Installed Fonts list now?
3. Return the "Show Only TrueType Fonts" check box to its former status and cancel the Fonts dialog box.
4. Open the Date & Time dialog box. What is the date format (M/D/Y, D/M/Y, etc.)? Is a 12-hour or 24-hour clock being used?
5. Cancel the Date & Time dialog box.
6. Open the International dialog box. What are the current <u>C</u>ountry, <u>L</u>anguage, <u>K</u>eyboard Layout, and <u>M</u>easurement settings?
7. Cancel the International dialog box.
8. Which, if any, "optional" (386 Enhanced, Network, MIDI Mapper) Control Panel icons appear in the window?

5.6   Other Ways to Customize Windows

All the customizing features you've seen so far in this chapter have been accessed from Control Panel. Windows provides several other ways to customize its operation. In this section, we will briefly describe these features.

Windows Setup

Customizing Using Windows Setup   Windows Setup is the program you run when installing Windows (see Appendix A). It can also be used when you want to make certain changes in the Windows environment. To start Setup from within Windows, choose its icon from Program Manager's Main group. The following dialog box will be displayed:

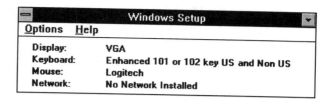

As you can see, this dialog box lists the current drivers for your video display adapter, keyboard, mouse, and network. The items on the Options menu allow you to:

■ Change the currently listed drivers by choosing the Change System Settings item.

■ Set up applications on your disk for use with Windows by choosing the Set Up Applications item.

■ Add or remove certain groups of files (components) from Windows. When you choose the Add/Remove Windows Components item, the following dialog box is displayed:

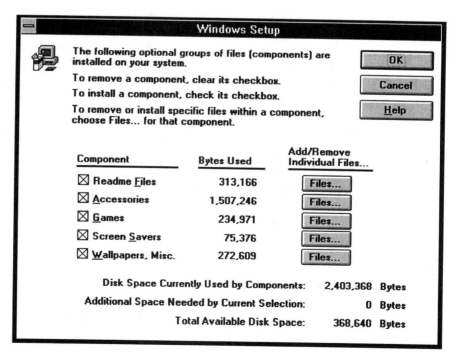

To add or remove the components listed (Readme Files, Accessories, etc.) or individual files within these components, follow the instructions at the top of the dialog box.

Customizing from Within an Application   As you have already seen in Program Manager and File Manager, you can customize Windows utilities and accessories by selecting menu items (usually from menus entitled Options, View, or Settings) or moving and resizing windows. This is also true for other Windows-based applications; here, the customizing features might also be chosen from a Preferences menu or from a Preferences item on the File menu.

Customizing by Editing Initialization Files   Initialization files, which have an INI extension and are located in the WINDOWS directory, are used by Windows and Windows-based applications to configure themselves when starting up. For example, when you start Windows, it determines the current desktop color scheme, pattern, and wallpaper from entries in a file called WIN.INI. It also determines your hardware configuration by "consulting" the SYSTEM.INI file. Other initialization files store your preferences for specific applications; for example, PROGMAN.INI for Program Manager and WINFILE.INI for File Manager.

Information is usually entered into initialization files by using user-friendly software within Windows or a specific application. For example, most of the entries in the WIN.INI file are the result of default settings or changes you have made to them using the Control Panel options. However, some entries in an INI file can only be changed by editing the file itself. For example, to change the size of the font used for Program Manager icon titles, you must edit the WIN.INI file.

Editing an initialization file is not for the faint of heart; improper entries can lead to unfortunate results, such as your computer *locking up* (refusing to respond to keyboard or mouse) when Windows is started. Nevertheless, if you're curious about the content of the INI files and how to edit them, see the manual for the Windows *Resource Kit*.

Chapter Summary

Key Terms   Bitmap image [page 175]

Control Panel [162]

Device driver [185]

Color scheme [164]

Desktop pattern [173]

Font [186]

Hue [168]

Luminosity [169]

Password [177]

Scalable font [187]

Solid color [170]

Wallpaper [175]

Initialization file [194]

Nonsolid color [170]

Saturation [168]

Screen saver [176]

TrueType font [187]

Windows Setup [192]

Topics
Covered

Control Panel Options and their Functions

Color	Selects existing color schemes. Creates new color schemes. Creates custom colors for use in new color schemes.
Date/Time	Sets the system date and time.
Desktop	Selects a desktop pattern. Creates new desktop patterns. Selects wallpaper. Selects and sets up a screen saver. Enables or disables Alt+Tab application switching. Changes the text cursor blink rate. Changes icon spacing and wraps titles. Changes window granularity and border width.
Drivers	Installs and sets up device drivers.
Fonts	Adds and removes fonts from Windows. Sets TrueType options.
International	Specifies international settings for country, language, keyboard layout, and system of measurement. Specifies the format for dates, times, currencies, and numbers.
Keyboard	Changes the repeat delay and repeat rate.
MIDI Mapper	Selects, changes, and creates MIDI setups.
Mouse	Sets the tracking speed. Sets the double-click speed. Swaps the left and right mouse buttons. Enables or disables pointer trails.
Network	Controls the way you access your network.
Ports	Specifies the settings for the computer's serial ports.

Printers   Adds and removes printers from Windows.
                         Specifies a printer's settings.
                         Selects a default printer.
                         Enables or disables Print Manager.

Sound   Enables or disables system sounds.
                         Assigns sounds to system events.

386 Enhanced   Specifies settings for 386 Enhanced mode operation.

Other Ways to Customize Windows

Windows Setup   Installs drivers for display adapter, keyboard, mouse,
                            and network.
                         Sets up applications to work with Windows.
                         Adds and removes Windows' components.

Windows-based   Sets preferences for that specific application.
   application

Initialization file   Edits the Windows' environment settings.

Chapter Exercises

***Short
Answer***

Complete each statement in Exercises 1 through 12.

1. To start Control Panel, choose its icon from the _____ group
    window.

2. The Color dialog box contains a list of predefined _____ .

3. You can create a custom color using the Custom Color Selector by
    specifying its hue, saturation, and _____ .

4. You can use Desktop to place _____ , a bitmap image, either
    tiled or centered on the desktop.

5. A _____ can be used to cause an animated image to appear
    on the screen after a specified period of inactivity.

6. To change the text cursor blink rate, choose the _____ icon
    from the Control Panel window.

7. To change the keyboard repeat rate, choose the _____ icon
    from the Control Panel window.

8. If you want the mouse to move more quickly across the screen when

you move it on the desk top, adjust its _____ using the Mouse option in Control Panel.

9. TrueType is a collection of _____ that are packaged with Windows.

10. If the Clock accessory is displaying the wrong time, you can reset the time by choosing the _____ icon from Control Panel.

11. The _____ utility can be used to add or remove Windows components.

12. The files that store the settings that Windows uses to configure itself when starting up are called _____ files.

In Exercises 13 through 25, determine whether each statement is true or false.

13. To change the screen colors for the Windows desktop, choose the Desktop icon from the Control Panel window.

14. To view the colors that make up a predefined color scheme, you must exit the Color dialog box.

15. In the Custom Color Selector, if you set Red, Green, and Blue to maximum levels, you will obtain the color white.

16. Desktop patterns are always displayed on a white background.

17. To view wallpaper you have just selected from the list in the Desktop window, you must first close this window.

18. To view a screen saver you have just selected from the list in the Desktop window, you must first close this window.

19. The text cursor blink rate can be changed by using the Keyboard option in Control Panel.

20. Using Control Panel, you can set up the mouse so that launching an application can be done by double-clicking the *right* mouse button on the appropriate icon.

21. A font is a collection of characters, all of which are the same point size.

22. The system date and time must be set every time you start Windows.

23. The International option in Control Panel is only available if your

computer was not manufactured in the United States.

24. The 386 Enhanced option in Control Panel is not available if you are using a computer with a 286 processor.

25. Windows Setup must be started from the DOS prompt.

In Exercises 26 through 34, choose the correct answer.

26. Which of the following is not a Control Panel option?

    a. Color.
    b. Desktop.
    c. Setup.
    d. International.

27. In the Custom Color Selector, you can specify a color by:

    a. Giving its hue, saturation, and luminosity.
    b. Using the color refiner box and the luminosity bar.
    c. Setting its red, green, and blue levels.
    d. Doing any of the above.

28. You cannot use the Desktop option in Control Panel to:

    a. Change the text cursor blink rate.
    b. Set the system date and time.
    c. Select a screen saver.
    d. Select wallpaper.

29. A screen saver:

    a. Only appears when your computer has been idle for a while.
    b. Cannot be used if a wallpaper has been selected.
    c. Will appear if you have been typing for a long time.
    d. Has all of the above properties.

30. A desktop pattern:

    a. May be tiled or centered.
    b. Is always the same color as the desktop.
    c. Can be edited to produce a new pattern.
    d. Has all of the above properties.

31. The Fonts option in Control Panel allows you to:

    a. Change the font used for icon titles in Program Manager.
    b. Change the font used in File Manager.
    c. Set a default font for your printer.

    d. Remove fonts from the Windows environment.

32. Which of the following can be used to customize Windows?

    a. The options available in Control Panel.
    b. The Windows Setup utility.
    c. Initialization files.
    d. All of the above can be used to customize Windows.

33. Which of the following Control Panel options is available only if your computer has the necessary hardware?

    a. Color.
    b. Network.
    c. Sound.
    d. All of the above.

34. Control Panel cannot be used to:

    a. Change the time on the computer's internal clock.
    b. Set up applications for use with Windows.
    c. Turn off (disable) the Print Manager utility.
    d. Turn off (disable) the computer's speaker.

Hands-On   In Exercises 35 through 40, start up Windows and Control Panel (if necessary) and perform the indicated tasks. To create a printed copy of your work, see Appendix B.

35. a. Open the Color dialog box (by choosing its icon) and expand it (by choosing the Color Palette button). What is the default color scheme?

    b. Select the "Windows Default" color scheme. How many different colors does it contain? (Either examine the sample screen or scroll through the Screen Elements while observing the Basic Colors selection cursor.)

    c. Try to remove this scheme. Can you?

    d. Now select the color scheme called "The Blues". Change the Inactive Title Bar to a light blue color and the Window Background to black. Can you still see the words "Window Text" in the sample screen?

    e. Select two contrasting colors for Button Shadow and Button Highlight. By examining the sample screen, describe the difference between these two screen elements.

    f. Choose the Cancel button to close the Color dialog box.

36. a. Open the Color dialog box (by choosing its icon) and expand it (by choosing the Color Palette button). Are any Custom Colors defined?

    b. Choose the Define Custom Colors button to open the Custom Color Selector window. What are the current values for Red, Green, and Blue?

    c. Drag the color refiner cursor across the bottom edge of the color refiner box. The value Sat should remain constant; what is it? What is the color all along the bottom edge?

    d. Set Red to 255, Green to 127, and Blue to 0. How would you describe this color? What is the closest solid color? (To answer both questions, check the Color/Solid box.)

    e. Assign the color specified in part d to the first Custom Colors box; assign the closest solid color to the second box.

    f. Choose the Close button.

    g. Cancel the expanded Color dialog box. Now, open it again. Do your custom colors still appear in their boxes?

    h. Cancel the Color dialog box to return to Control Panel.

37. a. Open the Desktop dialog box. What is the default desktop pattern?

    b. Choose the Edit Pattern button. What pattern is displayed in the Sample and Edit boxes?

    c. Select the "50% Gray" pattern. By examining the Sample box, it's probably clear why it's called 50% Gray, but based upon the Edit box, what's a better name for it?

    d. Edit the pattern by clicking on all the dark squares in *every other* row. How many mouse clicks did you use?

    e. Choose the OK button to return to the Desktop window. What is the default wallpaper?

    f. Select the "cars.bmp" wallpaper, select the Center option button, and choose OK.

    g. Reduce all running applications (including Program Manager) to icons. Do you see the desktop pattern, the wallpaper, neither, or both?

    h. Restore the Program Manager and Control Panel windows and open the Desktop window. Select the pattern and wallpaper that were in effect when you began this exercise. Then, close the Desktop dialog box.

38. a. Open the Desktop dialog box. What is the default screen saver? What is the delay time?

    b. Select the Blank Screen screen saver. What are the Setup

options?

c. Select the Mystify screen saver and Test it. How many rotating figures appear? How many sides does each have?

d. Choose the Setup button. What is the purpose of the Active check box? (If you can't figure it out, consult Help!)

e. Cancel the Mystify Setup dialog box and select the screen saver that was in effect at the beginning of this exercise.

f. Set the Cursor Blink Rate at its slowest and fastest settings. How many blinks per second occur at these two speeds? Return the blink rate to its original setting.

g. Set the Border Width to its maximum setting. What is this setting? Choose OK. How thick (in inches) do the Control Panel borders appear to be?

h. Open the Desktop dialog box, return the Border Width to its original setting (probably 3), and choose OK.

39. a. Open the Keyboard dialog box. Where are the Delay and Repeat Rate scroll boxes positioned on their scroll bars?

b. Set the repeat delay to be as short as possible and the repeat rate to be as fast as possible. Using the Test box, how many characters per second do you think are being displayed when you hold down a key?

c. Cancel the Keyboard dialog box.

d. Open the Mouse dialog box. Does it supply options to adjust tracking speed (or pointer speed) and double-click speed? What other options does it offer?

e. Cancel the Mouse dialog box.

f. Open the Sound dialog box. Are System Sounds enabled? How can you tell from this dialog box if your computer has a sound board installed?

g. Cancel the Sound dialog box.

40. a. Open the Fonts dialog box. Which fonts appear at the top and bottom of the list of Installed Fonts?

b. Choose the TrueType button to open its window. Which, if any of the check boxes are selected?

c. Choose Cancel to close the TrueType window and choose Cancel again to close the Fonts dialog box.

d. Open the Date & Time dialog box. Is time displayed using a 12-hour or a 24-hour clock?

e. Close the Date & Time dialog box by choosing Cancel.

f. Open the International dialog box. How many different language listings are there? What are the available systems of measurement?

g. Cancel the International dialog box.

Creative Writing

41. Control Panel provides more than 25 functions to customize Windows (see the list in the Chapter Summary). Which do you believe are the three most important customizing features? Justify your answers.

42. Describe one way that you would like to customize Windows that is currently not available in Windows. Give a name to this option and describe its features (being specific about the way they work).

43. Describe a procedure that could be used to perform each of the following tasks. (Begin with: "Choose the Desktop icon ...".)

    a. Edit an existing desktop pattern so that the new one replaces the original in the Desktop Name list.

    b. Remove an existing pattern from the Desktop Name list.

44. There are three Control Panel options (386 Enhanced, Network, and MIDI Mapper) that are available only if your computer has certain hardware installed. If your Control Panel window contains one of these icons, with the aid of Help and/or the Windows *User's Guide,* describe the features of this option.

6 Word Processing: Write and Notepad

OVERVIEW   Word processing was one of the first business-related applications available for personal computers and it is now probably the most popular. Windows supplies two applications whose primary purpose is to help you create text-based documents:

- **Write** is a medium-strength word processor. You can use it to write letters, memos, essays, and moderately complicated documents, such as reports and term papers.

- **Notepad** is a very simple word processor, a *text editor*. It is suitable for quick jobs such as writing notes and editing certain system files.

In this chapter, we will discuss the features of these two applications. You will learn:

1. To use Write to create a simple document: entering the text, saving it to disk, and printing it on a printer.

2. To use Write's editing features, such as search and replace.

3. About fonts and how to use them in Write documents.

4. To format a Write document, including setting margins, tabs, line spacing, and justification, and using headers and footers.

5. To insert and manipulate graphics in a Write document.

6. To use Notepad.

6.1   An Introduction to Write

Using a word processor to create a document involves several steps. You
have to:

1.   Enter the text that makes up the document.

2.   Edit the document to correct errors and improve its style.

3.   Format the document; for example, set margins and choose fonts.

4.   Save and print the document.

In this section, we will demonstrate how to use Write to enter text, make
corrections to it, and save and print the resulting document. Other features of Write will be discussed in the ensuing sections.

Entering Text in the Write Window

Write

To start Write, open the Accessories group window and choose the Write
icon (by, for example, double-clicking on it). This will open the window
shown in Figure 6.1.

FIGURE 6.1   The Write Window

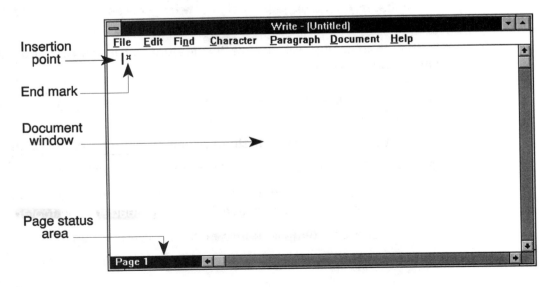

Entering text   Once you have started Write, you can type whatever you want on the keyboard, and the corresponding text will appear in the document window and be stored in RAM. The **insertion point** (or *text cursor*), the blinking vertical bar, indicates where the next character you type will appear on the screen. The **end mark** (see Figure 6.1) indicates the end of the document.

When you reach the end of a line, just keep typing; Write's **word wrap** feature will automatically continue the text at the beginning of the next line. To start a new line manually, press the Enter key, and the insertion point will move to the beginning of the next line. If you want to skip a line, press Enter again.

For example, suppose you have to write a report for your history class. You start Write and begin by typing the title and then press Enter twice to skip a line. Now, you type your name, your class, and the date, pressing Enter after each, so that these items appear on separate lines. The Write window should now resemble the one in Figure 6.2.

FIGURE 6.2   Text Entered into the Write Window

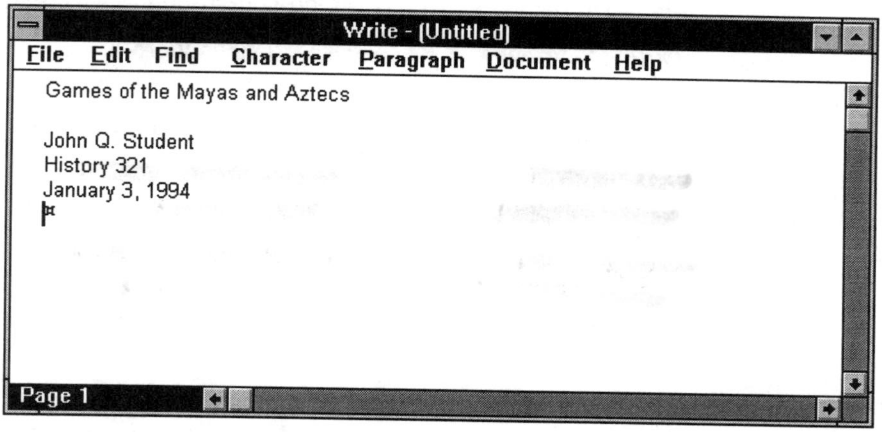

Write - (Untitled)
File   Edit   Find   Character   Paragraph   Document   Help
Games of the Mayas and Aztecs
John Q. Student
History 321
January 3, 1994
Page 1

Simple Editing

If you make a typing error, you can erase the character just to the left of the insertion point by pressing the Backspace (or ◄───) key; to delete the character just to the right of the insertion point, press the Delete (or Del) key. If you notice a mistake elsewhere on the screen, you can move the insertion point to this location using either the mouse or keyboard:

- To use the mouse, scroll the Write window, if necessary, until the desired location is visible on the screen. Then click on this location to move the insertion point there. (See "Working in a Window" in Section 1.3 for more information on using scroll bars.)

- You can also use the Arrow keys to move the insertion point left, right, up, or down and to scroll the window (see "Working in a Window" in Section 1.3). Certain other keys will often do the job faster, as detailed in Table 6.1. In this table, "5" refers to the 5 key on the numeric keypad *with Num Lock off*.

TABLE 6.1   Text Cursor Movement Keys

Key	Moves insertion point ...
Home / End	To beginning of a line / end of a line
Page Up / Page Down	One screen up / one screen down
Ctrl+Left Arrow / Ctrl+Right Arrow	To previous word / next word
Ctrl+Home / Ctrl+End	To beginning of document / end of document
5+Left Arrow / 5+Right Arrow	To previous sentence / next sentence
5+Up Arrow / 5+Down Arrow	To previous paragraph / next paragraph

For example, suppose that your screen looks like the one in Figure 6.2 and you realize you've made a mistake; your middle initial is "X", not "Q". To correct this error:

1. Either click the mouse pointer just before the Q to move the insertion point there, or press the Up Arrow key three times and the Right Arrow key five times to accomplish the same thing.

2. Press the Del key to delete the Q, and type an X.

3. Press Ctrl+End to move the cursor back to the end of the document.

The page number that appears in the page status area of the Write window (Figure 6.1) can be misleading. It will continue to read "Page 1", even after you have entered what seems to be many pages of text. This is because Write does not break a document into pages until you issue either the Print or Repaginate command from the File menu. When you do, the pagination process is done automatically and the beginning of a new page is indicated by a >> symbol in the left margin. To insert a page break manually, move the insertion point to the desired location and press Ctrl+Enter. A manual page break is indicated on the screen by a dotted horizontal line.

Once the document has been broken into pages, you can move the insertion point to:

- The previous page or next page by pressing 5+Page Up or 5+Page Down, respectively. (Here, "5" represents the middle key on the numeric keypad with Num Lock off.)

- Any desired page by choosing Go To Page from the Find menu (or pressing F4), typing the desired page number in the dialog box, and choosing OK.

Saving a Write Document

When you *save* a document, it is copied from its temporary location in RAM to a more permanent place on disk. The save operation provides a name, of your choosing, for the document, as well. If you don't save your document before exiting Write, the changes you have made to it since the last save will be lost.

Write provides two versions of the save operation:

- The Save command on the File menu saves the document under its current file name. The version of the document currently stored on disk under this name is *overwritten* (erased); the just-saved version, including all changes that you have made since the last save, replaces the former version.

- The Save As command on the File menu lets you select a file name for the document being saved, and then saves the document under this name. (If you don't specify an extension in the file name, Windows appends the extension WRI.) You would use the Save As command if your document has not yet been saved to disk, and consequently has no name, or if the document has a name but you want to create a new copy of it with a different name.

For a step-by-step description of how to issue the Save and Save As commands, see "Saving a Document" in Section 4.4. As an example, let's save the document in Figure 6.2 to the floppy disk in the A: drive:

1. Choose Save from the File menu. (The Save As dialog box appears because the file has never been saved.)

2. Select the a: drive from the Drives drop-down list.

3. Type TITLE-1 in the File Name text box.

4. Choose the OK button. (The file will be saved as A:\TITLE-1.WRI.)

When working on a document, it is generally wise to use the Save (or Save As) command frequently (perhaps every fifteen minutes or so) even if the document is not yet complete. Then, should disaster strike in the form of a power outage, a glitch in the system, or a mistake on your part, you won't have to recreate very much work. The last version of the document that was saved to disk is probably safe; you'll only have to redo the changes that were made since then.

Printing a Write Document

To print a copy of the document displayed in the Write window, make sure that the printer is on and ready to receive information from your computer. Then:

1. Choose the Print command from the File menu. When you do, the Print dialog box shown in Figure 6.3 will be displayed.

2. In this dialog box, select the desired options:

   ■ In the Print Range area, selecting the option button:
   All prints the entire document.
   Selection prints the currently selected text.
   Pages prints the range of pages specified in the From and To boxes.

   ■ Print Quality affects the way that graphics (pictures) in the document are printed. The higher the quality, the better they will look, but the slower they will print.

   ■ Selecting the Print to File check box causes the document, together with all printer codes, to be copied to disk.

FIGURE 6.3   The Print Dialog Box

```
┌────────────────────────────────────────────────────────┐
│ ─                          Print                         │
├────────────────────────────────────────────────────────┤
│ Printer:      Default Printer (HP LaserJet 4/4M          │
│               on LPT1:)                    ┌──────────┐  │
│  ┌─Print Range──────────────────────┐     │    OK    │  │
│  │ ⊙ All                            │     └──────────┘  │
│  │                                  │     ┌──────────┐  │
│  │ ○ Selection                      │     │  Cancel  │  │
│  │                                  │     └──────────┘  │
│  │ ○ Pages                          │     ┌──────────┐  │
│  │    From: │1│      To: │1│         │     │ Setup... │  │
│  └──────────────────────────────────┘     └──────────┘  │
│                                                          │
│  Print Quality:  │High            ▼│   Copies:  │1│      │
│  ☐ Print to File                     ⊠ Collate Copies    │
└────────────────────────────────────────────────────────┘
```

- You can select the number of Copies of each page to be printed and whether to Collate Copies (sort them).

- Choosing the Setup button provides additional options that are specific to the selected printer (see Section 4.5).

3. Choose the OK button.

Closing a Document and Quitting Write

If you are finished working on one document and want to start another, choose New from the File menu. This will remove the current document from RAM and clear the Write window. (If you've made changes to the current document after the last save, a warning message will be issued before the New command is carried out.)

When you are finished processing words, you can exit Write in the same manner you exit most Windows applications (see Section 2.6). The quickest ways are to double-click on the Control menu box or to press Alt+F4. You can also choose Exit from the File menu.

Hands-On 6.1

Start up Windows and Write, if necessary, and try the following exercise:

1. Clear the Write window, if it is not empty, by choosing New from the File menu.

2. Type the following text (skipping lines, as indicated):

> January 4, 1994
>
> Dear Pat,
>   Having a good time! Wish you were here.
>
> --- John

3. Print the resulting document.
4. Change the word "good" to "great".
5. Save this document to a floppy disk, giving it the name JOHN.LTR. Was it saved under this name or under JOHN.WRI?
6. Print the document.
7. Clear the Write window.

6.2   Editing a Write Document

In Section 6.1, we demonstrated how to **edit** (change) a Write document in a simple way: by using the Delete or Backspace keys and then typing new text. In this section, we will discuss more powerful editing features.

Opening a Write Document

When you *open* a document, it is copied from disk into RAM and (at least part of it) is displayed in the document window. To open a Write document, choose Open from the File menu. For a detailed description of the process, see "Opening a Document" in Section 4.4.

As an example, let's open the GAMES.WRI file in the WRITE directory on the Lab Projects diskette (assuming the disk is in the A: drive):

1. Choose Open from the File menu (displaying the Open dialog box).

2. Select the a: drive from the Drives list (by clicking on it) and the WRITE directory from the Directories list (by double-clicking on it).

3. Double-click on the GAMES.WRI name in the File Name list.

Selecting Text

To perform certain editing and formatting operations, you must first *select* text within a document. You can select any block of text by moving the insertion point just in front of the first character of the block and either:

- Dragging the mouse just past the last character in the block.

or

- Holding down the Shift key while using cursor movement keys to move the insertion point just past the last character in the block.

In either case, the selected text is highlighted on the screen.

Write also provides an easy way to select lines, paragraphs, or the entire document. These techniques make use of the **selection area** of the Write window — the region between the text and the left window border. When the mouse cursor enters the selection area, it changes shape from an I-beam to a pointer. Figure 6.4 shows the mouse pointer in the selection area and the second paragraph of the document selected.

FIGURE 6.4   Selecting Text Using the Selection Area

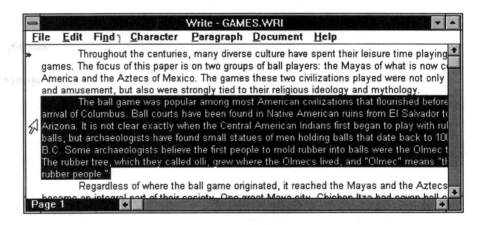

Using the selection area

To use the selection area technique:

- To select *a line* of text, move the mouse pointer into the selection area next to that line and click. To select *several lines*, drag the mouse through the selection area next to these lines.

- To select *a paragraph* of text, move the mouse pointer into the selection area next to that paragraph and double-click.

■ To select *the entire document*, move the mouse pointer into the selection area (anywhere), hold down the Ctrl key, and click.

As usual, the selected text will become highlighted.

To cancel a selection, if you change your mind, just press the Esc key or click the mouse anywhere on the screen. The previously-selected text will be restored to its normal appearance.

Deleting, Moving, and Copying Text

When you are trying to improve the style of a document, the ability to delete, move, and copy large blocks of text is a time-saving convenience. All these tasks can be performed with the aid of the Windows Clipboard, as explained in Section 2.4. We will briefly review these techniques here.

■ To *delete* a block of text, select the block and press the Delete key.

■ To *move* a block of text; that is, to delete it from its current location and place it somewhere else:

> Select the block.
> Choose Cut from the Edit menu (or press Ctrl+X).
> Move the insertion point where you want to place the text.
> Choose Paste from the Edit menu (or press Ctrl+V).

■ To *copy a block of text* — to transfer it to a new location without deleting it from the current one — follow the *move* procedure just described, but instead of cutting the text, choose Copy from the Edit menu (or press Ctrl+C).

For example, to interchange the first and second paragraphs in the GAMES.WRI document, select the second paragraph as shown in Figure 6.4, choose Cut from the Edit menu, move the insertion point to the beginning of the document (by, for example, pressing Ctrl+Home), and choose Paste from the Edit menu.

In editing a document, you will occasionally do something that you wish you hadn't, such as deleting a large and especially important block of text. Fortunately, Write provides the Undo command for just such situations. To undo the effect of your *last* editing (or formatting) change, choose Undo from the Edit menu or just press Ctrl+Z. The document will be restored to the way it was before the last modification.

Search and Replace

Another common editing operation involves replacing one or more occurrences of a word or phrase with another word or phrase. (For example, you might want to replace every occurrence of the word *loss* in a document with the word *profit*.) This operation is known as "search and replace." To perform a search and replace:

1. Position the insertion point where you want the search to begin, or select the text that you want searched, and choose Replace from the Find menu. The Replace dialog box will be displayed:

Replace	
Fi**n**d What: [ ]	**F**ind Next
Re**p**lace With: [ ]	**R**eplace
☒ Match **W**hole Word Only	Replace Se**l**ection
☐ Match **C**ase	C**l**ose

Select

2. Type the text you want to change in the **Fi**nd What box and type the text you want to replace it by in the **Replace With box**.

3. Select the Match **W**hole Word Only check box if you just want to replace entire words. For example, suppose your document contains the words *all*, *small*, and *allow*, and you type *all* in the Fi**n**d What box and *every* in the Replace With box. If the Match Whole Word Only check box is selected, only the word *all* will be replaced with *every*. On the other hand, if this check box is not selected, *all* will be replaced with *every*, *small* with *smevery*, and *allow* with *everyow*!

4. Select the Match Case check box if you just want to replace text that has the same combination of upper and lower case letters as the Fi**n**d What text. For example, if this check box is selected and you type *all* in the Fi**n**d What box, then *all* will be replaced, but not *All*; if this check box is not selected, both *all* and *All* will be replaced.

5. Choose one of the command buttons:

   - **Fi**nd Ne**x**t locates the next occurrence of the Fi**n**d What text and highlights it, but does not replace it.

   - **R**eplace replaces the next occurrence of the Fi**n**d What text with the Replace With text.

- Replace All replaces all occurrences of the Find What text.

- Close terminates the search and replace process.

If the Find What text is not found, a message to this effect will be displayed on the screen.

You can use the Replace command to find text without replacing it (by choosing the Find Next button in the Replace dialog box), but there is an easier way to do this: Choose Find from the Find menu and the following dialog box will appear:

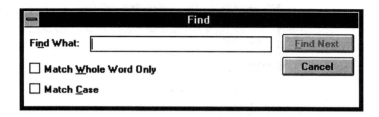

Then, type the text you want to locate in the Find What box and select either or both check boxes, if you want. You can use the *wildcard* **?** in the Find What text to represent any character. (It works the same way as the DOS wildcard character **?**, discussed in Section 3.3.) For example, *?all* will find *mall* and *ball*. Now, choose the Find Next button to locate the next occurrence of the specified text.

The Find dialog box will remain on the screen to allow you to locate additional occurrences of the specified text. As an alternative, you can choose Cancel to close the dialog box and then press F3 (or choose Repeat Last Find from the Find menu) to locate additional occurrences of the specified text.

Hands-On

6.2

Start up Windows and Write, if necessary, and try the following exercise:

1. If the Write window is not empty, clear it by choosing New from the File menu.
2. Insert the Lab Projects diskette in its drive.
3. Open the file GAMES.WRI in the WRITE directory on this disk.
4. Find all occurrences of the text *here* in this document. How many are there? How many of these occur in words other than "here"?
5. Select and delete the first paragraph of the document.
6. Move the last sentence to the beginning of the document.

7. Replace every occurrence of the word *found* with *discovered*.
8. Print the edited document.
9. Clear the Write window without saving the document.

6.3 Fun with Fonts

Nothing makes a bigger difference in the impact your words will have on the reader than the fonts you use to print them. In this section, we will discuss how to change fonts and font attributes in a Write document.

What is a Font?

A **font** is a collection of characters — letters, numerals, and other symbols — of a given design, size, and style.

- The *design* of a font refers to the general appearance of the characters, independent of their size, thickness, or other attributes. For example, Arial and Courier are two of the designs, or **typefaces**, supplied by Windows 3.1.

- The *size* of a font refers to its height, measured in *points*. There are 72 points per inch, so 12-point type is roughly 1/6-inch high. Here are some examples of different sizes of the Arial typeface:

8-point   12-point   18-point

- The *style* of a font refers to the attributes it has. The two most common styles are **bold** and *italic*.

Some fonts are distributed only in certain discrete sizes, such as 8-point, 10-point, and so on. Others, called **scalable fonts**, can be scaled to any size. Microsoft includes several scalable fonts, called *TrueType* fonts, with Windows. Other popular types of scalable fonts are the *PostScript* typefaces developed by Adobe Corporation.

WYSIWYG   When you launch the Write application and start typing, the text appears on the screen in the default font, typically 10-point Arial type. The text will also be printed in this font. When you change the font, it changes on both the screen and the printed page. We say that Write is a WYSIWYG (What You See Is What You Get, pronounced "whizzywig") word processor: WYSIWYG means that the appearance of the document on the screen, including fonts, spacing, graphics, and so on, generally previews the way it will be printed on your printer.

Changing the font

There are several ways of changing the font used by Write. With all techniques, the font change applies to either:

■ The currently selected text.

or

■ The text that you are about to type (if no text is currently selected).

The Fonts Command

The most flexible way to change the current font is to use the Fonts command. It allows you to change any combination of the typeface, style, and type size. To do so:

1. Choose the Fonts command from the Character menu. The Font dialog box shown in Figure 6.5 will be displayed.

FIGURE 6.5   The Font Dialog Box

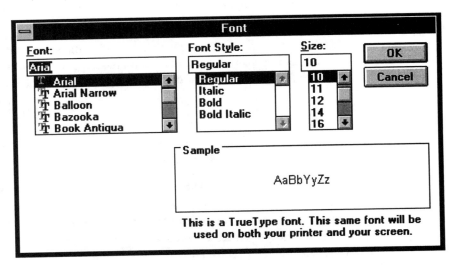

2. Select the desired typeface from the Font list.

3. Select a style from the Font Style list.

4. Select a size from the Size list. If the selected typeface is scalable

(for example, if it's a TrueType font), you can select any size supported by your printer, even if it does not appear on the Size list. Simply select one of the listed sizes and then type the size you want; it will appear at the top of the Size list.

5. Choose the OK button.

For example, in the document of Figure 6.2 on page 205 (which was saved as TITLE-1.WRI), to change the first line to 24-point Arial bold type, select this line and choose Fonts from the Character menu. Then, in the dialog box, select Arial from the Font list, Bold from the Font Style list, 24 from the Size list, and choose OK. The result is shown in Figure 6.6 on the next page.

Using the Character Menu

There are two quicker, though less flexible, ways of changing fonts in Write. Like the Fonts command, the changes apply to either the currently selected text or the characters you are about to type.

Adding a style

To add a style to the current font, choose the style you want from the Character menu:

bold   *italic*   <u>underline</u>   subscript   superscript

Bold, italic, and underline add emphasis to text; subscript and superscript are often used in scientific and mathematical formulas, such as H_2SO_4 and $f(x) = x^3 - 5x^2$. Note that Ctrl+B, Ctrl+I, and Ctrl+U are shortcut keys for bold, italic, and underline, respectively. They are easy to remember and will save you time.

Text may be given more than one style; those that are currently in effect (turned on) are indicated by check marks on the Character menu. You can turn off (cancel) a style by choosing it from the Character menu or by pressing its shortcut key; the check mark will also be removed from its menu item.

An easier way to cancel a style is to press F5 (or choose Regular from the Character menu). This method saves time if there is more than one style in effect. For example, suppose you have just typed **Shazam**. To turn off the bold and italic styles, all you need do is press F5 once! This technique works with both selected text and text that you are about to type.

**Enlarging or
reducing text**

To change the size of the current font, select Enlarge Font or Reduce Font from the Character menu. The text will be enlarged or reduced to the next larger or next smaller point size. (These sizes are set by Windows; they don't necessarily correspond to the sizes listed in the Fonts dialog box.)

For example, consider the last three lines on the screen of Figure 6.2 (page 205). If you want to change the style of this text from regular to bold and increase its size:

1. Select the three lines of text to be changed.

2. Press Ctrl+B or choose Bold from the Character menu.

3. Choose Enlarge from the Character menu.

Figure 6.6 shows the effects of making the font changes described in this section. (The document pictured here is stored in the WRITE directory on the Lab Projects diskette as TITLE-2.WRI.)

FIGURE 6.6   Changing the Font in a Document

Write - TITLE-2.WRI

File   Edit   Find   Character   Paragraph   Document   Help

Games of the Mayas and Aztecs

**John Q. Student
History 321
January 3, 1994**

Page 1

Hands-On

6.3

Start up windows and Write, if necessary, and try the following exercise:

1. Insert the Lab Projects diskette in its drive.
2. Open the file FONTS.WRI in the WRITE directory on this disk.
3. Follow the instructions on the screen.
4. Print the document.
5. Clear the Write window and remove the diskette from its drive.

6.4   Formatting Paragraphs

When you edit a document, you change, in some way, the text contained within it. When you **format** a document, the text itself is not affected, but the way it's arranged on the page changes. We will divide the topic of formatting into two parts: this section deals with *local* formatting — changes that affect the current paragraph or selected text. Section 6.5 will cover *global* formatting — procedures that apply to the entire document.

Some Basics

When you press the Enter key while entering text into a Write document, a *paragraph marker* code, which is not visible on the screen, is placed in the document file. A *paragraph*, as far as Write is concerned, is the text that lies between two paragraph markers, or between a paragraph marker and the beginning or end of the document. In other words, every time you press the Enter key, Write interprets this as the beginning of a new paragraph.

Paragraph formatting features

Write has several formatting features that apply to either the paragraph in which the insertion point is currently located or the paragraphs containing currently selected text. You can:

- Align the text with the left margin, the right margin, with both margins, or center it between the margins.

- Use single spacing, one-and-one-half line spacing, or double spacing between the lines.

- Indent the text on the left, right, or on both sides, a specified distance from the corresponding margin.

When you start typing a new paragraph, it automatically inherits all the formatting characteristics of the previous one. For example, suppose the current paragraph is double-spaced. If you press Enter and start typing, the new text will also be double-spaced.

Each paragraph formatting command can be issued in two ways:

1. By selecting the appropriate option from the Paragraph menu.

or

2. By making use of icons or markers on the Ruler.

The Ruler

The **Ruler** is displayed by choosing Ruler On from the Document menu. It is displayed at the top of the document window, as shown in

Figure 6.7. The Ruler contains a ruler, which measures distances from the left margin, and a variety of icons and markers which, when clicked or dragged, cause formatting changes.

FIGURE 6.7   The Ruler and Some of its Icons

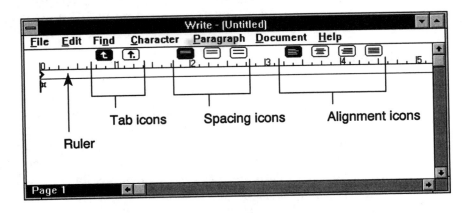

Although the Ruler can simplify certain formatting chores, it also takes up room on the screen. (It is *not* part of the document itself; in particular, it does not appear on the printed page.) To hide the Ruler, choose <u>R</u>uler Off from the <u>D</u>ocument menu.

Changing Text Alignment

Write provides four options for aligning (or **justifying**) the text within a paragraph:

This text is *left-justified*. All lines in the paragraph align on the left margin.

This text is *fully-justified*. All lines in the paragraph except the last one, align on both margins.

This text is *right-justified*. All lines in the paragraph align on the right margin.

This text is *center-justified*. All lines in the paragraph are centered between the margins.

The default alignment option is left-justification. The alignment option within any paragraph of a document is indicated by a check mark next to that item on the Paragraph menu. To change text alignment, place the insertion point in the desired paragraph or select the paragraphs to be changed, and either:

- Click the appropriate alignment icon above the Ruler.

or

- Choose the appropriate alignment option from the Paragraph menu. (For fully-justified text, choose Justified.)

For example, to center all the text in the document shown in Figure 6.6 (TITLE-2.WRI in the WRITE directory on the Lab Projects diskette):

1. Select the entire document by moving the insertion point into the left margin, holding down the Ctrl key, and clicking.

2. Choose Centered from the Paragraph menu (or display the Ruler and click on the center-justify icon).

Changing the Spacing Between Lines

Write provides three line spacing options: single spacing, one-and-one-half line spacing, and double spacing.

This is an example of single line spacing.

This is an example of one-and-one-half line spacing.

This is an example of double line spacing.

The default setting is single spacing. To change line spacing, place the insertion point in the desired paragraph or select the paragraphs to be changed and either:

- Choose the appropriate spacing option from the Paragraph menu.

or

- Click the appropriate spacing icon above the ruler.

Changing Paragraph Indentation

As you will see in Section 6.5, all page margins apply to the entire document. To change the left and/or right margin for a particular paragraph, you change its *indentation* relative to the given margin(s). Write's indentation feature also allows you to change the amount the first line of a paragraph is indented relative to the rest of the paragraph.

For example, in Figure 6.8:

- The first paragraph is not indented (the left, right, and first line indents are all 0 inches).

- The second paragraph is indented 1 inch on the left, 0.5 inches on the right, and the first line indent is 0 inches. Since the first line indent is measured relative to the rest of the paragraph, the first line aligns with the rest of the paragraph.

- The third paragraph is indented 1 inch on the left, 0.25 inches on the right, and the first line indent is -0.5 inches Since the first line indent is *negative* and measured relative to the rest of the paragraph, it is one-half inch to the *left* of the rest of the paragraph. (This kind of indentation is called a *hanging indent*.)

FIGURE 6.8   Examples of Indented Paragraphs

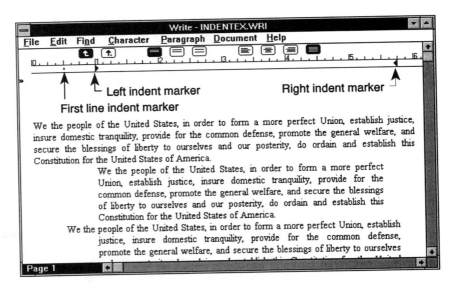

To change indentation, place the insertion point in the desired paragraph or select the paragraphs to be changed and either:

- Choose Indents from the Paragraph menu, which opens the following dialog box:

```
┌─────────────────────────────────────────────┐
│ ▬                    Indents                 │
├─────────────────────────────────────────────┤
│ Left Indent:    │0.00"│      ┌──────────┐    │
│                               │    OK    │    │
│ First Line:     │0.00"│      └──────────┘    │
│                               ┌──────────┐    │
│ Right Indent:   │0.00"│      │  Cancel  │    │
│                               └──────────┘    │
└─────────────────────────────────────────────┘
```

Now, type the desired Left Indent, First Line indent, and Right Indent, and choose OK.

or

■ On the Ruler, drag the left, right, and first line indent icons to the desired positions (see Figure 6.8, where they are set for the third paragraph).

Inserting Optional Hyphens

At times, you may notice a large gap occurring at the end of a line within a paragraph. This happens when a long word doesn't fit into the space remaining at the end of a line, and is therefore wrapped to the beginning of the next line. The overall appearance of a document will be improved if you hyphenate such words, so that they are "broken" between the two lines, as illustrated here:

> This is an example of an unhyphenated word leaving a "tremendous" gap at the end of a line (the one above this one).

> This is an example of a hyphenated word not leaving a "tremendous" gap at the end of a line.

The best way to hyphenate a word in a Write document is to move the insertion point to where you want to break that word and press Ctrl+Shift+Hyphen. This inserts an optional hyphen (*soft hyphen*); if that word would normally be wrapped to the next line, Write will hyphenate it and display the hyphen. On the other hand, if you edit the document so that the word in question no longer falls at the end of the line, no hyphen will appear.

Hands-On

6.4

Start up Windows and Write, if necessary, and try the following exercise:

1. Insert the Lab Projects diskette in its drive.
2. Open the PREAMBLE.WRI file in the WRITE directory on this disk.
3. Center the title.

4. Fully justify the rest of the document, using one-and-one-half line spacing, with a left indent of 1.0" and a first line indent of -0.8".
5. Print the resulting document.
6. Clear the Write window and remove the diskette from its drive.

6.5   Formatting the Document as a Whole

Write provides several formatting features that apply to the document as a whole. When these commands are issued, it does not matter where the insertion point is positioned or if text is currently selected. These commands affect all text that has already been typed and that will be typed in the current document. Write's document formatting features allow you to:

■ Use headers and/or footers in your document.

■ Determine the position and kind of tab stops in the document.

■ Set the widths of all margins in the document.

Using Headers and Footers

A **header** is text that is positioned at the top of every page of a document. Similarly, a **footer** is text that appears at the bottom of every page. Documents use headers and/or footers to provide page numbers and general information, such as the title of the document. For example, this book uses headers to give the current page number and the chapter number and title; it does not contain footers.

If you want, Write will automatically place a header and/or a footer in the margin(s) of every page of your document. Or, at your option, the header or footer can be omitted from the first page and appear on all the rest.

You may use any text you want in a header or footer, and it can extend over several lines. If you wish, the text can contain (or consist entirely of) the current page number. Moreover, all font and paragraph formatting features discussed in Sections 6.3 and 6.4 can be applied to header and footer text. For example, you can center the text, set it in italics, and use a larger font for the page number.

We will now describe how to insert a header into a Write document. Footers are used in a similar way.

1. Choose Header from the Document menu. The HEADER window

and Page Header dialog box (Figure 6.9) will both be displayed.

FIGURE 6.9 The Header and Page Header Windows

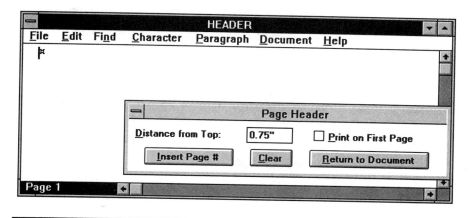

2. Type the desired text in the HEADER window, using any fonts and formatting features you like. (If you want to delete all text and start over, choose the Clear button from the Page Header window.)

3. If you want to insert a page number, click on the Insert Page # button in the Page Header window. The word *page*, enclosed in parentheses, then appears at the insertion point in the HEADER window. When the document is printed, the current page number will appear at this location (without parentheses).

4. By default, the header prints 3/4-inch below the top edge of the paper on all pages of the document except the first. To change these settings, in the Page Header window:

   ■ Type the desired value in the Distance from Top text box.

   ■ Select the Print on First Page check box.

5. When you're done, choose the Return to Document button.

The header (and/or footer) is not displayed in the Write window but will appear in the printed document.

As an example, let's add a header and footer to the GAMES-2.WRI document in the WRITE directory of the Lab Projects diskette. (This is basically a double-spaced version of the GAMES document with larger margins.) This header will contain the document's title and the footer, a page number. If you want to follow along, open this file and:

- Create the header by choosing Header from the Document menu and, in the HEADER window, typing "Games of the Mayas and Aztecs". To bold and center the text, select it, press Ctrl+B, and choose Centered from the Paragraph menu. Finally, choose the Return to Document button.

- Create the footer by choosing Footer from the Document menu and, in the Page Footer window, choosing the Insert Page # button. Then, center the page number by choosing Centered from the Paragraph menu. Finally, choose the Return to Document button.

Changing the Tab Settings

When you press the Tab key while working on a Write document, the insertion point moves to the next tab setting (or **tab stop**). By default, the tab stops are set at half-inch intervals across the document. For example, if the insertion point is at the left margin, pressing the Tab key twice moves it to a position one inch to the right of the left margin.

Write provides two kinds of tab stops: *left-aligned* and *decimal*. They are useful for aligning columns of text or numbers, respectively. Figure 6.10 shows how this works. Here, a left-aligned tab stop is set at 1 inch and a decimal tab is set at 3 inches. (Notice the corresponding tab markers on the Ruler.) The text on each line is typed by pressing Tab, typing the name, pressing Tab, typing the number, and pressing Enter.

Setting
tab stops

To set or change the tab stops, do one of the following:

- Choose Tabs from the Document menu, which opens the Tabs dialog box:

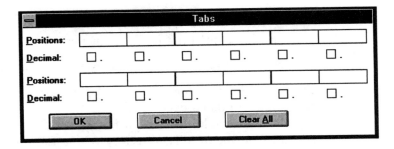

Now, select a Positions text box and type the desired setting. (If

FIGURE 6.10 Creating Columns using Tabs

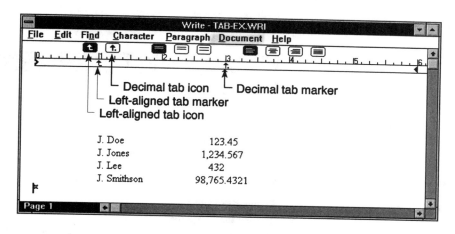

there is a value in this box already, it can be overwritten, changing the corresponding tab stop.) If you want to set a decimal tab at the given position, select its check box. Then choose the OK button.

■ Or select the appropriate icon (left-aligned or decimal) above the Ruler and click on the desired position on the Ruler; the corresponding marker will appear on the Ruler as shown in Figure 6.10 (the default tab stops do not appear on the Ruler). To move a tab stop, drag its marker to a new position on the Ruler.

Removing tab stops

To remove a tab stop, either:

■ Drag its marker off the Ruler.

or

■ In the Tabs dialog box, select its Positions box and delete its value; to remove all specified tabs (and return to the defaults), choose Clear All. Then, choose OK.

Setting Margins

By default, Write sets the following margins for each document: one inch at the top and bottom and 1.25 inches at the left and right. Thus, on a standard 8 1/2" × 11" piece of paper, all text is enclosed in an imaginary box that is six inches wide and nine inches high.

To use different margins for the current document:

1. Choose Page Layout from the Document menu. The following dialog box will be displayed:

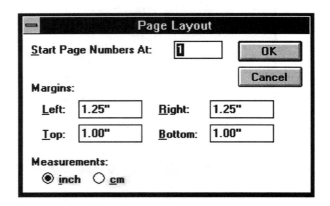

2. For each margin to be changed, select the appropriate text box and type in the new value.

3. Choose the OK button.

The Page Layout dialog box contains two other (infrequently used) items:

- If you are numbering pages (in a header or footer), use the Start Page Numbers At box to specify the number for the first page of the document; the default value is 1.

- If you want to change the unit of measurement from inches to centimeters, select the cm option button. This change will apply, not only to this dialog box, but also to the other Write dialog boxes that contain measurements and to the markings on the Ruler.

Hands-On 6.5

Start up Windows and Write, if necessary, and try the following exercise:

1. Insert the Lab Projects diskette into its drive and open the GAMES-2.WRI file in the WRITE directory.

2. Set all margins to 1.5".

3. Create a header containing your name and your class, right-justified and single-spaced on separate lines on all pages except the first.

4. Create a footer containing only the page number, centered in bold type, and appearing on all pages.

5. Set a left-aligned tab stop at 0.3". Does this cause any reformatting of the text?

6. Print the document.

7. Clear the Write window and remove the diskette from its drive.

6.6 Using Graphics in a Write Document

Write lets you do more than just process words. You can insert **graphics** (pictures) into a Write document, and then move and size them. In this section, we will demonstrate how to perform these operations.

Inserting a Graphic into a Write Document

To place a graphic in a Write document:

1. Use a graphics program, such as Paintbrush (described in Chapter 7), to create the picture or to open an existing graphics file.

2. Copy the graphic to the Clipboard.

3. Switch to Write.

4. Position the insertion point at the beginning of the line on which you want the upper-left corner of the graphic to be located. If the cursor is not positioned at the beginning of the line, the graphic will appear at the left margin on the next line.

5. Choose Paste from the Edit menu (or press Ctrl+V). The graphic will be displayed in your document.

In addition to Paste, there are two other commands on the Edit menu (Paste Special and Paste Link) that can be used in step 5 to transfer the graphic from the Clipboard to Write. When in doubt, use Paste; it's usually the best choice. All three commands, when they are available, will insert the picture into Write. They differ in the way that the graphic in Write is linked to the application that created it. This, in turn, affects the way that you edit the graphic within the Write document. We will discuss editing next.

Editing a Graphic within Write

A graphic that has been inserted into a Write document can be deleted, edited, moved, and resized.

Deleting a
graphic

To delete a graphic from a Write document:

1. Select the graphic by clicking on it. It will change color as a visual indication that it has been selected.

2. Press the Delete key.

OLE

The procedure for editing a graphic from within Write depends on the command you used to insert the graphic into the Write document in the first place. This command determines whether you can use Windows' **Object Linking and Embedding** (or **OLE**) feature to edit it. We will discuss OLE briefly here and in more detail in Section 9.1.

Let's assume that a graphic has been copied to the Clipboard from Paintbrush. Then, any of the following commands can be used to paste the picture into Write:

■ Paste *embeds* the graphic in Write. An embedded picture (or *object*) can be edited by double-clicking on it, which starts Paintbrush and opens the graphic's file. When you're done editing the picture, choose "Exit and Return to" from the Paintbrush File menu and the modified graphic will be copied into Write.

■ Paste Link *links* the Write document and the graphic file, so that when a new version of the graphic is saved in Paintbrush, the copy in Write is modified, as well. To edit a linked graphic, double-click on it, which starts Paintbrush. Then, modify the graphic, save it, and switch back to Write, which will display the revised picture.

■ Paste Special opens a dialog box that, in general, gives you the choice of embedding the graphic object, linking the graphic file, or (by selecting Bitmap) just transferring the graphic into Write. In the last case, the only way to edit the picture is to delete it from the Write document, modify it in Paintbrush, and re-insert it into Write.

Moving or Copying a Graphic

A graphic can be moved or copied *vertically* through a Write document (always clinging to the left margin) in the same way as a block of text. To transfer the graphic to a new position at the left margin:

Moving and copying vertically

1. Select the graphic by clicking on it.

2. Either *copy* the graphic, so that it appears in both the original and the new locations, or *move* the graphic, which deletes it from the original location and transfers it to the new one.

   ■ To copy the graphic, choose <u>C</u>opy from the <u>E</u>dit menu (or press Ctrl+C).

   ■ To move the graphic, choose Cu<u>t</u> from the <u>E</u>dit menu (or press Ctrl+X).

3. Move the insertion point to the new location.

4. Choose <u>P</u>aste from the <u>E</u>dit menu (or press Ctrl+V).

To move a graphic *horizontally*:

Moving horizontally

1. Select the graphic by clicking on it.

2. Choose <u>M</u>ove Picture from the <u>E</u>dit menu. The cursor will change to a "square within a square," positioned within the graphic like this:

Cursor ⎯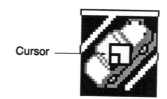

3. Move the mouse (do *not* click or drag it) horizontally. As you do, a rectangular outline will indicate the new position of the graphic:

4. When the graphic is positioned as you want, click the mouse to complete the move.

Resizing a Graphic

To enlarge or reduce the size of a graphic within a Write document:

1. Select the graphic by clicking on it.

2. Choose <u>S</u>ize Picture from the <u>E</u>dit menu. The cursor will change to a "square within a square," positioned within the graphic.

3. Move the mouse (do *not* click or drag it) horizontally or vertically to resize the graphic's width or height, respectively. Move it diagonally to change the height and width at the same time. As you move the mouse, a rectangular outline indicates the new size of the graphic:

4. When the graphic is the size you want, click the mouse to complete the operation.

Hands-On 6.6

Start up Windows and Write, if necessary, and try the following exercise:

1. Resize the Write window so that it's as small as possible.
2. Press Alt+Print Screen to copy this window to the Clipboard.
3. Maximize the Write window and choose <u>P</u>aste from the <u>E</u>dit menu to transfer the captured window (the graphic) into the Write document. What other paste options were available in this case?
4. Double-click on the graphic to attempt to edit it. Is this graphic an embedded or linked object?
5. Move the graphic horizontally to the center of the window.
6. Enlarge the graphic, keeping its dimensions in proportion, until its right edge touches the right window border.
7. Print this document. Did it print properly?
8. Exit Write.

6.7 Using Notepad

Notepad is a *text editor*, a very simple word processor, and lacks many of the features of Write. Nevertheless, as you will see, it has its own special uses.

Starting Notepad

Notepad

To start Notepad, choose its icon from the Accessories group. The Notepad window (Figure 6.11) will open. Notice that the insertion point appears in the upper-left corner, but there is no end mark.

FIGURE 6.11   The Notepad Window

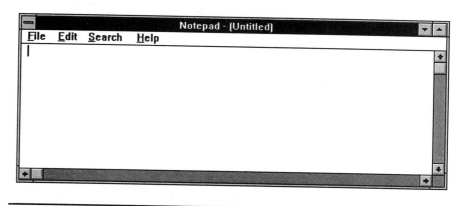

Notepad's Features

Although Notepad does have a few unique features of its own, most of its capabilities are similar to those of Write. So, to provide an overview of Notepad, let's begin by considering Write's features and see how (if at all) they are implemented in Notepad.

Basic Operations   You enter text into a Notepad document in the same way as Write — just type, and the words appear on the screen — with one major exception: In Write, text always automatically wraps to the next line. In Notepad, you can turn this feature on or off (for the entire document) by choosing Word Wrap from the Edit menu. A check mark next to this item indicates that it's in effect.

- If word wrap is on, when text reaches the right edge of the *window*, it wraps to the next line. Thus, with word wrap on, the width of the Notepad window determines the width of the lines on the printed page.

- If word wrap is off, a line of text continues until you press the Enter key. When the text is printed, long lines will wrap at the right page margin, usually in the middle of a word!

The New, Open, Save, Save As, and Exit commands on Notepad's File menu work the same general way they do in Write. However, when using Save As, if you don't provide an extension for the file name, Windows adds the extension TXT instead of WRI.

Notepad's Print command is especially simple. When you choose Print from the File menu, the entire document is printed immediately; a dialog box does not appear as it does in Write. On the other hand, Notepad's Print Setup command (also on the File menu) provides the same options as the corresponding command in Write.

Editing Text   Notepad's editing capabilities are less powerful than those of Write. The Backspace and Delete keys work exactly the same way, as does the Undo command on the Edit menu. However, Notepad has far fewer cursor movement keys: The only ones available are the Arrow keys, and the Home, End, Ctrl+Home, and Ctrl+End keys (for moving the insertion point to, respectively, the beginning of the current line, the end of the current line, the beginning of the document, and the end of the document).

There are two ways to select text in Notepad:

1. Drag the insertion point from the first character in the block to be selected to its last character (or position the insertion point at its first character, hold down the Shift key, and move the insertion point to the last character).

2. Choose Select All from the Edit menu to select all the text in the document.

Once selected, text can be copied, cut, and pasted by using the appropriate commands on the Edit menu.

Notepad has Find and Find Next commands on its Search menu that are similar to those of Write. However, it does not have automatic search and replace capability.

Fonts   Notepad has no font capability; all text is printed in the default font of the current printer. Styles, such as bold and italic, are not available.

Local Formatting   Notepad has no local formatting features. Text must be single-spaced and left-justified. Optional hyphens and indents are not available. There is no Ruler.

Global Formatting   Tabs are preset every one-half inch and cannot be changed. However, you can set margins and use headers and/or footers, if you want. These features are accessed by choosing Page Setup from the File menu, which opens the following dialog box:

```
┌──────────────────────────────────────────────┐
│ ─ │              Page Setup                   │
│                                               │
│   Header:   [&f            ]    ┌──────────┐  │
│                                 │    OK    │  │
│   Footer:   [Page &p       ]    └──────────┘  │
│                                 ┌──────────┐  │
│  ┌─Margins────────────────┐     │  Cancel  │  │
│  │ Left:  [.75]   Right:  [.75] └──────────┘ │
│  │                                           │
│  │ Top:   [1  ]   Bottom: [1  ]              │
│  └───────────────────────────────────────┘   │
└──────────────────────────────────────────────┘
```

Margins are set the same way as in Write. To have Notepad automatically insert a header or footer on every page of the document:

1. Type the desired text (up to 39 characters) in the appropriate box: Header or Footer. You may include the following codes in this text:

   - &c   centers text that follows this code;
   - &d   inserts the current date in place of this code;
   - &f   inserts the document's file name in place of this code;
   - &l   left-justifies text that follows this code;
   - &p   inserts the current page number in place of this code;
   - &r   right-justifies text that follows this code;
   - &t   inserts the current time in place of this code.

2. Choose the OK button.

   For example, if you type &lPage &p &rDate: &d in the Header box of the Page Setup dialog box and choose OK, Notepad places a header similar to the following one at the top of every page of your document:

        Page 1   Date: 1/3/94

Using Graphics   Graphics cannot be inserted into a Notepad document.

Special Uses for Notepad

Because of its simplicity, many Windows users prefer Notepad to Write for writing short notes or making lists. Notepad is also commonly used for the following special purposes.

Keeping a Log   A *log* is a diary, a chronological (ordered by time) list of events. Notepad makes it especially easy for you to create and use a log document. To create the document, start Notepad, type .LOG (a period, followed by the capital letters LOG) and save the file. Then, every time you open this document, Notepad automatically inserts the time and date on a new line at the end of the document. You can then type whatever notes you wish. If you want to enter the current time and date, but don't want to close and reopen the document, choose Time/Date from the Edit menu or press F5. (This technique inserts the time and date into *any* Notepad document.)

Editing System Files   System files, such as SYSTEM.INI and WIN.INI are stored in ASCII (pronounced "askey") format. **ASCII,** which stands for American Standard Code for Information Interchange, is the simplest and most universal format for storing text files. It is the format used by Notepad, but not by Write.

Thus, Notepad is the ideal tool for editing a system file. In fact, the extension INI is associated with the Notepad application, so all you need do to open an INI file is to double-click on it in File Manager (see Section 4.3). This will start Notepad and open the desired document. Then, make your changes and save the document.

Editing system files can be hazardous to your system's well-being, so it's not wise to experiment here. Make sure you understand what you are doing and *always make a backup* of the original version.

Hands-On 6.7

Start up Windows and Notepad (if necessary) and try the following:

1. Set all margins to 1.5".
2. Create a header that contains your full name aligned with the left margin, the page number centered, and the date aligned with the right margin.
3. With word wrap off, type the sentence (without pressing Enter):

> We hold these truths to be self-evident, that all men are created equal, that they are endowed by their Creator with certain unalienable Rights, that among these are Life, Liberty and the pursuit of Happiness.

4. Print the document.
5. Turn word wrap on and print the document.
6. Exit Notepad.

Chapter Summary

Key Terms

ASCII text [page 236]

End mark [205]

Footer [224]

Graphic [229]

Insertion point [205]

Notepad [203]

OLE [230]

Scalable font [215]

Tab stop [226]

Word wrap [205]

Edit text [210]

Font [215]

Format [219]

Header [224]

Justified text [220]

Object Linking and Embedding [230]

Ruler [219]

Selection area [211]

Typeface [215]

Write [203]

Topics Covered

Basic Operations in Write

To start Write	Choose the Write icon from the Accessories group.
To enter text	Type the text at the keyboard.
To start a new paragraph	Press the Enter key.
To start a new page	Press Ctrl+Enter.

To open a document	Choose Open from the File menu.
To print a document	Choose Print from the File menu.
To save a document	Choose Save or Save As from the File menu.
To clear the Write window	Choose New from the File menu.

Selecting Text in Write

To select a block of text	Position the insertion point at the beginning of the block. Then, drag it to the end of the block; or hold down the Shift key as you move the insertion point to the end of the block.
To select a line	Click in the selection area next to the line.
To select a paragraph	Double-click in the selection area next to the paragraph.
To select the entire document	Hold down the Ctrl key and click anywhere in the selection area.

Editing Text in Write

To delete text	Press the Delete key to delete the selected text or the character that follows the cursor; press Backspace to delete the selected text or the character in front of the cursor.
To copy/move selected text	Choose Copy/Cut from the Edit menu, position the insertion point in the new location, and choose Paste from the Edit menu.
To find text	Choose Find from the Find menu.
To replace text	Choose Replace from the Find menu.
To undo the last change	Choose Undo from the Edit menu, or press Ctrl+Z.

Changing Fonts in Write

To change the typeface	Choose Fonts from the Character menu and select the typeface from the Font list.
To change the style	Choose Bold, Italic, Underline, Superscript, or Subscript from the Character menu; or select an available Font Style from the Font dialog box.

To change the size	Choose Enlarge Font or Reduce Font from the Character menu; or select a Size from the Font dialog box.

Formatting Text in Write

To display the Ruler	Choose Ruler On from the Document menu.
To change text alignment	Choose an alignment option from the Paragraph menu; or select an alignment icon above the Ruler.
To change line spacing	Choose a line spacing option from the Paragraph menu; or select a line spacing icon above the Ruler.
To change indentation	Choose Indents from the Paragraph menu; or drag the indent markers along the Ruler.
To insert an optional hyphen	Press Ctrl+Shift+Hyphen.
To paginate the document	Choose Repaginate from the File menu; or print the document.
To set tab stops	Choose Tabs from the Document menu; or select a tab icon above the Ruler and click on the desired location on the Ruler.
To set margins	Choose Page Layout from the Document menu and specify the margins in the dialog box.
To create a header or footer	Choose Header or Footer from the Document menu.

Using Graphics in Write

To paste a graphic from the Clipboard	Choose Paste, Paste Special, or Paste Link from the Edit menu.
To select a graphic	Click on it.
To copy/move a graphic vertically	Select the graphic, choose Copy/Cut from the Edit menu, reposition the insertion point, and choose Paste from the Edit menu.
To move a graphic horizontally	Select the graphic, choose Move Picture from the Edit menu, move the mouse to reposition the graphic, and click.
To resize a graphic	Select the graphic, choose Size Picture from

the Edit menu, move the mouse to resize the graphic, and click.

Special Notepad Features

The following Notepad features are similar to the corresponding ones for Write: Clearing the window; opening, saving, and printing the document; selecting a block of text; deleting, copying, moving, and finding text; and exiting the application.

To turn word wrap on or off	Choose Word Wrap from the Edit menu.
To select the entire document	Choose Select All from the Edit menu.
To set margins	Choose Page Setup from the File menu.
To create a header or footer	Choose Page Setup from the File menu.
To insert the current time and date	Choose Time/Date from the Edit menu, or press F5.
To create a log	Start Notepad, type ".LOG", and save the document.

Chapter Exercises

Short Answer   Complete each statement in Exercises 1 through 15.

1. To start Write, choose its icon from the _____ group.

2. While entering text in Write, you begin a new paragraph by pressing the _____ key.

3. To move the insertion point to the end of a document in Write or Notepad, press _____ .

4. To select a paragraph in a Write document, move the mouse pointer into the selection area and _____ .

5. To *move* a selected paragraph to a new location in a Write document, begin by choosing _____ from the Edit menu.

6. To print type that is about one inch high, use a _____ point size.

7. To change the current typeface in Write, choose _____ from

the Character menu.

8. To insert an optional (soft) hyphen in a word, press _____ .

9. To display write's Ruler, choose Ruler On from the _____ menu.

10. A _____ is text that appears at the bottom of every page (except possibly the first) of a document.

11. To create a table containing three two-inch wide columns of text, set _____ at 2", 4", and 6".

12. To move a selected graphic horizontally within a Write document, begin by choosing _____ from the Edit menu.

13. The feature of Windows that allows graphics to be edited from *within* a Write document is called _____ .

14. In Notepad, all text is _____ -justified with _____ line spacing.

15. To create a header in Notepad that contains the current page number, type the symbols _____ in the Header box of the Page Setup dialog box.

In Exercises 16 through 30, determine whether each statement is true or false.

16. A Write document must be saved using a file name with a WRI extension.

17. When a Write document is printed, it is automatically paginated (broken into pages).

18. To select an entire Write document, double-click anywhere in the selection area.

19. To locate all five-letter words that begin with "b" and end with "t", type b?t in the Find dialog box.

20. Subscripts and superscripts normally appear in a smaller size than regular type.

21. To change the typeface from Times New Roman to Arial in Write, you must open the Font dialog box.

22. If you have not selected an alignment option for a Write document, all text will be left-justified.

23. To indent the first line of a paragraph one-quarter inch to the left of the rest of the paragraph, set the first line indent to 0.25 inches in the Indents dialog box.

24. Each paragraph in a Write document can have different tab settings.

25. If you use a header in your Write document, then it must appear on *every* page.

26. To edit a graphic that has been embedded in a Write document, begin by double-clicking on it.

27. A graphic cannot be resized from within a Write document.

28. If word wrap has been turned off in a Notepad document, then you must press Enter to begin a new line.

29. To select an entire Notepad document, hold down Ctrl and click anywhere in the selection area.

30. All text in a Notepad document is printed in the same font.

In Exercises 31 through 40, choose the correct answer.

31. Using the Print command on Write's File menu, you can:
    a. Select the printer font to be used for the document.
    b. Select the range of pages to be printed.
    c. Select single, double, or one-and-one-half line spacing.
    d. Select all of the above.

32. To delete selected text from one location and transfer it to another, begin by:
    a. Choosing Cut from the Edit menu.
    b. Choosing Copy from the Edit menu.
    c. Choosing Paste from the Edit menu.
    d. Pressing the Delete key.

33. The Find command on the Find menu can be used to:
    a. Locate all occurrences of *rich* in a document.
    b. Replace all occurrences of *rich* with *poor*.
    c. Replace the first occurrence of *rich* with *poor*.
    d. Do all of the above.

34. The Font dialog box in Write cannot be used to:
    a. Change the current typeface.

    b.   Change the size of the current font.

    c.   Change to underlined text.

    d.   Change to italicized text.

35. Which formatting feature is not available in Write?

    a.   Changing tab settings.

    b.   Changing margin widths.

    c.   Changing line spacing.

    d.   Changing page orientation.

36. Assuming that no text has been selected, which of the following actions applies to the entire Write document?

    a.   Choosing margin widths.

    b.   Selecting a text alignment (justification) option.

    c.   Choosing indentation amounts.

    d.   Selecting a line spacing option.

37. Once a graphic is inserted into a Write document, you can:

    a.   Enlarge or reduce its size.

    b.   Move it to the right.

    c.   Move it to the top of the document.

    d.   Do all of the above.

38. In Write, you cannot:

    a.   Turn word wrap off.

    b   Start a new page whenever you want.

    c.   Hyphenate a word that is wrapped to the next line.

    d.   Print just the current page of the document.

39. Using the Print command on Notepad's File menu, you can:

    a.   Select the printer font to be used for the document.

    b.   Select the range of pages to be printed.

    c.   Select single, double, or one-and-one-half line spacing.

    d.   Not do any of the above.

40. Which formatting action is possible in Notepad?

    a.   Selecting double line spacing.

    b.   Selecting right-justified text.

    c.   Setting a tab stop at 0.3".

    d.   Setting top and bottom margins to 1.5".

Hands-On In Exercises 41 through 47, start up Windows (if it's not already running) and perform each of the indicated tasks.

41. a. Start Write.
    b. Type your name, your class, and the date on separate lines. Then, skip a line, press Tab and type: Exercise 41
    c. Save this document to a floppy disk under the name Ch6-Ex41. What extension, if any, did Windows append to this name?
    d. Print the document.
    e. Type the current time on the same line as the date.
    f. Use the Save As command to save the edited version of the document under the same name, but select the Backup check box. What are the names of the two files?
    g. Print the revised document and quit Write.

42. Perform the tasks described in Exercise 41 using Notepad (with word wrap off) instead of Write, *except*:
- In parts b and c, type 42 instead of 41.
- In part e, have Notepad add the time and date by issuing the appropriate command from the Edit menu.
- In part f, do not select Backup. (Notepad does not provide this option!)

43. a. Start Write, insert the Lab Projects diskette in its drive, and open the TITLE-3.WRI document in the WRITE directory on this disk.
    b. Enlarge the graphic about 50 per cent in such a way that the ball remains round.
    c. Center the graphic between the left and right margins. (The Ruler is useful here.)
    d. Center all the text.
    e. Make any other adjustments to the picture or text that you believe improves the layout of the title page.
    f. Print the document.
    g. Clear the document window. (Do not replace TITLE-3.WRI.)
    h. Remove the diskette from its drive.

44. a. Start Write, insert the Lab Projects diskette in its drive, and open the PREAMBLE.WRI document in the WRITE directory on this disk.
    b. By using the Font dialog box, determine the two fonts used in this document.
    c. Break the title into two lines (after "Constitution") and center both lines.

    d. Change the font for the entire title to 18-point Arial bold.

    e. Change the size of the font in the rest of the document to 10-point type.

    f. Within the preamble:
- Bold the phrase *We the people.*
- Italicize the word *Constitution.*
- Underline the last four words — *United States of America.*

    g. Print the document.

    h. Clear the document window. (Do not replace PREAMBLE .WRI.) Remove the diskette from its drive.

45. a. Start Write, insert the Lab Projects diskette in its drive, and open the PREAMBLE.WRI document in the WRITE directory on this disk.

    b. Delete the title and the blank line that follows it.

    c. Find all occurrences of the text *or*. How many are there? How many are complete words?

    d. Replace all occurrences of the complete word *and* with *or*.

    e. Insert an optional hyphen in the word justice (between the "s" and the "t"). Is the word now hyphenated on the screen?

    f. Skip a line at the end of the text and copy the entire document to the new end mark location.

    g. Print the document.

    h. Clear the document window. (Do not replace PREAMBLE .WRI.) Remove the diskette from its drive.

46. a. Start Write, insert the Lab Projects diskette in its drive, and open the GAMES.WRI document in the WRITE directory on this disk.

    b. Format the first paragraph so that the text is right-justified with one-and-one-half line spacing and every line is indented one inch on both the left and right.

    c. Format the rest of the document so that the text is fully-justified with double line spacing. Set the first line indent for the second paragraph to one inch. With the aid of the Ruler, determine the actual first line indent. Explain this discrepancy.

    d. Create a header which displays (on every page) the page number, your name, your class, and the date on separate centered lines.

    e. Print the document. What problem has the header caused?

    f. Change the top margin to correct the problem in part e.

    g. Print the revised document.

    h. Clear the document window. (Do not replace GAMES.WRI.)

47. a. Start Notepad and begin a log document by typing .LOG in the upper-left corner of the window.

b. Create a header containing your name aligned with the left margin, the page number centered, and your class aligned with the right margin.

c. Save the document to a floppy disk.

d. Add three entries to this log by repeatedly opening the document, entering whatever text you want, and saving it.

e. Print the log.

f. Clear the Notepad window.

Creative Writing

48. Compare using Write to using a standard typewriter. Discuss the following topics: entering text, editing text, font availability, formatting features, and graphics capability.

49. Compare using Notepad to using a standard typewriter. (Discuss the topics listed in Exercise 48.)

50. Compare using Write to using Notepad. (Discuss the topics listed in Exercise 48.)

51. Describe the steps you would take in using Write to create a title page for a report. Use a paper that you have written for English or History as an example.

52. In the Overview to this chapter, we referred to Write as a "medium-strength" word processor. Describe some features that could be improved and some additional features that could be added to Write to increase its power. (It may help if you imagine that you want to use Write to create a newsletter or a book.)

Creating Graphics: Paintbrush

OVERVIEW   Often, the best way to communicate a large amount of information in a small amount of space is to use a **graphic** — a picture, diagram, graph, chart, or other kind of illustrative material. Windows supplies a drawing program called **Paintbrush** to help you create graphics. In this chapter, we will describe how to use this application. You will learn:

1. To select the colors, drawing widths, and tools needed in creating a Paintbrush graphic.

2. To save and print graphics, and to open graphic files.

3. To use the Paintbrush drawing tools, such as the Line, Curve, Brush, and those that create various geometric shapes.

4. To use the Paintbrush editing tools, such as the Scissors, Pick, Eraser, and Color Eraser.

5. To copy, move, flip, resize, and tilt cutouts.

6. To place text in a graphic.

7. To change the default drawing size, palette, and page setup.

7.1   An Introduction to Paintbrush

Creating a graphic in Paintbrush is not unlike creating one using conventional artist's tools. In fact, many Paintbrush tools have familiar names, such as *brush*, *scissors*, and *eraser*. To produce a graphic using Paintbrush, you have to:

1. Draw the graphic using Paintbrush's drawing tools.

2. Edit the graphic using Paintbrush's editing tools, together with other editing features such as copy, move, and resize.

3. Place text in the graphic, if appropriate.

4. Save and print the graphic.

In this section, we will provide an overview of the graphics-creation process. The remaining sections of this chapter will discuss it in considerably more detail.

Starting Paintbrush

Paintbrush

To start Paintbrush, choose its icon (by double-clicking on it) from the Accessories group. The Paintbrush window, shown in Figure 7.1, will open. In addition to the usual components, such as the title and menu bars, the Paintbrush window contains four main areas:

1. The **Toolbox** contains icons that represent the tools you use to create the graphic. The names of the various tools are given in Figure 7.2. We will describe how these tools work in the next few sections of this chapter.

2. The **Linesize box** displays the available drawing widths. Its pointer indicates the current drawing width, which determines the thickness of the lines and curves that you're about to draw.

3. The **Palette** displays the available colors. The current foreground and background colors are indicated to its left.

4. The **drawing area** is the region in which you compose the graphic. Often, the graphic is larger than the drawing area, so only part of it is displayed. In these cases, you can view other parts of the graphic by using the scroll bars. To minimize scrolling, you can increase the size of the drawing area in the following ways:

FIGURE 7.1   The Paintbrush Window

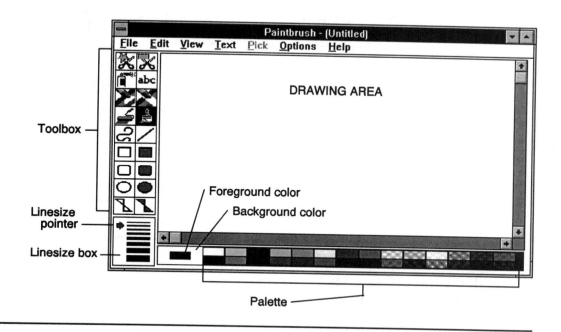

FIGURE 7.2   The Paintbrush Tools

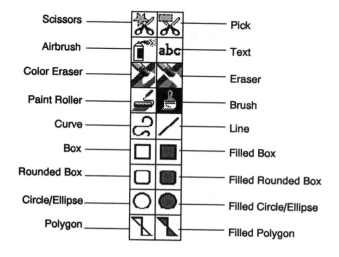

Increasing the
drawing area

- Maximize the Paintbrush window.

- Choose <u>T</u>ools and Linesize from the <u>V</u>iew menu to remove the Toolbox and Linesize box from the screen. They can be restored by choosing this item again.

- Choose <u>P</u>alette from the <u>V</u>iew menu to remove the Palette from the screen. It can be restored by choosing this item again.

- Choose Zoom <u>O</u>ut from the <u>V</u>iew menu, or press Ctrl+O, to display the entire graphic in the drawing area. To return to the normal view, press the Escape key or choose Zoom <u>I</u>n from the <u>V</u>iew menu (or press Ctrl+N).

- Choose <u>V</u>iew Picture from the <u>V</u>iew menu, or press Ctrl+P, and the drawing area will occupy the entire screen. (Unfortunately, you cannot do any work on your graphic in this mode.) To restore the Paintbrush window, click the mouse or press any key.

Drawing a Graphic

Using Paintbrush to draw a graphic involves these general steps:

1. Select a **background color**, the color of the drawing area, by clicking the *right* mouse button on the desired color in the Palette. This color is displayed in the box to the left of the Palette (see Figure 7.1). Then, choose <u>N</u>ew from the <u>F</u>ile menu, which clears the drawing area and colors it as you specified.

2. For the object you are about to draw:

   - Select a drawing width by clicking on one of the lines in the Linesize box.

   - Select a **foreground color**, the color with which the object will be drawn, by clicking the *left* mouse button on the desired color in the Palette. This color is displayed in the box to the left of the Palette. Some tools require that you select a background color, as well; this does not affect the color of the drawing area.

3. Draw the object:

   - Select a drawing tool by clicking on its icon in the Toolbox. (This icon becomes highlighted).

   - Position the cursor at the location in the drawing area where you want to begin drawing.

- Hold down the mouse button and move the mouse (that is, *drag the cursor*) to draw the object. When you're done, release the button.

4. Repeat steps 2 and 3 until your drawing is complete.

As an example, let's create a graphic image of a signature:

- Leave the foreground and background colors at their defaults: black and white, respectively.

- Set the drawing width to a relatively thin setting by clicking on the second line from the top in the Linesize box.

- Select the Brush tool by clicking on its icon in the Toolbox (see Figure 7.2).

- Move the cursor into the drawing area, hold down the mouse button and drag the cursor to form your first name. When you're done, release the button.

- Position the cursor where you want your last name to begin, drag the cursor to complete your signature, and release the mouse button.

It takes some practice to use the Brush tool effectively. To start over again, choose Undo from the Edit menu, or just press Ctrl+Z. If your name were John Hancock, the completed graphic might look like this:

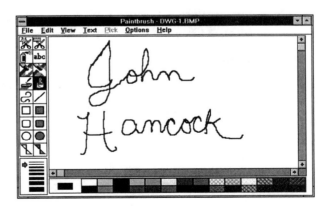

Saving a Graphic

If you want to keep a permanent copy of your graphic on disk, you must *save* it. When you save a graphic, it is copied from RAM to disk, but continues to be displayed in the drawing area. The save operation provides a name, of your choosing, for the graphic, as well. If you don't save your graphic before exiting Paintbrush or starting a new graphic, the changes you have made to it since the last save will be lost.

Paintbrush provides two versions of the save operation:

■ The Save command on the File menu saves the graphic under its current file name. The version of the graphic currently stored on disk under this name is *overwritten* (erased); the just-saved version, including all changes that you have made since the last save, replaces the former version.

■ The Save As command on the File menu lets you select a file name for the graphic being saved, and then saves the graphic under this name. (If you don't specify an extension in the file name, Windows adds the extension BMP.) You would normally use the Save As command when your graphic has not yet been saved to disk (and consequently has no name), or if the graphic has a name but you want to store a new copy of it on disk with a different name.

For a step-by-step description of how to issue the Save and Save As commands, see "Saving a Document" in Section 4.4. As an example, let's save the "signature" graphic we just created to the floppy disk in the A: drive. To do so:

1. Choose Save from the File menu. (The Save As dialog box appears because the graphic has never been saved.)

2. Select the a: drive from the Drives drop-down list.

3. Type namesign in the File Name text box.

4. Choose the OK button. (The file will be saved as A:\NAMESIGN .BMP.)

When working on a graphic, it is generally wise to use the Save command frequently, perhaps every fifteen minutes or so. Then, should disaster strike in the form of a power outage, a glitch in the system, or a mistake on your part, you won't have to recreate very much work. The last version of the graphic that was saved to disk is probably safe; you'll only have to redo the changes that were made since then.

Opening an Existing Graphic File

When you want to display a graphic in the drawing area that is currently stored on disk, you must *open* its file, which copies it from disk to RAM. To open a Paintbrush graphic file, choose Open from the File menu. For a detailed description of the process, see "Opening a Document" in Section 4.4.

As an example, let's open the FACTORY.BMP file in the PAINT directory on the Lab Projects diskette (assuming this disk is in the A: drive):

1. Choose Open from the File menu (displaying the Open dialog box).

2. Select the a: drive by clicking on it in the Drives list and the PAINT directory by double-clicking on it in the Directories list.

3. Double-click on the FACTORY.BMP name in the File Name list.

If there is a graphic in the drawing area when you open a file, it will be replaced on the screen by the one you just opened. If changes to the former graphic have not been saved, a warning message will be displayed informing you of this fact.

Printing a Graphic

To print a copy of the graphic displayed in the drawing area, make sure that the printer is on and ready to receive information from your computer. Then:

1. Choose the Print command from the File menu. When you do, the Print dialog box, shown in Figure 7.3 on the next page, will open.

2. In this dialog box, choose the desired options:

Printing
options

-   In the Quality area, select Draft to print the graphic more quickly than with Proof, but at a lower resolution.

-   Select the Number of copies to be printed.

-   Select a Scaling factor relative to the graphic's size on the screen. For example, if you type 200 (percent), the graphic will be printed roughly twice the size it appears on the screen.

-   Selecting the Use Printer Resolution check box translates one pixel (dot of light) on the screen into one dot of ink produced by your printer. This option may produce a better-proportioned

FIGURE 7.3   Paintbrush's Print Dialog Box

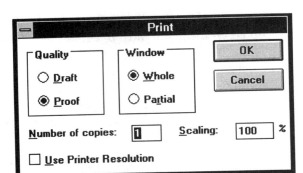

printout of the graphic, but it may also appear much smaller on paper than it did on the screen.

- In the Window area, select <u>W</u>hole to print the entire graphic or Pa<u>r</u>tial to print just the part of the graphic you want.

3.   Choose the OK button. The Print dialog box will close, and:

- If the <u>W</u>hole option button is selected, printing begins.

- If the Pa<u>r</u>tial option button is selected, the drawing area zooms (if necessary) to show the entire graphic. Now, enclose the part of the graphic you want to print in a rectangular box by positioning the cursor (cross hairs) in one corner of this rectangle and dragging it to the opposite corner. When you release the mouse button, printing begins.

Clearing the Drawing Area; Quitting Paintbrush

If you are finished working on one graphic and want to start another, choose <u>N</u>ew from the <u>F</u>ile menu. This will remove the current graphic from RAM and clear the drawing area. If you've made changes to the current graphic after the last save, a warning message will be issued before the New command is carried out.

When you are finished using Paintbrush, you can exit it in the same manner you exit most Windows applications (see Section 2.6). The fastest ways are to double-click on the Control menu box or to press Alt+F4. You can also choose E<u>x</u>it from the <u>F</u>ile menu.

Start up Windows and Paintbrush (if necessary) and try the following:

Hands-On 7.1

1. Select the Brush tool.
2. Draw eight horizontal lines, each with a different drawing width.
3. Print the graphic.
4. Save this graphic to a floppy disk under the name LINES. Was it stored under this name, or LINES.BMP, or something else?
5. Insert the Lab Projects diskette into its drive and open NAMESIGN .BMP in its PAINT directory.
6. Print only the part of this graphic containing the first name.
7. Remove the Lab Projects disk from its drive and clear the drawing area.

7.2   Using the Drawing Tools

In this section, we will describe how to use each of the drawing tools supplied by Paintbrush: the Brush, Airbrush, Line, Curve, Paint Roller, and the various Box, Circle/Ellipse, and Polygon tools. Their locations in the Toolbox are shown in Figure 7.2 on page 249. We will create graphics that make use of these tools in Sections 7.3, 7.4, and 7.5.

There is a lot of material in this section, but you don't have to master it all at once. The best way to learn to use the drawing tools is to "play" with them; start up Paintbrush and try them out!

The Brush Tool

The Brush tool is used like an artist's paint brush; it creates free-form curves in any available foreground color and drawing width. Recall that we used this tool in Section 7.1 to draw the "signature" graphic.

To use the Brush tool:

1. Select a foreground color and drawing width (see Section 7.1).

2. Select the Brush tool by clicking on its icon in the Toolbox (see Figure 7.2).

3. Select a *brush shape* by choosing Brush Shapes from the Options menu. The following dialog box will open:

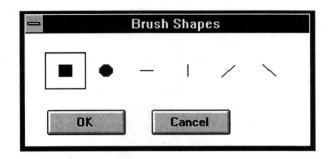

4. The effect of using the various shapes is illustrated in Figure 7.4. Here, each brush shape is shown above the three strokes made by it. (The differences among the brush shapes are most noticeable in the thicker drawing widths.) Click on the desired shape and choose OK to close the Brush Shapes dialog box.

FIGURE 7.4   The Six Available Brush Shapes

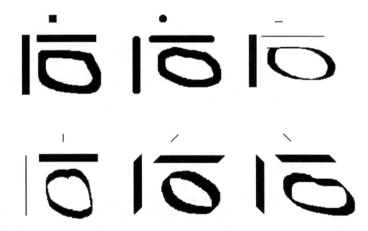

5. Position the cursor (a box the size of the current drawing width) in the drawing area where you want to begin painting, press the mouse button, and drag the cursor to form the desired curve.

To paint a perfectly horizontal or vertical line, hold down the Shift key while dragging the cursor in a horizontal or vertical direction.

6. Release the mouse button (and the Shift key, if necessary) when the curve or line is complete.

The Airbrush Tool

The Airbrush tool works in a similar way to the Brush tool; as you drag the cursor, a curve is formed by its path. However, unlike the Brush, which draws a continuous, solid curve, the Airbrush produces a spray of dots in the current foreground color and drawing width. This tool is useful for creating special effects, such as shading.

To use the Airbrush tool:

1. Select a foreground color and drawing width.

2. Select the Airbrush tool from the Toolbox.

3. Position the cursor (cross hairs) in the drawing area where you want to begin spraying, press the mouse button, and drag the cursor to form the desired curve. The faster you move the mouse, the finer is the resulting spray pattern:

Slow

Medium

Fast

4. Release the mouse button when the curve is complete.

The Line Tool

The Line tool draws straight lines in the current foreground color and drawing width. To use the Line tool:

1. Select a foreground color and drawing width.

2. Select the Line tool from the Toolbox.

3. Position the cursor (cross hairs) in the drawing area where you want the line to begin, press the mouse button, and drag the cursor to the location of the other endpoint. As you do, a "flexible" line is displayed, joining the starting point to the current cursor position.

To draw a horizontal, vertical, or diagonal (inclined at a 45° angle) line, hold down the Shift key and drag the cursor in a horizontal, vertical, or diagonal direction.

4. When the line is positioned correctly, release the mouse button (and the Shift key, if necessary). A straight line joining the end points, with the specified color and drawing width, will appear.

The Curve Tool

The Curve tool draws smooth curves, in the current foreground color and drawing width, between two points. This tool requires practice to master, but it's worth the effort. The resulting curves are usually much smoother than those produced by the Brush tool.

To use the Curve tool to create a curve, you first construct a line that defines its endpoints, and then deform this line into a curve by "bending" it once or twice with the aid of the mouse. To be more specific:

1. Select a foreground color and drawing width.

2. Select the Curve tool from the Toolbox.

3. Position the cursor (cross hairs) in the drawing area where you want the curve to begin, press the mouse button, and drag the cursor to the desired end point. A straight line now connects the starting point and the current cursor position.

4. Release the mouse button to anchor the straight line in place.

5. Drag the cursor away from the line in the direction you want it to bend. As you do, you will see a curve take shape. Continue to drag the cursor until this part of the curve looks the way you want, then release the button. If the curve's appearance is satisfactory, double-click the mouse to complete the operation.

6. If you want the curve to bend in a second direction, drag the cursor in that direction. When the curve has the desired appearance, release the mouse button to complete the operation.

The curve is drawn in the specified foreground color and drawing width.

Let's try an example. Select the Curve tool and draw a vertical line about two inches long (Figure 7.5a). Now, position the cursor about one-half inch from the top of the line and drag it to the right as indicated in Figure 7.5b. Notice how the curve bends to the right. Release the mouse button. Then, position the cursor about one-half inch from the bottom of the curve, and drag the cursor to the left (Figure 7.5c). Notice that the bottom of the curve bends back to the left. Finally, release the mouse button to complete the operation and anchor the curve in place.

FIGURE 7.5 Using the Curve Tool

a. Draw a vertical line   **b.** Drag the top of the line to the right   **c.** Drag the bottom of the curve to the left

More complicated curves can be constructed by using the Curve tool repeatedly, taking the starting point for each new curve to be the ending point of the previous one. In this way, a series of curves is constructed that has the appearance of one long, intricate curve.

The Box Tools

The Toolbox contains four box tools (see Figure 7.2):

 1. The tool labeled Box draws a hollow (*unfilled*) square or rectangle in the current foreground color and drawing width.

 2. The Filled Box tool draws a square or rectangle that is filled with the current foreground color, and has a border that is the current background color and drawing width.

 3. The Rounded Box draws a hollow (*unfilled*) square or rectangle with rounded corners, in the current foreground color and drawing width.

4. The Filled Rounded Box tool draws a square or rectangle with rounded corners that is filled with the current foreground color, and has a border that is the current background color and drawing width.

Here are examples of each of these four shapes:

| Box | Filled Box | Rounded Box | Filled Rounded Box |

To use the Box or Rounded Box tool:

1. Select a foreground color and drawing width.

2. Select the appropriate tool from the Toolbox.

3. Position the cursor (cross hairs) in the drawing area where you want one corner of the box, press the mouse button, and drag the cursor to the location of the opposite corner. A "flexible" rectangle is displayed, connecting the starting point and the current cursor position, expanding or contracting as you move the cursor.

   To draw a *square* or rounded *square*, hold down the Shift key while dragging the cursor.

4. Release the mouse button. A box will be drawn with the specified color and drawing width.

To draw a Filled Box or a Filled Rounded Box, follow the same procedure, but also select a background color in step 1. After you complete the procedure, a box will be drawn, filled with the *foreground* color, and with a border of the specified *background* color and drawing width. To draw a filled box without a border, use the same foreground and background colors.

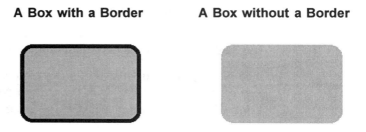

A Box with a Border   **A Box without a Border**

The Circle/Ellipse Tools

   The Toolbox contains two Circle/Ellipse tools: the (hollow) Circle/Ellipse and the Filled Circle/Ellipse. Both create, at your option, either a circle or an ellipse (an oval). Here are some examples:

To use the Circle/Ellipse tool:

1. Select a foreground color and drawing width.

2. Select the Circle/Ellipse tool from the Toolbox.

3. The circle or ellipse will be drawn inside an imaginary box that you outline on the screen. Position the cursor (cross hairs) in the drawing area where you want the upper-left corner of this box, press the mouse button, and drag the cursor. As you do, a "flexible" circle or ellipse moves with it.

   To draw a perfect circle, hold down the Shift key while you drag the cursor.

4. When the shape is satisfactory, release the mouse button (and Shift key, if necessary). A circle or ellipse will be drawn with the specified foreground color and drawing width.

The procedure for using the Filled Circle/Ellipse tool is similar to the one just given, but also select a background color in step 1. When you complete the process, a circle or ellipse is drawn on the screen with a border in the specified background color and drawing width, and filled with the foreground color.

The Polygon Tools

  A *polygon* is made up of straight line segments joined together to form a closed figure. The Toolbox contains two Polygon tools, the (hollow) Polygon and the Filled Polygon. Here are a few examples:

To use the Polygon tool:

1. Select a foreground color and drawing width.

2. Select the Polygon tool from the Toolbox.

3. Position the cursor (cross hairs) in the drawing area where you want one of the sides to begin, press the mouse button, drag the cursor, and release the mouse button to form a side of the polygon.

    To draw a perfectly horizontal, vertical, or diagonal side, hold down the <u>Shift key</u> while you drag the cursor in the appropriate direction.

4. Repeat step 3 for all but the last side.

5. To draw the last side (the one that closes the figure), without moving the cursor from the endpoint of the last line drawn, double-click the mouse. The polygon will be displayed in the specified color and drawing width.

    The procedure for using the Filled Polygon tool is similar to the one just described, but also select a background color in step 1. When you complete the process, a polygon is drawn on the screen with a border in the specified background color and drawing width, and filled with the foreground color.

The Paint Roller

All the tools we have discussed so far draw objects on the screen. The Paint Roller does not; it fills an existing enclosed figure with color. For example, drawing a rectangle with the Box tool and using the Paint Roller to fill it with color has the same effect as using the Filled Box tool. Of course, the usefulness of the Paint Roller is that it can fill *any* enclosed region, not just a box, circle, or polygon.

For the Paint Roller to work properly, the object to be colored must be completely enclosed. If it isn't, the fill color will "leak out" and cover the entire screen. If this happens, choose <u>U</u>ndo from the <u>E</u>dit menu, or just press Ctrl+Z, to remedy the situation.

Sometimes it may look as if a region is completely enclosed, when there is actually an indiscernible gap in its boundary. To locate and close this gap, you can use the Zoom In command, as described in Section 7.3.

To use the Paint Roller:

1. Select a foreground color; it will be used to color the object.

2. Select the Paint Roller tool from the Toolbox.

3. Position the cursor (a paint roller) inside the region you want to fill with color. For small regions, make sure that the lower-left corner of the cursor is inside the region.

4. Click the mouse button. The region will be filled with the foreground color.

The Paintbrush drawing tools give you a great deal of power to create graphics. Here are some additional hints on using them effectively:

1. While dragging the cursor to form a figure, press the *right* mouse button to cancel the operation.

2. To draw a filled figure (box, circle, ellipse, or polygon) without a border, use the same foreground and background colors.

3. To align figures more precisely, choose <u>C</u>ursor Position from the <u>V</u>iew menu. A small window will open on the right end of the menu bar to display the current *cursor coordinates*, like this: [200 . 0] The first number measures the horizontal distance (in pixels) from the left edge of the drawing area; the second number measures the distance down from its top edge. For example, when the position is 200,0 (as shown above), the cursor is 200 pixels from the left edge and is at the top edge of the drawing area.

Hands-On 7.2

Start up Windows and Paintbrush (if necessary) and try the following:

1. Select foreground and background colors of black and white, respectively, and select the thinnest drawing width.

2. Use the Line, Box, Circle/Ellipse, and Curve tools to create a graphic that looks like the floppy disk pictured on the next page.

Remember that:
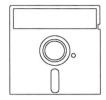
- Clicking the right mouse button while dragging the cursor cancels the operation.
- Choosing <u>U</u>ndo from the <u>E</u>dit menu erases everything you've drawn since the current tool was selected.

3. Print the graphic.
4. Save the graphic on a floppy disk and clear the drawing area.

7.3   Editing the Graphic

After you have drawn part of your graphic, you will probably want to **edit** it — alter the graphic to correct mistakes or improve its looks. We have already described one way to edit a graphic: You can use the <u>U</u>ndo command on the <u>E</u>dit menu to erase all the work you've done since the current tool was selected. This section discusses other, more specialized, editing features of Paintbrush.

The Eraser Tool

The Eraser is the editing tool you're likely to use the most. It works on your electronic graphic the way an ordinary eraser works on a conventional drawing. As you drag its cursor across the graphic, the Eraser wipes out everything in its path. More specifically, to use the Eraser:

1. Select the Eraser tool from the Toolbox.

2. Select a drawing width; it determines the size of the eraser, the width of the path it cuts through the object to be edited.

3. Select a *background* color. When the Eraser "erases," it changes every foreground color in its path to this background color.

4. Move the cursor (a hollow square) into the drawing area, position it where you want to start erasing, and drag it to erase everything in its path.

   To move the cursor perfectly horizontally or vertically, hold down the Shift key while dragging the cursor in a horizontal or vertical direction.

5. When you're done erasing, release the mouse button.

Paintbrush contains another kind of eraser that is a little more selective than the Eraser tool. To select it, press the Backspace key. The cursor will become a square with a X inside. Then, select a drawing width and drag the cursor to erase. The process works like the one just described for the Eraser tool with two important exceptions:

- The Backspace eraser changes everything in its path to the *original* background color, the color of the blank drawing area.

- The Backspace eraser erases only those objects that have not yet been *pasted down*. Once drawn, an object is pasted down by selecting a tool from the Toolbox, using a scroll bar, resizing the drawing area, or switching to another application.

You can use the Backspace eraser to your advantage by pasting down objects that you're fairly sure you won't want to change. Then, they will not be accidentally erased if you use the Backspace eraser on nearby newly-drawn objects.

The Color Eraser Tool

The Color Eraser tool works in the same general way as the Eraser tool, but only erases the specified color in its path. To use this tool:

1. Select the Color Eraser tool from the Toolbox.

2. Select a drawing width; it determines the size of the eraser, the width of the path it cuts through the object to be edited.

3. Select a foreground and background color. When the Color Eraser "erases," it changes every occurrence of the selected foreground color in its path to the specified background color.

4. Move the cursor (a square with cross hairs inside) into the drawing area, position it where you want to start erasing, and drag it to erase every occurrence of the selected foreground color in its path.

   To move the cursor perfectly horizontally or vertically, hold down the Shift key while dragging the cursor in a horizontal or vertical direction.

5. When you're done erasing, release the mouse button.

   Here's an example that illustrates the difference between the Eraser and the Color Eraser. Before using the erasers on the object below, the background color was set to white.

Eraser

Color Eraser
with foreground:

Gray   Black

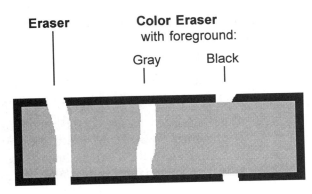

The Color Eraser tool can be used in another powerful way — in one step, it can change *every* occurrence of a given color in the drawing to another specified color. To do so:

1. Select a foreground and background color; the selected background color will replace *every* occurrence of the specified foreground color.

2. Double-click on the Color Eraser icon in the Toolbox.

Be careful with this technique; it can make major changes to your work. If your graphic is larger than the drawing area, don't forget to scroll or zoom out (Ctrl+O) to check the entire graphic before double-clicking. And remember: If you don't like the effect of the change, undo it (Ctrl +Z) immediately.

Zooming In to Edit Detail

At times, you may want to change small details in a graphic; for example, the shape of the dog's nose in Figure 7.6a. For just such situations, Paintbrush provides the Zoom In command, which allows you to magnify a small portion of the graphic and edit it pixel by pixel. (Recall that *pixels* are the tiny dots of light on the screen that make up the graphic; they are also called *pels*, for "picture elements.")

To use the Zoom In command:

1. Choose Zoom In from the View menu, or press Ctrl+N. The cursor becomes a rectangular box.

2. Position the box over the region you want to magnify. In Figure 7.6a, it is positioned over the top of the dog's nose.

3. Click the mouse button. The drawing area then displays the selected region as a collection of colored squares, each representing one pixel in the graphic. The upper-left corner of the drawing area shows the region being magnified (see Figure 7.6b).

FIGURE 7.6 Using the Zoom In Command

a. Select the Region to be Magnified   **b. Edit the Magnified Image**

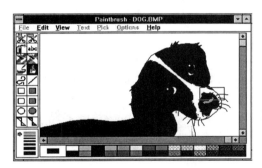 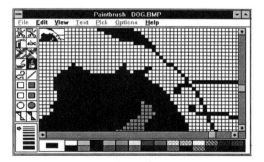

Editing the magnified region

4. You can now edit the magnified region in the following ways:

   ■ Click on a square with the *left* mouse button to change that pixel to the current *foreground* color.

   ■ Click on a square with the *right* mouse button to change that pixel to the current *background* color.

   ■ Press the left or right mouse button and drag the cursor over the squares in any region to change those pixels to the current foreground or background colors, respectively.

   ■ Use the Paint Roller to change the color of enclosed areas in the same way it is used with non-magnified graphics (see Section 7.2).

5. When you are done, choose Zoom Out from the View menu, or press Ctrl+O, to return to the normal drawing area.

The Cutout Tools: Scissors and Pick

One of the major advantages of Paintbrush over conventional drawing is its ability to move, copy, and resize any object in the graphic. To perform these operations, you must first select the object to be manipulated; in Paintbrush parlance, you must "define a cutout." A **cutout** is a region in the graphic that has been selected by using either the Scissors tool or the Pick tool.

The Scissors tool (its icon is in the margin on the left) defines an irregularly shaped cutout; the Pick tool (its icon is on the right) defines a rectangular cutout. Pick is easier to use, but Scissors is more versatile. Figure 7.7 illustrates the two types of cutouts.

FIGURE 7.7   **Using the Cutout Tools**

a. A Cutout Created by Pick   **b. A Cutout Created by Scissors**

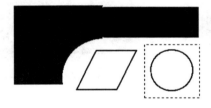 

To use the Pick tool to define a rectangular cutout:

1. Click on the Pick icon in the upper-right corner of the Toolbox.

2. Position the cursor at one corner of the cutout, the region that contains the object(s) to be manipulated.

3. Press the mouse button and drag the cursor to the opposite corner of the cutout. As you drag, a "flexible" box will move with the cursor, indicating the selected region.

4. When the cutout is defined as you want, release the mouse button. The selected region is then enclosed in a dotted rectangular box (see Figure 7.7a).

To use the Scissors tool to define an irregularly shaped cutout:

1. Click on the Scissors icon in the upper-left corner of the Toolbox.

2. Position the cursor in the drawing area where you want to start the cutout, the region that contains the object(s) to be manipulated.

3. Press the mouse button and drag the cursor, creating a curve that defines the cutout.

4. Release the mouse button. The selected region is then enclosed in a dotted curve (see Figure 7.7b).

Notice that the Scissors tool is used to select the parallelogram in Figure 7.7b. Pick cannot be used in this case without also selecting part of the black area around the parallelogram.

Deleting a cutout   Here's a simple example of how cutouts are used: Suppose you want to delete an object from a graphic; say, the circle in Figure 7.7. To do so, define a cutout that contains the circle, as in Figure 7.7a, and choose Cut from the Edit menu. The cutout will be deleted from your graphic, taking the circle with it. We will discuss many other ways to manipulate cutouts in Section 7.4.

An Example

We will illustrate some of the material in the last two sections by drawing the truck shown in Figure 7.8. To draw this graphic:

FIGURE 7.8   The "Truck" Graphic

1. Select black as the foreground color, white as the background color, and click on the second-thinnest drawing width.

2. To draw the road, select the Line tool, hold down the Shift key (for a horizontal line), and drag the cursor across the drawing area, about one-half inch from the bottom.

3. Select the Airbrush and a medium drawing width to add the shading under the road. (Hold down the Shift key to get a horizontal "line.")

4. To draw the rear wheel, select the Circle/Ellipse tool, set the drawing width to its maximum setting (to make the tire), position the cursor on the road, hold down the Shift key (for a circle), and drag the cursor to form a wheel about one inch in diameter.

5. Use the Cursor Position coordinates to help draw a front wheel that's the same size as the rear one. First, determine the value of the second coordinate at the top of the rear wheel. Then, as you drag the cursor to draw the front wheel, stop when you reach that height.

6. To draw the truck's trailer, select the Filled Box tool with a foreground of light gray and a background of black, and return the drawing width to its second setting. Start near the rear wheel and make the rectangle about 4" high and 5" long.

7. Return the foreground and background colors to black and white, respectively, and select the Line tool to draw all the straight lines that make up the cab of the truck. Consult Figure 7.8 for their relative positions.

8. Select the Curve tool to draw the front of the cab; just drag the flexible line, near its top, a little to the right.

9. Use the Paint Roller to fill the entire cab, except the window area, with dark gray. (You need to click in two different places.) If the paint leaks, use the Undo command, and then Zoom In on all the line joints to make sure they're solid.

The graphic in Figure 7.8 is stored in the PAINT directory of the Lab Projects diskette as TRUCK1.BMP.

Hands-On 7.3

Start up Windows and Paintbrush (if necessary) and try the following:

1. Insert the Lab Projects diskette in its drive and open the TRUCK1 .BMP file from its PAINT directory.

2. Change the color of the trailer from gray to dark blue.

3. Add another wheel just in front of the rear one.
4. Add a handle to the cab door.
5. Redraw the cab windows using thicker lines.
6. Save the modified graphic as TRUCK3 to a floppy disk.
7. Print the modified graphic.

7.4 Manipulating Cutouts

Once you have *defined a cutout* — selected a region in the graphic — using either the Scissors or Pick tool as described in Section 7.3, Paintbrush allows you to:

1. Cut or copy the cutout to the Clipboard.

2. Save the cutout in a graphic file on disk.

3. Move, copy, or sweep the cutout to another part of the graphic.

4. Flip the cutout horizontally or vertically and invert its colors.

5. Tilt and resize the cutout.

In this section, we will describe how to perform these operations.

Basic Operations on Cutouts

Cut, copy, and paste   A cutout, like any other selected information, can be cut or copied to the Clipboard, and then pasted into Paintbrush or another Windows application (see Section 2.4). Recall that when information is *cut* to the Clipboard, it is deleted from the current graphic, but when it is *copied* to the Clipboard, the current graphic remains unchanged. Here's how these procedures work in Paintbrush.

■ To *cut* a cutout to the Clipboard, choose Cut from the Edit menu. The cutout will be deleted from the current graphic.

■ To *copy* a cutout to the Clipboard, choose Copy from the Edit menu.

■ To *paste* a cutout from the Clipboard into a Paintbrush graphic, choose Paste from the Edit menu. The cutout is pasted into the upper-left corner of the drawing area and remains *active*, as indicated by the curve or box enclosing it. An active cutout can continue to be manipulated; in particular, it can be moved (as described shortly) to another location in the drawing area.

In general, once it is selected, a cutout remains active until it is *pasted down* — anchored in place. To paste down a cutout, perform any of the following actions:

- Click the mouse outside the cutout.

- Define (select) a new cutout.

- Select any tool from the Toolbox.

When a cutout is anchored in place, the enclosing curve or box, constructed when you defined the cutout, disappears.

Saving and retrieving cutouts

Paintbrush allows you to save a cutout as a separate file on disk. It can then be opened at any later time as a graphic of its own or as part of another graphic. In this way, you can create a *library* of graphic components. For example, if you frequently draw pictures of houses, you can create and save types of windows, doors, and other "house components" for use in all your drawings.

To save an active cutout to disk:

1. Choose Copy To from the Edit menu. The Copy To dialog box, which is virtually identical to the Save As dialog box discussed earlier, is displayed.

2. Proceed as you would to save any file to disk.

If you want to *insert* a graphic that is stored on disk into your current drawing, you must use the Paste From command on the Edit menu to retrieve it. If you use the Open command, the new graphic *replaces* the current one in the drawing area. To insert a graphic file on disk into the current graphic:

1. Choose the Paste From command from the Edit menu. The Paste From dialog box, which is virtually identical to the Open dialog box discussed earlier, is displayed.

2. Proceed as you would to open any file stored on disk.

The retrieved graphic will be pasted, as an active cutout, into the upper-left corner of the current graphic. You can then move it anywhere in the drawing area, as we will now demonstrate.

Moving, Copying, and Sweeping a Cutout

Paintbrush makes it very easy to transfer a cutout from one location in the drawing area to another. There are three types of "transfer" operations:

Move   1.   When you *move* a cutout, it is transferred to the new location and deleted from the original one. To move an active cutout, position the cursor inside the cutout, press either mouse button, drag the cutout to the new location, and release the mouse button.

Copy   2.   When you *copy* a cutout, it is transferred to the new location without being deleted from the original one. To copy an active cutout, follow the *move* procedure, but hold down the Ctrl key as you drag the cutout.

Sweep   3.   When you *sweep* a cutout, it is transferred to the new location, leaving a series of copies in its path. To sweep an active cutout, follow the *move* procedure, but hold down the Shift key as you drag the cutout. Here is the result of sweeping a square from one location to another:

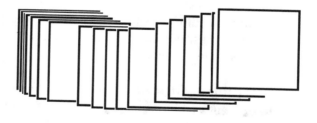

When you perform a transfer operation (move, copy, or sweep), the copy of the cutout may obscure whatever is beneath it. We refer to this as an *opaque* transfer. When the part of the graphic lying beneath the copy shows through, we call it a *transparent* transfer.

Figure 7.9 (on the next page) illustrates the difference between the two types of transfers. The original figures, circles, are shown on the left. They were selected with the Pick tool and copied over the picture of the car on the right. In Figure 7.9a, the copy is opaque — the entire cutout obscures the graphic; in Figure 7.9b, the copy is transparent — the car shows through the copied circle.

To transfer a cutout opaquely, select a background color that is different from the current one before moving, copying, or sweeping the cutout. To transfer a cutout transparently, select the background color that matches the current one.

FIGURE 7.9   Opaque versus Transparent Transfer

a. Opaque Copying   **b. Transparent Copying**

Using the Pick Menu

The Pick menu provides several additional operations that can be performed on cutouts. Although the name of this menu might seem to imply that you must use the Pick tool to define the cutout, the Scissors tool can be used here as well.

Flipping a Cutout   If you want to flip an active cutout from left to right, choose Flip Horizontal from the Pick menu; to flip it from top to bottom, choose Flip Vertical from the Pick menu. The cutout is flipped "in place"; it is not copied. Here is an example of each type of flip — in the graphic, the triangle on the right *replaces* the one on the left.

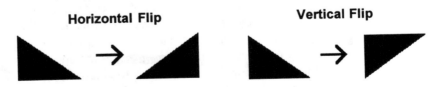

Horizontal Flip   **Vertical Flip**

Inverting the Colors in a Cutout   To reverse all colors in an active cutout, choose Inverse from the Pick menu. This command turns black into white, reds into greens, and blues into browns or yellows.

In the example below, the object on the left has a blue border, black interior and white stripes. When it is selected and the Inverse command is applied, the object on the right, with brown border, white interior, and black stripes, replaces it.

Inverting Colors

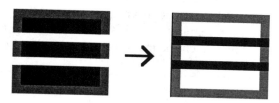

Resizing a Cutout   A copy of a cutout can be made that is larger or smaller than the original. To resize an active cutout:

1.   Choose Shrink + Grow from the Pick menu.

2.   Position the cursor (cross hairs) where you want to place the upper-left corner of the resized copy and drag the cursor to create it. A "flexible" box is displayed, indicating the size and shape of the copy.

     If you want the resized copy of the cutout to have the same proportions as the original, hold down the Shift key as you drag the cursor.

3.   Release the mouse button. The resized copy is then drawn in the specified area.

In the example shown below, the polygon on the left has been enlarged as it was copied to form the figure on the right:

A cutout remains active after the resize operation is complete, so you can repeat the process to make as many resized copies of the original as you like. To turn Shrink + Grow off, choose it again from the Pick menu or anchor the cutout. A check mark next to Shrink + Grow on the menu indicates that it's in effect.

If you want to *replace* the original cutout with the resized copy, you could follow the procedure just given and then delete the original. This can be done in one step by choosing Clear from the Pick menu, setting the current background color to that of the cutout to be deleted, and choosing Shrink + Grow. In effect, choosing Clear changes the Shrink + Grow command from a *copy* operation to a *move* operation. The Clear option remains in effect until the cutout is anchored or you choose Clear again. A check mark next to this item on the Pick menu indicates that it's in effect.

Tilting a Cutout   A copy of a cutout can be made that is *tilted* — skewed to the left or right — relative to the original. To tilt an active cutout:

1. Choose Tilt from the Pick menu.

2. To automatically delete the original cutout after creating the tilted copy, choose Clear from the Pick menu.

3. Position the cursor (cross hairs) where you want the upper-left corner of the tilted cutout to be placed and press the mouse button. A "flexible" box, the size of the active cutout, is displayed.

4. To tilt the copy to the left or right, drag the cursor in the appropriate direction. The further you drag it horizontally, the more the tilt.

5. Release the mouse button when the box is positioned as you want. The tilted copy of the cutout is then drawn in the specified area.

In the example shown here, the circle on the left was tilted as it was copied to form the two figures on the right:

A cutout remains active after the tilt operation is completed, so you can repeat the process to make additional tilted copies of the original. To turn Tilt off, choose it again from the Pick menu or anchor the cutout. A check mark next to Tilt on the menu indicates that it's in effect.

An Example

We will illustrate some of the techniques of this chapter by drawing the graphic shown in Figure 7.10.

FIGURE 7.10   The "Factory" Graphic

To construct this graphic:

1. Set the foreground color to black, the background color to white, and click on the second-thinnest drawing width.

2. Select the Box tool and draw the factory building.

3. Select the Filled Box tool and draw the smokestack.

4. Draw the right-most window by using the Box tool to construct its frame and the Line tool for the horizontal and vertical crosspieces. (The cursor coordinates are useful in centering these lines.)

5. Use the **Shrink + Grow** command to create a smaller copy of this window on the left end of the factory.

6. Select the Line tool and create the triangular piece above the left window.

7. Select the Pick took and copy the trapezoid-shaped left window, placing the copy just to its right. (Don't forget to hold down Ctrl.)

8. With the newly-created middle window still selected, choose the Flip Horizontal command to orient it in the proper direction.

9. Select a gray foreground color and a medium drawing width and draw the smoke with several strokes of the Airbrush.

10. Select the Paint Roller and click inside the factory building (but not inside any window) to color it gray.

The graphic in Figure 7.10 is stored in the PAINT directory on the Lab Projects disk as FACTORY.BMP.

Hands-On 7.4

Start up Windows and Paintbrush (if necessary) and try the following:

1. Create the "traffic light" graphic shown at the right. Use the copy and horizontal flip techniques to minimize your work. What drawing tools did you use in creating your graphic?
2. Save your graphic to a floppy disk.
3. Print the graphic.

7.5 Placing Text in a Graphic

Although a graphic can often convey a thought without using any explanatory text, sometimes it needs a few words to clarify the message. In this section, we will describe how to insert text into a graphic in your choice of color, design, style, and size.

Selecting a Font

When you insert text into a Paintbrush graphic, the characters appear on the screen in the current **font**, a certain design, style, and size of type. To select a font for your text, choose Fonts from the Text menu. The Font dialog box will be displayed:

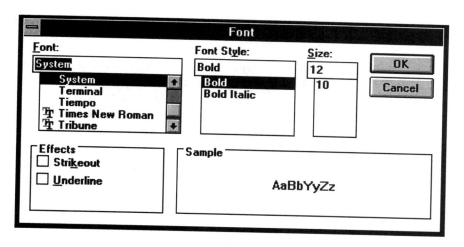

The currently selected font is displayed in the Sample box, which allows you to view the effects of changes in the font without closing the Font dialog box. In selecting a font, you specify the following characteristics:

Typeface
1. The font *design* or *typeface* is the overall "look" of the characters, independent of size or special effects. To change the typeface, select one from the Font list.

Font style
2. A font *style* refers to special effects applied to the font. These vary according to the typeface selected, but usually include:

Regular   **Bold**   *Italic*   <u>Underline</u>   ~~Strikeout~~

Some styles are selected from the Font Style list; others by using the Effects check boxes.

Point size
3. The font *size* is, roughly speaking, the height of the tallest characters. The size of a font is measured in *points*, with one point equal to 1/72 of an inch. Thus, 36-point type is about one-half inch high. To change the font size, select one from the Size list, or type the size you want in the Size text box.

To put a font into effect, choose the OK button to close the dialog box. The font change affects all text that you type until the next change, as well as all text in the graphic that has not yet been *pasted down*. Text is pasted down by performing any of the following actions:

Pasting
down text
- Selecting a tool from the Toolbox.

- Repositioning the text cursor.

- Scrolling or resizing the drawing area.

■ Switching to another application.

To change the typeface or size of the current font, you must use the Font dialog box. You can change aspects of its style, however, from the Text menu. This menu allows you to choose Bold, Italic, Underline, Outline, and Shadow styles (when they are available for the current typeface).

A check mark appears on the Text menu next to each selected style. Instead of opening the Text menu, you can choose Bold, Italic, or Underline styles by pressing the shortcut keys Ctrl+B, Ctrl+I, or Ctrl+U, respectively. To cancel a style, choose it again or choose Regular, which cancels all styles currently in effect.

Inserting Text into a Graphic

To insert text into a graphic:

1. Select a foreground color; this will be the color of the inserted text.

2. Select the Text tool from the Toolbox.

3. Select a font (as described earlier in this section).

4. Position the text cursor (an I-beam) in the drawing area where you want to begin typing text.

5. Type characters at the keyboard. They will be displayed in the specified color and font on the screen.

6. To start a new line, press Enter. Text does not automatically *wrap* in Paintbrush; when you reach the right edge of the drawing window, you will not be able to insert more text into the graphic until you press Enter or reposition the cursor.

Editing Text within a Graphic

Paintbrush has very limited text editing capabilities. The text itself can only be edited before it is pasted down and only by using the Backspace key. So, to modify text that has not yet been anchored in place, press the Backspace key until the errant text is erased and then retype it correctly. Remember: You *cannot use the mouse to reposition the cursor and then use the Backspace key*; repositioning the cursor pastes down the text!

After text has been pasted down, it can be erased (using the Eraser or Color Eraser) or moved to another location in the drawing (using the Pick tool). These tools provide editing capabilities of a sort, but are not easy to use on individual characters. To avoid some potential frustration, try to find all mistakes in your text *before* pasting it down.

An Example

To illustrate the material in this section, let's return to the "Truck" graphic of Figure 7.8 (page 269). We will insert text into this graphic, creating the "Lettered Truck" graphic shown in Figure 7.11.

FIGURE 7.11   The "Lettered Truck" Graphic

To create the modified graphic:

1. Open the "Truck" graphic; it is stored in the PAINT directory of the Lab Projects diskette under TRUCK1.BMP.

2. Set the foreground color, which will be the color of the lettering, to black.

3. Select the Text tool from the Toolbox.

4. Select the Arial Bold 24-point font from the Font dialog box. (You may use a more interesting font, if one is available.)

5. Position the text cursor near the top of the truck and type: SAM'S Don't worry about the exact positioning, you can always move it later using the Pick tool.

6. Position the cursor for the next line of lettering, turn Bold off (by

pressing Ctrl+B), and type: Delivery Service

7. Reposition the cursor, select the Times New Roman Italic 14-point font, and type: We Deliver

8. Reposition the cursor and type: Call

9. Reposition the cursor (to paste down *Call*), turn off italics by pressing Ctrl+I, and type: 555-5555

10. Change the background color to light gray, select the Pick tool, and move any block of text, as needed.

The new graphic is stored in the PAINT directory of the Lab Projects diskette as TRUCK2.BMP.

Hands-On 7.5

Start up Windows and Paintbrush (if necessary) and try the following:

1. Insert the Lab Projects diskette in its drive and open the TRUCK1 .BMP file from its PAINT directory.

2. Use the Text tool to create your own sign on the side of the truck. Use at least four lines of text in two fonts of your choosing. Try to position the text in a pleasing manner.

3. Save the modified graphic as TRUCK4 on a floppy disk.

4. Print the modified graphic.

7.6 Other Paintbrush Features

In this section, we will describe how to change some of the default settings we've used in all our graphics so far. These include:

- The size of the drawing.

- The colors on the Palette.

- The page setup for the printed graphic.

Changing the Drawing Size

7″ × 5″   Paintbrush uses a default drawing size that is roughly seven inches wide and five inches high. To change this setting:

1.   Choose Image Attributes from the Options menu. The following dialog box will be displayed:

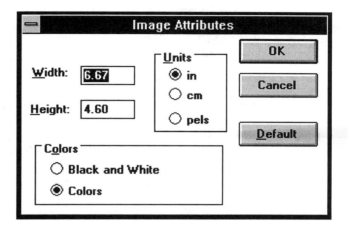

2.   If you would rather measure using centimeters or pixels, select cm or pels, respectively, in the Units section of the dialog box.

3.   Type the new Width and Height in their text boxes.

4.   Choose the OK button.

The new dimensions take effect when you begin your next drawing, assuming there is enough memory (RAM) available to store a graphic of the size you have selected. If the new dimensions are *smaller* than the drawing area, a rectangular box will be displayed in the upper-left corner, marking off the specified drawing area. To return to the original width and height set by Paintbrush, choose the Default button from the Image Attributes dialog box.

Changing the Palette Colors

The colors available on the Palette can be changed in two ways:

■ By electing to use black-and-white patterns instead of colors.

■ By replacing existing colors with your own custom colors.

Using black-and-white patterns   When the colors in a graphic are printed on a non-color printer, they are rendered as shades of gray (actually, as blocks of black dots of various densities). With some printers, using black-and-white patterns in the graphic, instead of colors, produces a more pleasing result. To display a Palette that contains these patterns:

1. Choose Image Attributes from the Options menu.

2. In the Colors section of the Image Attributes dialog box, select the Black and White option.

3. Choose the OK button.

The new Palette will be displayed when you begin your next drawing.

Using custom colors   Paintbrush allows you to replace any color on the Palette with a *custom color* — one of your own choosing. You can even do this in the middle of a drawing without affecting the color of the objects you have already drawn. To place a custom color in the Palette:

1. Select the color to be replaced as the foreground color.

2. Choose Edit Colors from the Options menu. The following dialog box will be displayed:

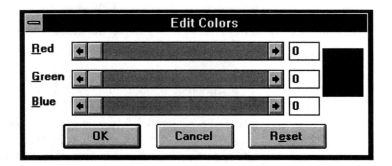

You create a custom color using this dialog box by specifying the intensity of the red, green, and blue (RGB) components of which it is made. For example, white consists of maximum amounts of all three colors, while bright yellow is made up of maximum amounts of red and green but no blue.

3. Use the Red, Green, and Blue scroll bars to vary the intensity of each of these colors, moving the scroll box to the right to strengthen a color. As you scroll, the value of each component appears in the corresponding text box and the resultant color is displayed in the box to the right of the text boxes.

4. When you achieve the desired color, choose the OK button. The

dialog box will close and the custom color will appear on the Palette instead of the original one.

The new Palette remains in effect until you exit Paintbrush. (The default Palette appears every time you start Paintbrush.) To save the new Palette so that it can be used in future sessions, choose the Save Colors item on the Options menu. To retrieve a previously-saved Palette, choose the Get colors item on the Options menu.

Setting Up the Printed Page

Before printing a graphic, you may want to alter the default margins (one-half inch all around) or insert a header or footer above or below the graphic. To take either action, choose Page Setup from the File menu, which opens the following dialog box:

```
┌─────────────────────────────────────────────────────────┐
│ ▬              Page Setup                                 │
├─────────────────────────────────────────────────────────┤
│                                           ┌───────────┐  │
│  Header: ┌──────────────────┐             │    OK     │  │
│          └──────────────────┘             └───────────┘  │
│                                           ┌───────────┐  │
│  Footer: ┌──────────────────┐             │  Cancel   │  │
│          └──────────────────┘             └───────────┘  │
│  ┌─Margins────────────────────────────────────────┐     │
│  │                                                 │     │
│  │  Top: [0.50]    Bottom: [0.50]                  │     │
│  │                                                 │     │
│  │  Left: [0.50]   Right:  [0.50]                  │     │
│  └─────────────────────────────────────────────────┘     │
└─────────────────────────────────────────────────────────┘
```

(This is the same dialog box used by the Notepad accessory — see Section 6.7.)

Setting margins
The margin settings determine the size of the blank border around your graphic. To change the margin widths, just type the desired values in the Top, Bottom, Left, and Right text boxes. The new settings take effect when you choose the OK button.

If the margins are so *large* that the drawing cannot fit in its allotted space on the page when the graphic is printed, it will be continued on to additional pages. If the margins are so *small* that they leave "too much" space for the specified drawing size, the graphic will be printed in the upper-left corner of its allotted space on the page.

Headers
and footers

A **header** is text that is positioned at the top of every page of a document. Similarly, a **footer** is text that appears at the bottom of every page. To have Paintbrush automatically insert a header and/or footer on every page of the printed graphic, in the Page Setup dialog box:

1. Type the desired text in the Header and/or Footer text boxes. You may include the following codes in this text:

    &c   centers text that follows this code;
    &d   inserts the current date in place of this code;
    &f   inserts the graphic's file name in place of this code;
    &l   left-justifies text that follows this code;
    &p   inserts the current page number in place of this code;
    &r   right-justifies text that follows this code;
    &t   inserts the current time in place of this code.

2. Choose the OK button.

Headers and footers are printed in the top and bottom margins in the default printer font. For example, if you type &lPage &p &rDate: &d in the Header box (and choose OK), Paintbrush will place text similar to the following in the top margin of every page of the printed graphic:

Page 1   Date: 1/3/94

Chapter Summary

Key Terms

Background color [page 250]   Cutout [268]

Drawing area [248]   Edit a graphic [264]

Font [278]   Foreground color [250]

Footer [286]   Graphic [247]

Header [286]   Linesize box [248]

Paintbrush [247]   Palette [248]

Toolbox [248]

Topics Covered

General Features of Paintbrush

To hide the Toolbox and   Choose Tools and Linesize from the View
  the Linesize box   menu.

To hide the Palette	Choose Palette from the View menu.
To view the graphic full-screen	Choose View Picture from the View menu; or press Ctrl+P.
To zoom out	Choose Zoom Out from the View menu; or press Ctrl+O.
To zoom in	Choose Zoom In from the View menu; or press Ctrl+N.
To change the drawing size	Choose Image Attributes from the Options menu and set the new Height and Width in the dialog box.
To replace Palette colors with black-and-white patterns	Choose Image Attributes from the Options menu and select the Black and White option from the dialog box.
To create a custom color for the Palette	Select the color to be replaced on the Palette, choose Edit Colors from the Options menu, and specify the new color in the dialog box.

Paintbrush Tools

	Scissors	Defines an irregularly shaped cutout.
	Pick	Defines a rectangular cutout.
	Airbrush	Draws a free-form figure with a spray of dots.
	Text	Inserts text into the graphic.
	Color Eraser	Erases the specified color in its path.
	Eraser	Erases everything in its path.
	Paint Roller	Fills an enclosed region with color.
	Brush	Draws a free-form figure.
	Curve	Draws a curve.
	Line	Draws a line.
	Box	Draws a hollow rectangle.
	Filled Box	Draws a rectangle and fills it with color.
	Rounded Box	Draws a rectangle with rounded corners.
	Filled Rounded Box	Draws a rectangle with rounded corners and fills it with color.

 Circle/Ellipse	Draws a circle or ellipse.
Filled Circle/Ellipse	Draws a circle or ellipse and fills it with color.
Polygon	Draws a polygon.
Filled Polygon	Draws a polygon and fills it with color.

Operations on Cutouts

Cut to Clipboard	Choose Cut from the Edit menu.
Copy to Clipboard	Choose Copy from the Edit menu.
Paste from Clipboard	Choose Paste from the Edit menu.
Save to disk file	Choose Copy To from the Edit menu.
Retrieve from disk file	Choose Paste From from the Edit menu.
Flip horizontally/vertically	Choose Flip Horizontal/Flip Vertical from the Pick menu.
Reverse colors	Choose Inverse from the Pick menu.
Resize	Choose Shrink + Grow from the Pick menu.
Tilt	Choose Tilt from the Pick menu.

Changing the Current Font

To change the font color	Select a foreground color from the Palette.
To change the typeface	Choose Fonts from the Text menu and select a typeface from the dialog box.
To change the font style	Choose Fonts from the Text menu and select a style from the dialog box; or choose Bold, Italic, Underline, Outline, or Shadow from the Text menu.
To change the point size	Choose Fonts from the Text menu and select a size from the dialog box.

Selecting Printing Options

To set margins	Choose Page Setup from the File menu and type the values in the dialog box.
To create a header or footer	Choose Page Setup from the File menu and type the Header or Footer in the dialog box.
To print a partial graphic	Choose Print from the File menu and select

the Partial option in the dialog box.

To print a scaled graphic   Choose Print from the File menu and type a Scaling factor in the dialog box.

Chapter Exercises

Short Answer

Complete each statement in Exercises 1 through 15.

1. To expand the drawing area to the entire screen, choose _____ from the View menu.

2. To select red as the background color, click the _____ button on that color in the Palette.

3. To draw a rectangle filled with the color blue using the Filled Box tool, select blue as the _____ color.

4. To draw a line inclined at a 45° angle with the Line tool, hold down the _____ key while dragging the cursor.

5. If a figure is completely enclosed by curves, it can be filled with color using the _____ tool.

6. To erase a green circle enclosed in a red square with the Color Eraser, set the foreground color to _____ .

7. To define an irregularly shaped cutout, use the _____ tool.

8. To magnify a small area of your graphic, use the _____ command.

9. To sweep a cutout, hold down the _____ key while dragging the cursor.

10. To flip a cutout from top to bottom, choose _____ from the Pick menu.

11. To save a cutout on disk, choose _____ from the Edit menu.

12. To change the point size of the current font, you must open the _____ dialog box.

13. Text can be edited using the _____ key, as long as it has not yet been pasted down.

14. You can replace the colors in the Palette with black-and-white patterns by choosing _____ from the Options menu.

15. A _____ is text that appears at the top of every page of a document.

In Exercises 16 through 30, determine whether each statement is true or false.

16. When the drawing area has been expanded to the entire screen, you cannot use the Line tool.

17. To print part of a graphic, you must use the Pick tool before opening the Print dialog box.

18. The Brush tool cannot draw perfectly straight horizontal lines.

19. To draw a box filled with blue and having no border, select blue for both the foreground and background colors.

20. To draw a perfect square with the Box tool, hold down the Shift key while dragging the cursor.

21. The Polygon tool cannot be used to draw a rectangle.

22. To change every occurrence of green in your graphic to the current background color, double-click on green in the Palette.

23. While "zoomed in" on part of your graphic, you can use the Paint Roller to fill an enclosed region with color.

24. To define a cutout that is the same shape as a circle, use the Pick tool.

25. To move a cutout transparently, choose Clear from the Pick menu before dragging the cursor.

26. To automatically delete a cutout as it is resized, choose Clear from the Pick menu before performing the resize operation.

27. A change in the current font cannot apply to text that is already on the screen.

28. A block of text can be moved using the Pick tool.

29. If a graphic is too large to fit within the current margins, they will be changed automatically when you issue the Print command.

30. To print a header with the page number centered, type &c&p in the Header text box of the Page Setup dialog box.

In Exercises 31 through 40, choose the correct answer.

31. To increase the size of the drawing area:

    a. Choose Zoom In from the View menu.
    b. Choose Tools and Linesize from the View menu.
    c. Set smaller margins using the Page Setup dialog box.
    d. Select the Whole option in the Print dialog box.

32. To select red as the background color:

    a. Click the left mouse button on red in the Palette.
    b. Double-click the left mouse button on red in the Palette.
    c. Click the right mouse button on red in the Palette.
    d. Double-click the right mouse button on red in the Palette.

33. Which tool cannot draw an "L-shaped" pair of lines?

    a. The Polygon tool.
    b. The Line tool.
    c. The Brush tool.
    d. The Airbrush tool.

34. To fill an irregularly shaped region with color:

    a. Double-click on the fill color on the Palette.
    b. Use the Filled Box tool.
    c. Use the Color Eraser tool.
    d. Use the Paint Roller tool.

35. To draw a perfect circle with the Circle/Ellipse tool, while dragging the cursor, hold down:

    a. The Shift key.
    b. The Control key.
    c. The Spacebar.
    d. The Circle key.

36. To copy a cutout from one location to another:

    a. Drag it to the new location.
    b. Drag it to the new location while holding down the Ctrl key.
    c. Drag it to the new location while holding down the Shift key.
    d. Drag it to the new location while holding down the Spacebar.

37. Which operation on cutouts cannot be issued from the Pick menu?

    a. Tilting a cutout.
    b. Flipping a cutout.

    c. Rotating a cutout.

    d. Resizing a cutout.

38. To paste down (anchor) a cutout:

    a. Choose <u>C</u>lear from the <u>P</u>ick menu.

    b. Reposition the cursor.

    c. Move the cutout.

    d. Click outside the cutout.

39. To paste a graphic file into the current drawing:

    a. Choose <u>P</u>aste from the <u>E</u>dit menu.

    b. Choose Paste <u>F</u>rom from the <u>E</u>dit menu.

    c. Choose <u>C</u>opy from the <u>E</u>dit menu.

    d. Choose C<u>o</u>py To from the <u>E</u>dit menu.

40. Which text characteristic cannot be changed in the Font dialog box?

    a. The design of the font (the typeface).

    b. The font style.

    c. The point size.

    d. The font color.

Hands-On   In Exercises 41 through 46, start up Windows and Paintbrush (if necessary) and perform each of the indicated tasks.

41. a. Insert the Lab Projects diskette in its drive and open the CAR .BMP file from its PAINT directory.

    b. Use the Paint Roller to color the car a medium gray. (Select a pattern that most looks like gray.)

    c. Use the Eraser to make the car look like a convertible.

    d. Using a foreground color of black and the Line and Curve tools, add a front door and door handle to the car.

    e. Save the modified car as CAR1 on a floppy disk.

    f. Print the CAR1 graphic.

42. a. Create a drawing that resembles the blue-and-white Greek flag shown at the right.

    b. Use the 24-point Arial Bold font to insert the title Greek Flag above your drawing.

    c. Create a header for the graphic containing your name, your class, and the date.

    d. Save your graphic on a floppy disk as FLAG.

    e. Print the FLAG graphic.

43. a. Insert the Lab Projects diskette in its drive and open the GRAPH1.BMP file in its PAINT directory.

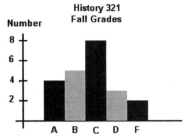

b. Add text to this graphic so that it looks like the one at the right. (Use 10-point Arial bold type for all text.)

c. Create a header for your graphic that contains your name, your class, and the date.

d. Save your graphic on a floppy disk as GRAPH2.

e. Print the GRAPH2 graphic.

44. To test your printer's color handling capabilities:

a. Create the "Palette" graphic shown below. (Each box contains one of the colors from the actual Palette.) How did you get the boxes to all be the same size?

b. Save your graphic on a floppy disk as PALETTE.

c. Print the PALETTE graphic.

45. a. Create a drawing that resembles the house shown at the right.

b. Use the Courier 12-point font to insert your name, your class, and the date on separate lines below the drawing.

c. Save your graphic on a floppy disk as HOUSE.

d. Print the HOUSE graphic.

46. a. Create a drawing that resembles the locomotive shown at the right.

b. Create a header for the graphic that contains your name, your class, and the date.

c. Save your graphic on a floppy disk as TRAIN.

d. Print the TRAIN graphic.

Creative Writing

47. In naming its graphics application *Paintbrush*, Microsoft seems to view it as an electronic form of *painting*. Do you feel as if you're painting when you use Paintbrush, or does it feel more like using crayons, colored pencils, pastels, or some other medium? In one or two paragraphs, justify your answer.

48. Discuss the advantages and disadvantages of using Paintbrush compared to drawing or painting with conventional artist's tools.

49. Paintbrush allows you to perform many operations on cutouts: copy, move, resize, tilt, and so on. Which of these operations do you believe are the most valuable? Which could you do without? Are there other operations on cutouts that you wish were available?

50. Discuss a few features that are not available in Paintbrush but that you wish it offered. Be specific about the way they would work.

Using Other Windows Accessories

OVERVIEW In Chapters 6 and 7, we discussed three of the applications, or *accessories*, included with Windows: Write, Notepad, and Paintbrush. In this chapter, we will describe how to use other Windows accessories. More specifically:

- Section 8.1 discusses Clock and Calculator, which are Windows' versions of these devices, and Character Map, which allows you to insert special characters into a document.

- Section 8.2 covers Cardfile, a simple database that provides the electronic equivalent of a box of index cards.

- Section 8.3 describes how to use Calendar to keep track of your appointments.

- Section 8.4 covers Recorder, which allows you to record keystrokes and mouse actions that can be played back any time you want.

- Section 8.5 discusses how to use Terminal to communicate with a remote computer.

- Section 8.6 briefly describes the functions of the remaining Windows accessories: Media Player, Sound Recorder, and Object Packager.

8.1 Clock, Calculator, and Character Map

In this section, we will discuss the simplest Windows accessories: Clock and Calculator, which provide on-screen versions of their namesakes, and Character Map, which allows you to insert special characters into Windows documents.

Clock

Clock

The **Clock** accessory accesses the computer's internal clock to display the current date and time. To start Clock, choose its icon from the Accessories group. Either a *digital clock* (using numbers) or an *analog clock* (using hands) is then displayed, depending on which setting was active when Clock was last exited. The two clocks are shown in Figure 8.1. To switch between them, choose either <u>D</u>igital or <u>A</u>nalog, as desired, from the <u>S</u>ettings menu.

FIGURE 8.1 The Two Types of Clock Displays

Digital

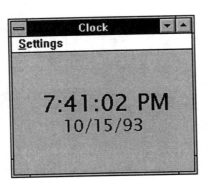

Analog

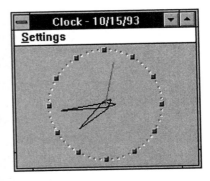

The Clock <u>S</u>ettings menu also provides the following features:

**Features
of Clock**

■ You can change the time display to show only hours and minutes by choosing <u>S</u>econds from the <u>S</u>ettings menu. To turn seconds back on, choose it again.

■ You can turn off the date display by choosing Da<u>t</u>e from the <u>S</u>ettings menu. To turn the date display back on, choose it again.

- You can hide the menu and title bars by choosing <u>N</u>o Title from the <u>S</u>ettings menu, or double-clicking in the Clock window, or pressing the Escape key. To make the title and menu bars reappear, double-click in the Clock window or press Escape.

- You can change the *font* used by the digital clock — the appearance of the characters that make up the time and date. To do so, choose Set <u>F</u>ont from the <u>S</u>ettings menu, select the desired font in the resulting Font dialog box (a few characters of the selected font will be displayed in the Sample box), and choose the OK button. The size of the selected font is determined by the size of the Clock window.

Clock has another useful feature; one that does not appear on the <u>S</u>ettings menu. If you want to keep Clock from being covered by other application windows, choose <u>A</u>lways on <u>T</u>op from the Control menu. Then, Clock will be visible at all times, until you choose this menu item again.

When Clock is minimized, it continues to display the time and date. Moreover, if Always on <u>T</u>op is in effect, this icon is always visible. You can take advantage of these features to create an unobtrusive, ever-present time display by turning on Always on <u>T</u>op, minimizing Clock, and moving its icon to the title bar of the application in which you are working.

Quitting Clock

You can quit Clock in the same manner in which you exit most Windows applications. The quickest ways are to double-click on the Control menu box or press Alt+F4.

Calculator

Calculator

Windows' **Calculator** accessory provides both a basic *standard* calculator and a more versatile *scientific* calculator. To start Calculator, choose its icon from the Accessories group. The type of calculator displayed — standard or scientific — depends on which setting was in effect the last time Calculator was exited. To switch from one type to the other, choose <u>S</u>cientific or S<u>t</u>andard, as desired, from the <u>V</u>iew menu. We will only discuss the standard calculator here; it is shown in the Calculator window of Figure 8.2 on the next page.

FIGURE 8.2   Calculator in Standard Mode

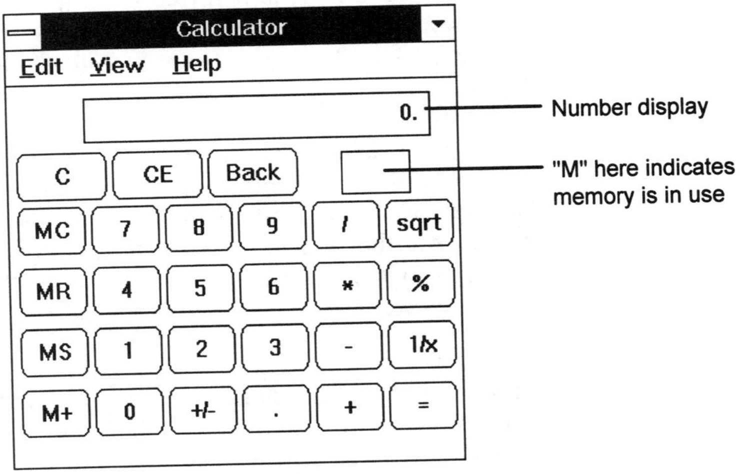

If you can use a conventional calculator, then you can use Windows Calculator; it works in an analogous way. Instead of pressing a button with your finger, click on that button with the mouse. For example, to multiply 365 by 23:

1. Click on the 3, 6, and 5 buttons. As you do, the corresponding digits appear in the display, just as they do with a conventional calculator.

2. Click on the multiplication key (*).

3. Click on the 2 and 3 buttons; 23 appears in the display.

4. Click on the equals key (=). The product, 8395, appears in the display.

You can also use the keyboard to enter numbers and operation symbols, which can be useful if you have a lot of figures to enter and you're adept at using the computer's numeric keypad. If you do use the numeric keypad, don't forget to turn on Num Lock first by pressing this key; the Num Lock light indicates that it is in effect. When Num Lock is turned on, all digits, the decimal point, and the four basic operations (+, -, *, and /) can be entered from the numeric keypad. You can also execute *equals* by pressing Enter.

The standard calculator contains all the keys usually found on a basic calculator, including clear (C), clear entry (CE), square root (sqrt), percentage (%), and reciprocal (1/x). It also provides one "memory" with memory add (M+), memory store (MS), memory recall (MR), and memory clear (MC). When a number is stored in memory, an M is displayed in the box to the right of the Back button.

Special features of Calculator

Calculator provides one atypical key: clicking on the Back button deletes the right-most digit in the number displayed. This feature allows you to correct the number just entered without clearing it and reentering the entire number. For example, if you've just entered the number 365 and meant to enter 367, click on Back to delete the 5 and then click on 7 to make the correction.

Scientific Calculator features ??

If you want to transfer numbers between Calculator and another Windows application, you can copy the number displayed to the Clipboard (see Section 2.4) or paste a number from the Clipboard into the display. These operations are accomplished in the usual way — by choosing Copy or Paste, respectively, from the Edit menu.

Quitting Calculator

You can quit Calculator in the same manner in which you exit most Windows applications. The quickest ways are to double-click on the Control menu box or press Alt+F4.

Character Map

Character Map

Character Map allows you to insert special symbols into a document contained within another Windows application. To start Character Map, choose its icon from the Accessories group. The window shown in Figure 8.3 will open.

FIGURE 8.3   The Character Map Window

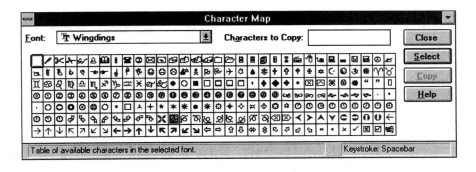

To use Character Map to insert characters into a document:

1. Select a *font*, a collection of characters of similar design, from the Font drop-down list. The characters available in that font will be displayed in the window.

2. Select a character from those displayed by double-clicking on it or by highlighting it with the Arrow keys and choosing the Select button. The character selected will appear in the Characters to Copy box.

3. If you want, repeat step 2 to select additional characters.

4. Choose the Copy button to copy the selected characters to the Clipboard.

5. Switch to the document in which you want to insert the characters.

6. Position the cursor where the characters are to be inserted, *select the same font* as the one used in Character Map, and choose Paste from the Edit menu.

You can obtain a magnified view of a character displayed in the Character Map window by either:

- Pointing at the character and pressing and holding down the mouse button.

or

- Using the Arrow keys to move from character to character, magnifying each as it is selected. By repeatedly pressing the Right Arrow key, you can obtain magnified views of all the displayed characters.

Start up Windows, if necessary, and try the following exercise. To create a printed copy of your work, see Appendix B.

1. Start up Clock. Is the displayed clock analog or digital?
2. Switch, if necessary, to the digital clock. Turn off the date display, turn on the seconds display, and hide the title and menu bars.
3. Select the Arial font. Did you have to display the title/menu bars to do this?
4. Switch to the analog clock and turn off the seconds display. How did the appearance of the clock change?
5. Exit Clock and start Calculator.

6. Switch to the standard calculator, if necessary. Can you maximize the Calculator window?
7. Use Calculator to find 512 / 23. Place this number in the calculator's memory.
8. Now, find the square root of 70 and press MS. What number is stored in memory now?
9. Clear the calculator display and exit Calculator.

8.2   Cardfile: Managing Data

Cardfile

Cardfile is a simple **database manager**, a program that organizes the information entered into it in a way that facilitates its retrieval. For example, you could use Cardfile to create a personal phone directory or to store a collection of recipes. To start Cardfile, choose its icon from the Accessories group. The window shown in Figure 8.4 will then open.

FIGURE 8.4 The Cardfile Window (in *Card View*)

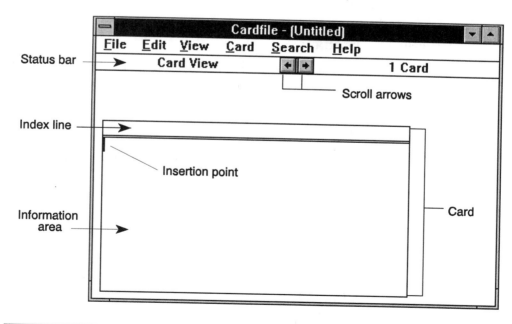

In Cardfile, the **database** — the entire collection of data — consists of a sequence of *cards*, each of which contains information about a single entity. For example: if the database consists of employee records, each card would hold information about a single employee; if the data consists of recipes, each card would hold a different recipe. In learning to use Cardfile, it is useful to think of these electronic cards as actual index cards residing in a file box. By analogy, Windows refers to the database created by Cardfile as a *card file*.

A card is divided into two parts (see Figure 8.4):

■ The *index line*, at the top of the card, contains text that is used to sort the cards. This text is usually a name, title, or number that uniquely identifies the card.

■ The *information area* can contain text and/or graphics (pictures); it supplies information about the entity mentioned on the index line.

As an example, suppose that you want to use Cardfile to create an electronic address book consisting of the names, addresses, and telephone numbers of people you know. In this case, each card would contain information about a different person (or couple), with the name on the index line and the address, phone number, and any other data occupying the information area.

Creating a Database

To use Cardfile to create a database — a card file — you simply fill in the cards, one by one, and add them to the database. To do so:

1. Choose <u>A</u>dd from the <u>C</u>ard menu or press F7. This displays the Add dialog box:

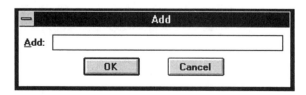

2. Fill in the index line for the card to be added by typing its text in the <u>A</u>dd box and then choosing the OK button. This closes the dialog box and positions the *insertion point*, the blinking vertical bar, in the upper-left corner of the information area.

3. Type the desired data into the information area. Each line on the

card can contain up to 40 characters. When you reach the end of one line, text will automatically *wrap* to the beginning of the next line.

You can correct an error in the usual way: Move the insertion point to the error by clicking on its location (or by using the Arrow keys); then, use the Backspace or Del key to delete the incorrect characters, and type the correct ones.

4. Repeat steps 1 - 3 for each card you want to add to the database. As a card is added, it becomes the *current card*, the one positioned in the front of the card file.

After you add the first card using this procedure, you will notice a blank card behind it:

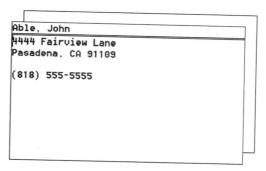

```
Able, John
4444 Fairview Lane
Pasadena, CA 91109

(818) 555-5555
```

To delete the blank card, click on it, which brings it to the front, choose <u>D</u>elete from the <u>C</u>ard menu, and then confirm the deletion in the resulting dialog box. (This process can be used to delete *any* card from the card file.)

To avoid adding the blank card to the database in the first place, alter steps 1 and 2 *for the first card only*: Choose <u>I</u>ndex from the <u>E</u>dit menu instead; then, type the first card's index line in the Index dialog box and choose OK.

The cards in the database are always arranged in alphabetical order, starting with the current card. When the card at the end of the alphabet is reached, the cards continue with those at the beginning of the alphabet (see Figure 8.5 on the next page).

Saving the database   The entire database is stored in a single file. To save this file to disk, choose Save <u>A</u>s from the <u>F</u>ile menu. (Choose <u>S</u>ave if you have modified an already-saved card file and want to replace the original ver-

FIGURE 8.5 Cards Arranged in a Card File

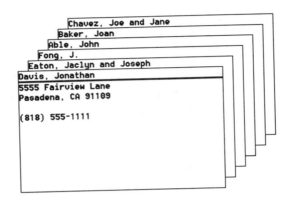

sion.) The usual Save As dialog box will open (see Section 4.4), allowing you to select a drive, directory, and file name for the card file. If the file name you choose does not have an extension, Windows will add a CRD extension to it. To retrieve a saved database, choose Open from the File menu, select the appropriate file name in the resulting dialog box, and choose OK. (For more information about opening files, see Section 4.4.)

Quitting Cardfile   When you are done working on the database, you can quit (exit) Cardfile in the same manner that you exit any Windows application. The quickest ways are to double-click on its Control menu box, or press Alt+F4, or choose Exit from the File menu.

Selecting Cards: Viewing the Database

Once you have created the database (card file), you will want to access its information. Since you can only view the *current card*, the one in front, Cardfile provides several ways of *selecting* a card from the database; that is, making it the current card. To select a card from the open card file, perform any of the following actions:

■ If any part of the card is visible, click on it.

■ Cycle through the cards in alphabetical order or reverse alphabetical order by repeatedly clicking the right or left scroll arrow, respectively, until the desired card is in front.

You can use the keyboard to select a desired card, sometimes more quickly than with the mouse.

Pressing Page Down or Page Up selects the next or previous card.

Pressing Ctrl+Home selects the first card in the database; Ctrl+End selects the last card.

Pressing Ctrl+Shift+*letter* selects the first card beginning with the specified letter; for example, Ctrl+Shift+S selects the first card beginning with S. This is especially useful in moving through a large database.

Searching for text on the index line

- To select a card by the text on its index line:

  1. Choose <u>G</u>o To from the <u>S</u>earch menu or press F4.

  2. Type enough of the index line text in the resulting dialog box to distinguish the desired card from the others.

  3. Choose the OK button.

  For example, for the card file in Figure 8.5, if you press F4, then type Joe in the dialog box and choose OK, the "Chavez, Jane and Joe" card will be brought to the front.

The Go To command described above uses the index line text to locate a card. Another, more user-friendly, way to select a card by using its index line is to switch Cardfile to *List View* mode. To do so:

1. Choose <u>L</u>ist from the <u>V</u>iew menu. The Cardfile window changes to look like this:

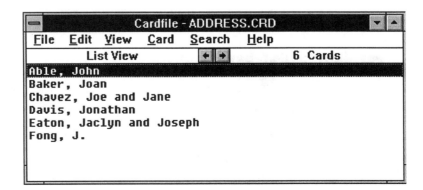

2. Select the desired index by clicking on it, or by using the scroll arrows or Arrow keys to highlight it.

3. Choose Card from the View menu to return to Card View mode with the selected card in front.

Searching
for text
on the card

■ To select a card by the text in its information area:

1. Choose Find from the Search menu. The following dialog box will be displayed:

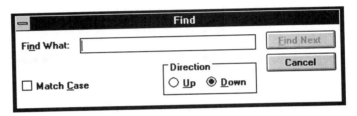

2. Type the text you want to locate in the Find What box.

3. Select the Match Case check box if you want to distinguish uppercase letters from lowercase letters in the search. For example, with Match Case selected, typing cat in the text box will *not* find Cat on a card.

4. Choosing the Up option button searches forward through the card file; choosing Down searches backwards.

5. Choose the Find Next button to select the first card that contains the specified text. To search for other cards with this text, choose Find Next again, or choose Cancel to end the search. (After the dialog box closes, you can find additional cards containing the specified text by choosing Find Next from the Search menu or by pressing the F3 function key.)

Editing the Database

To change the information on a card, first select it using one of the techniques just described. Then, to change text *on the index line*:

1. Choose Index from the Edit menu, or press F6.

2. Make the desired changes in the resulting dialog box and choose the OK button.

To change text *in the information area*, use the Backspace or Del keys to delete individual characters. You can also select text, and cut or copy it to the Clipboard, or paste it from the Clipboard into the information area. The procedures, which are described in more detail in Section 2.4, work like this:

Cut, copy, and paste procedures

- To *select* a block of text on a card, position the insertion point at the beginning of the block, then drag the mouse to the end of the block and release the button.

- To *copy* selected text to the Clipboard, choose Copy from the Edit menu.

- To *cut* selected text to the Clipboard (deleting it from its original location in the process), choose Cut from the Edit menu.

- To *paste* selected text from the Clipboard to a card, position the insertion point where you want to insert the text and choose Paste from the Edit menu.

If you change your mind, you can cancel any changes you make to the current card by choosing Restore from the Edit menu.

Sometimes you can speed up the process of creating a database by copying some or all of the information on an existing card to a new one.

- You can copy some of the information on one card to another by using the usual *copy and paste* process described above.

- You can make a copy of *all* the information (including the index line) on an existing card by selecting it and choosing Duplicate from the Card menu. Cardfile will place the duplicate card at the front of the stack. Now, edit the new card as needed.

The "copy and paste" procedure can also be used to insert text or even graphics from another application onto a particular card.

Merging two card files

It is a simple matter to merge two card files into a single database. To do so:

1. Open one of the files to be merged.

2. Choose Merge from the File menu. The Merge dialog box, which is virtually identical to the Open dialog box, will be displayed.

3. In the dialog box, select the file to be merged with the current one and choose OK (or double-click on the filename). The two files will be merged — sorted in alphabetical order by their index line text.

You can now use the Save As command on the File menu to save the merged database under a new file name or to overwrite either of the existing card files.

Printing

You can use Cardfile to print a single card or the entire database.

- To print a single card, select the card to be printed and choose Print from the File menu.

- To print the entire card file, choose Print All from the File menu. (Several cards will be printed on each page.)

Headers and footers

In either case, you may notice that on each page printed, the name of the file appears in the top margin and the current page number appears in the bottom margin. The text that appears at the top is called a *header*; the text that appears at the bottom is called a *footer*. To change the header and footer printed by Cardfile, or to eliminate either or both:

1. Choose Page Setup from the File menu. The following dialog box will then open:

```
┌─────────────────────────────────────────────┐
│ ▬           Page Setup                       │
│                                              │
│  Header:   [&f        ]      ┌────────────┐  │
│                              │    OK      │  │
│                              └────────────┘  │
│  Footer:   [Page &p   ]      ┌────────────┐  │
│                              │   Cancel   │  │
│  ┌─Margins──────────────────────────────┐   │
│  │ Left:  [.75  ]    Right:  [.75  ]     │   │
│  │                                       │   │
│  │ Top:   [1.00 ]    Bottom: [1.00 ]     │   │
│  └───────────────────────────────────────┘  │
└─────────────────────────────────────────────┘
```

2. Type the desired text (up to 39 characters) in the appropriate box: Header or Footer. (To omit headers and/or footers, delete all text in the appropriate box or boxes.) You may include the following codes in header or footer text:

[handwritten margin note: Q. What if I wish to print all data in one sheet ?]

&c centers text that follows this code;

&d inserts the current date in place of this code;

&f inserts the database's file name in place of this code;

&l left-justifies text that follows this code;

&p inserts the current page number in place of this code;

&r right-justifies text that follows this code;

&t inserts the current time in place of this code.

3. Choose the OK button.

For example, the default text shown in the Page Setup dialog box prints the file name at the top of each page and the word *Page*, followed by a space and the page number, at the bottom. As another example, if you type &lPage &p &rDate: &d in the Header box, Cardfile will print a header like the following one on each page of output:

```
Page 1                          Date: 1/3/94
```

Setting
margins

Notice that you can also specify all four margins in the Page Setup dialog box. Here, *margin* refers to the margin on the printed page, not on the individual cards.

Hands-On 8.2

Start Windows and Cardfile (if necessary) and try the following exercise.

1. Insert the Lab Projects diskette in its drive and open the ADDRESS .CRD card file in its root directory.
2. Add a card to this card file with your name and address on it.
3. Use the Search menu to find all cards that have addresses on Fairview Lane. How many are there?
4. Select the card for Joan Baker and duplicate it.
5. Change the index line on the duplicate card to Baker, Jessica. Make up an address and phone number for Jessica.
6. Create a header containing your name, your class, and the date.
7. Print the entire card file.
8. Exit Cardfile without saving the changes.

8.3 Calendar: Keeping Track of Appointments

The **Calendar** application provides a day-by-day electronic appointment book together with a month-by-month calendar. They are used in much the same way as their non-electronic counterparts, but have one important advantage: in Calendar, you can set "alarms" to remind you of upcoming appointments.

Calendar

To start Calendar, choose its icon from the Accessories group. The Calendar window will open, displaying its appointment book — the *Day view* (Figure 8.6). The *status bar*, near the top of the window, displays the current time and date; the *appointment area* is where you type text describing the appointments; and the *scratch pad*, at the bottom of the window, provides an area in which to type notes.

FIGURE 8.6   The Calendar Window in *Day View*

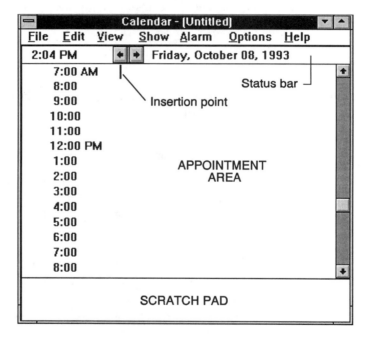

Entering Appointments

Entering appointments into Calendar is done in a very intuitive way:

1. Select the day on which your appointment is to be scheduled by clicking on the scroll arrows until the desired date appears on the

status bar. Alternatively, you can choose P̲revious or N̲ext from the S̲how menu to move to the day prior to, or following, the one on the status bar.

To select a date that's not close to the current one, choose D̲ate from the S̲how menu (or press F4), type the desired date in the resulting dialog box, and choose OK. For example, to select September 24, 1996, type 9/24/96 or 9-24-96 in the dialog box and choose the OK button. (To quickly return to the present day, choose T̲oday from the S̲how menu.)

2. Move the insertion point to the desired appointment time by scrolling the window, if necessary, and then clicking on the time. (As an alternative, you can use the Up and Down Arrow keys to move the insertion point.) If the exact time for the appointment is not listed, see the TIP below.

3. Type the text that describes the appointment. You can enter up to 80 characters; the text will scroll to the right, if necessary. If you make a mistake, use the Backspace or Del key to delete the incorrect text and retype it correctly.

4. If you want, you can type additional information on the scratchpad. Just click in this area and type; when you reach the end of a line, the text will automatically *wrap* to the beginning of the next line.

When Calendar is started for the first time, the appointment times are listed in one-hour intervals with a "starting time" of 7:00 AM at the top of the window. You can change these defaults by choosing D̲ay Settings from the O̲ptions menu. The following dialog box will be displayed:

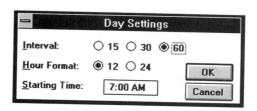

You can now change the I̲nterval between appointment times by selecting the appropriate option button; or specify a new S̲tarting Time by typing it in the text box. If you want, you can also switch to a 24 H̲our Format by selecting this option button. If you do so, times will be displayed as, for example, 14:30 instead of 2:30 PM.

If a particular appointment time does not match one of the times listed in the appointment area, you can display this particular time by choosing Special Time from the Options menu or by pressing the F7 function key. Then, type the desired time in the resulting dialog box, choose the Insert button, and this time will be listed in the appropriate place on the current day. (The Special Time dialog box can also be used to delete a previously-inserted "special time.")

Removing appointments

The simplest way to remove an appointment is to select the day on which it is scheduled, move the insertion point to the appropriate line, and repeatedly press the Backspace or Del key to delete it. To delete *all* appointments on a day, or on several consecutive days, it is easier to:

1. Choose Remove from the Edit menu. The following dialog box will be displayed:

2. In the From box, type the first date for which you want to remove appointments. (The current date is displayed.)

3. In the To box, type the last of the consecutive dates on which you want to remove appointments. You can leave this box blank if you only want to remove appointments on one day.

4. Choose the OK button.

Setting an Alarm

If you want Calendar to remind you of particular appointments, you can set alarms to be activated at these times. In order to make use of the alarm feature, Windows and Calendar must be running on your computer (and you have to be nearby) when the alarm goes off.

Unless you change the default settings, as described shortly, the computer will issue a "beep" at the appointment time. In addition:

- If Calendar is the active window, the Alarm dialog box appears, informing you of the appointment.

- If Calendar has been reduced to an icon, the icon flashes.

- If Calendar is an inactive window, its title bar flashes.

To turn off the alarm when it is activated, switch to the Calendar window (if necessary) and choose OK in the Alarm dialog box.

To set an alarm:

1. Move the insertion point to the appointment time.

2. Choose Set from the Alarm menu or press the F5 function key. An alarm symbol, pictured below, will appear next to the appointment time.

$$\text{Alarm set} \longrightarrow \triangle \quad \begin{array}{l} \text{12:00 PM} \\ \text{1:00} \\ \text{2:00} \end{array} \quad \text{Appointment with President Clinton.}$$

To remove an alarm, after it has been set but before it goes off, select the alarm time and choose Set from the Alarm menu again. The alarm symbol will disappear.

If you want an alarm to be activated a few minutes before the given appointment time or you do not want the beep to sound, choose Controls from the Alarm menu. The following dialog box will be displayed:

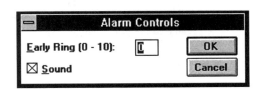

To have the alarm go off from one to ten minutes before the appointment time, type the desired value in the Early Ring text box. If you do not want the computer to beep when the alarm is activated, deselect the Sound check box. Choosing OK puts these changes into effect for all alarms.

Using the Month View

You can use Calendar to view monthly calendars by switching to the *Month view*. This is done by performing one of the following actions:

- Choose Month from the View menu.

- Press the F9 function key.

- Double-click on the date on the status bar.

The Calendar window in Month view, as shown in Figure 8.7, will replace the Day view. Notice that Day view's current date is highlighted.

FIGURE 8.7   The Calendar Window in *Month View*

Calendar - (Untitled)						
File Edit View Show Alarm Options Help						
10:16 AM ◄ ► Friday, October 08, 1993						
October 1993						
S	M	T	W	T	F	S
					1	2
3	4	5	6	7	**8**	9
> 10 <	11	12	13	14	15	16
17	18	19	20	21	22	23
24	25	26	27	28	29	30
31						

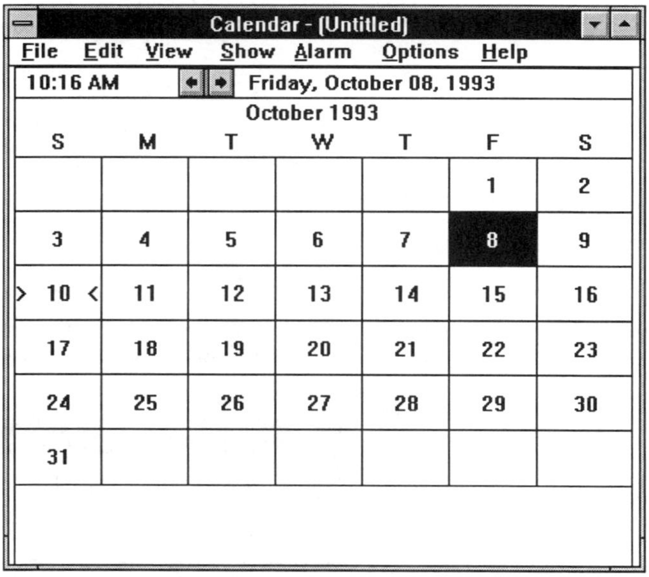

You can change the current (highlighted) date in several ways:

- To select another day in the current month, click on it or use the Arrow keys to highlight it.

- To select the previous month or the next month, click on the left or right scroll arrow, or press Page Up or Page Down, respectively.

(Choosing Previous or Next from the Show menu will accomplish the same thing.)

■ To select any month from 1980 to 2099, choose Date from the Show menu, (or press F4), type any date in the desired month in the resulting dialog box, and choose OK. For example, typing 5/1/96 in this dialog box and choosing OK, brings up May of 1996.

You cannot write text on the calendar itself in Month view, but you can use the scratchpad below it to enter notes as you would in Day view. Moreover, Windows supplies five different symbols for marking important days (such as pay days) on the calendar. To mark a day with a symbol:

Marking days on the calendar

1. Select the day to be marked.

2. Choose Mark from the Options menu or press the F6 function key to open the Day Markings dialog box:

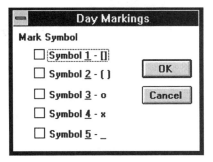

3. Select the check boxes corresponding to the symbol or symbols you want to apply to the current day.

4. Choose the OK button.

To remove symbols marking a day, select that day, open the Day Markings dialog box, deselect the appropriate check boxes, and choose OK.

Switching back to Day view

To switch back to Day view, perform any of the following actions:

■ Choose Day from the View menu or press the F8 function key.

■ Double-click on a calendar day or on the date on the status bar.

Calendar will return to Day view, showing the day that was current when Month view was exited.

Managing Calendar Files

You can use Calendar to save your appointments to disk, to open this file at a later time, and to print the appointments on a printer. All of these operations are performed in much the same way as in any other Windows application. To be more specific:

Saving files
■ To save your appointments, scratchpad notes, and day markings to disk, choose <u>S</u>ave or Save <u>A</u>s from the <u>F</u>ile menu. (For more information on saving files, see Section 4.4.) If you do not type an extension for the file to be saved, Windows will add the extension CAL to the file name.

Opening files
■ To open a previously saved Calendar file, choose <u>O</u>pen from the <u>F</u>ile menu. (For more information on opening files, see Section 4.4.)

Printing files
■ To print your appointments and scratchpad notes, choose <u>P</u>rint from the <u>F</u>ile menu. The following dialog box will open:

```
┌─────────────────────────────────────┐
│ ▬          Print                     │
│ Print Appointments:                  │
│                                      │
│ From:  │10/08/93│      ┌────────┐    │
│                        │   OK   │    │
│ To:    │        │      └────────┘    │
│                       ┌────────┐     │
│                       │ Cancel │     │
│                       └────────┘     │
└─────────────────────────────────────┘
```

Now, type the first and last dates of the consecutive days for which you want to print appointments in the <u>F</u>rom and <u>T</u>o boxes, respectively. (If you only want to print one day's appointments, you can leave the <u>T</u>o box blank.) Then choose OK to close the dialog box and begin printing.

You can change margin settings and type headers and/or footers on the printed page by choosing Page Se<u>t</u>up from the <u>F</u>ile menu, which opens the Page Setup dialog box. For more information on using this dialog box, see the material entitled "Printing" in Section 8.2.

Quitting Calendar
You can quit the Calendar application in the same manner in which you exit most Windows applications. The quickest ways are to double-click on the Control menu box, or press Alt+F4, or choose E<u>x</u>it from the <u>F</u>ile menu.

Hands-On 8.3

Start up Windows and Calendar (if necessary) and try the following exercise. To create a printed copy of your work, see Appendix B.

1. Enter appointments for one week from today at:
    - 1:00 PM for "Lunch."
    - 3:00 PM for "Meeting with the boss."
2. Type a note on the following day's scratchpad saying "Today's the day!".
3. Print the appointments for these two days.
4. Enter an appointment for today, a few minutes after the current time (according to the clock on the status line), using the Special Time item on the Options menu. Call the appointment "Meeting."
5. Set an alarm for the time used in part 4. Wait until the alarm goes off. What was the message in the dialog box? Turn off the alarm.
6. Switch to Month view. What day of the week is January 1, 2000?
7. Mark January 1, 2000 with a box and an "x".
8. Exit Calendar without saving the changes.

8.4   Recorder: Using Macros

Recorder is a Windows accessory that allows you to assign a sequence of keystrokes and/or mouse actions to a shortcut key, such as F10 or Ctrl+A. This process is called "defining a **macro**." Once a macro has been defined, it can be *played back*: press the shortcut key, and the sequence of keystrokes and mouse actions will be executed automatically.

Defining and playing back a macro is a good way to take the drudgery out of repetitive actions. For example, suppose you are typing an essay in the Write word processor that contains many occurrences of the phrase "United States of America." In this case, it would make sense to use Recorder to assign this phrase to a macro key such as Ctrl+A. Then, instead of typing the phrase each time it comes up, just press Ctrl+A and let Recorder type it for you.

Recorder

To start Recorder, choose its icon from the Accessories group. The window shown in Figure 8.8, on the next page, will then open.

FIGURE 8.8   The Recorder Window

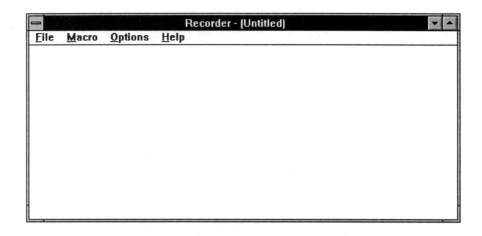

Defining a Macro

Defining a macro involves two basic steps. You must:

- Select a name or shortcut key for the macro.

and

- *Record* the macro: type the keystrokes and perform the mouse actions to be executed when you play back the macro.

To carry out this process using Recorder:

1. Start, or switch to, the application in which you want the macro to be carried out. For example, to create a macro that will automatically type the phrase United States of America in a Write document, make Write the active window.

2. Start up, or switch to, Recorder.

3. Choose Record from the Macro menu, which displays the Record Macro dialog box shown in Figure 8.9.

4. Identify the macro. Recorder allows you to designate a macro by a name and/or a shortcut key. Either designation may be omitted, but it's a good idea to include both. These identifiers will be displayed when the macro is listed in the Recorder window.

FIGURE 8.9   The Record Macro Dialog Box

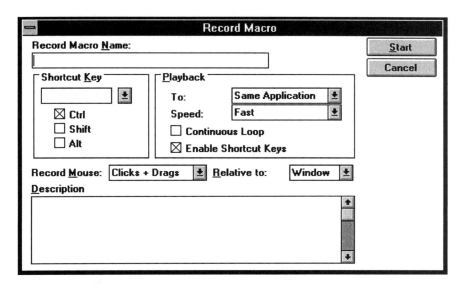

■ Type text (up to 40 characters, including spaces) in the Record
Macro Name text box that appropriately names the macro. For
example, the macro that types the phrase United States of
America could be called Type USA Text.

■ Select a shortcut key by typing a character in the Shortcut Key
text box and selecting any combination of the Ctrl, Shift, and
Alt check boxes. For example, if you type U in the text box and
select Ctrl, then the macro can be played back by pressing
Ctrl+U.

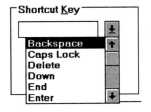

Some special keys, such as F10, can be used instead of
characters. To use one of these, select it from the Shortcut Key
drop-down list, shown at the left. For example, to use Ctrl
+Alt+F10 as a shortcut key, select F10 from the list (you have
to scroll first) and select the Ctrl and Alt check boxes.

5. In the Playback area of the dialog box, select either:

■ Same Application (the default), if you want the macro to apply
only to the application that was active before you switched to
Recorder. For example, the Type USA Text macro will only
make sense in Write, so Same Application is the appropriate

option for this macro.

or

■ Any Application, if you want to allow the macro to be played back in all applications. You would select this option, for example, in creating a macro that maximizes a window.

Normally, the other settings in the Record Macro dialog box can be kept at their default values. See the Windows *User's Guide* for more information on the other options.

6. If you want, type a description of the macro in the Description area of the dialog box. The description can be useful if you forget the function of a macro or where it can be applied.

7. Choose the Start button to begin the recording process. Recorder will be reduced to a flashing icon. Windows will now switch to the application that was active when you switched to Recorder.

8. Type the keystrokes and/or perform the mouse actions that you want to be able to play back. For example, type United States of America.

9. When you are done, click on the flashing Recorder icon or press Ctrl+Break. (The Break key is usually the same as the Pause key.) The following dialog box will appear:

Select Save Macro to stop the recording process, Resume Recording to continue the recording process, or Cancel Recording to abort the current macro definition.

10. Choose the OK button and the macro definition is complete.

If you now switch back to Recorder, you will see that the name and shortcut key for the macro just defined are displayed in the Recorder window, like this:

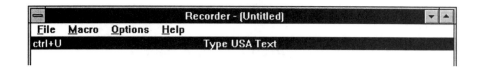

 Contrary to usual Windows practice, when defining a macro, it is advisable to use keystrokes rather than mouse actions; macros play back more reliably when you minimize the use of the mouse in recording them. So, instead of mouse clicks, use cursor movement keys to move the cursor (see Section 1.3) and choose menu items using the Alt key or shortcut keys (see Section 1.2).

Many of the problems with the mouse occur when a window is resized or moved between the definition and play back of a macro. So, if you must use a mouse while creating a macro, maximize the application window before starting the macro definition and playback.

Playing Back a Macro

Once a macro has been defined, you can make use of it by following this procedure:

1. Make sure that Recorder is running and that the macro you want to use is displayed in the Recorder window. (This may necessitate opening the file in which it is contained; more on this later.)

2. Switch to the application in which you want to use the macro.

3. If necessary, position the cursor where you want playback to begin. For example, for the Type USA Text macro, position the insertion point where you want the text to be typed in the Write document.

4. To play back the recorded keystrokes and/or mouse actions, do any of the following:

   ■ If you selected a shortcut key for the macro, press this key or key combination.

   or

   ■ Switch back to Recorder and double-click on the macro in the list displayed in the window.

   or

   ■ Switch back to Recorder, select the macro from the displayed list (by clicking on it or using the Arrow keys to highlight it), and choose <u>R</u>un from the <u>M</u>acro menu.

Changing the Properties of a Macro

Once a macro is defined, you cannot edit the keystrokes and mouse actions that comprise its definition. To modify a macro, you have to define it all over again. However, you can change the *properties* of an existing macro, including its name, shortcut key, and description. To change the properties of a macro:

1.   Select the macro in the Recorder window.

2.   Choose <u>P</u>roperties from the <u>M</u>acro menu. The Macro Properties dialog box, which is very similar to the Record Macro dialog box, will open (Figure 8.10).

FIGURE 8.10   The Macro Properties Dialog Box

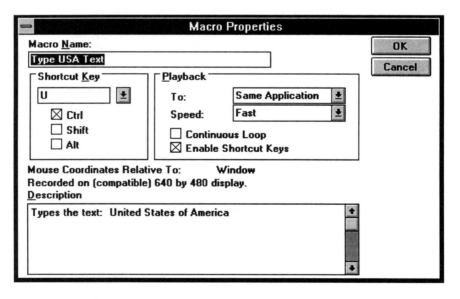

3.   Notice that the settings that were specified for this macro are listed in the appropriate places. Change any settings, as desired.

4.   Choose the OK button.

Managing Recorder Files

Saving a macro

When you define a macro, it is listed in the Recorder window, but *not* saved to disk. If you want to use this macro in future Windows sessions, you must save it in a file. To do so, choose the Save As command from the File menu and follow the usual procedure for saving a file (see Section 4.4). If you don't type an extension when naming the file, Windows will add a REC extension to it. For example, if you name the file to be saved SAMPLE, then it will be saved as SAMPLE.REC.

All macros listed in the Recorder window will be saved in the same file. This provides a natural way of grouping related macros together. For example, it is common practice to save all macros that apply to a given application in the same REC file.

Opening a macro file

To load the macros contained within a file into RAM and display them in the Recorder window, open the file by choosing Open from the File menu. The Open dialog box will be displayed. Now, follow the usual procedure for opening a file (see Section 4.4).

Adding and deleting macros

If some of the macros listed in the Recorder window have already been saved in a file, the file name will appear on the title bar. To *add* newly-defined macros to this file, just choose Save from the File menu. To *delete* a macro from the list in the Recorder window, select it, choose Delete from the Macro menu, and then choose OK in the resulting confirmation dialog box. Now, save the contents of the window to delete that macro from its file.

Merging macro files

When two files are *merged*, they are saved as a single file. To merge two macro files:

1. Open one of the two files to be merged, which displays its macros in the Recorder window.

2. Choose Merge from the File menu. The Merge dialog box, which looks virtually identical to the Open dialog box, will appear.

3. In the File Name list, double-click on the file to be merged, or select it and choose the OK button. The macros in this file are then displayed in the Recorder window, together with those already there.

4. Choose Save As from the File menu to save the merged file under whatever name you want.

Quitting
Recorder

You can quit Recorder in the same manner in which you exit most Windows applications. The quickest ways are to double-click on the Control menu box, or press Alt+F4, or choose E<u>x</u>it from the <u>F</u>ile menu.

Hands-On 8.4

Start up Windows and Recorder, if necessary, and try the following exercise. To create a printed copy of your work, see Appendix B.

1. Define a macro to *minimize* the active application. In the Record Macro dialog box:
   - Name this macro Minimize.
   - Specify the shortcut key Ctrl+Alt+F10.
   - Type a description of the macro.
   - Set the playback to Any Application.
   Start recording.
2. Use the keyboard to minimize the active application:
   - Open its Control menu by pressing Alt+Spacebar.
   - Choose Mi<u>n</u>imize by pressing the N key.
   Then, stop recording by pressing Ctrl+Break and save the macro.
3. Switch to Program Manager.
4. Play back the Minimize macro by pressing Ctrl+Alt+F10.
5. Insert a floppy disk in its drive and save the Minimize macro to this diskette under the name GENERIC.
6. Clear the Recorder window (by using the New command).
7. Switch to Program Manager and press Ctrl+Alt+F10. Why didn't the macro work this time?
8. Switch back to Recorder and exit it.

8.5   Terminal: Communicating with Another Computer

By now, you have worked with a personal computer long enough to appreciate how powerful and versatile it is. Its capabilities can be extended even further by using it to access information on other computer systems. Using computer-to-computer communication:

1. You can access the vast quantities of data on an *on-line information service*, such as CompuServe or Prodigy. Depending on the particular service you call, you might be able to use encyclopedias, get stock market quotations, make airline reservations, or even get the latest ball scores.

2. You can post messages on electronic *bulletin boards* and read messages posted there by others.

3. You can send and receive *electronic mail* — communicate with anyone whose computer is connected to a worldwide system of computer networks known as the Internet.

4. You can connect to your campus mainframe, and use the software and data on it that has been authorized for public access.

Some Communications Basics

When you create a link between your computer and another system, the latter is known as the *remote* or *host* computer. In order to "talk to" a remote computer, your system must contain, or have access to, some special hardware and software. You need:

■ A **modem**, a device that translates computer-generated data into signals that can be sent to another computer, usually over ordinary telephone lines. The modem can be an *internal* one, located on a circuit board within the system unit, or an external one, in a small case connected by a cable to one of your computer's serial ports.

■ A nearby telephone jack. The modem is connected to the telephone lines by the same kind of wire and connectors as your telephone.

■ **Communications software**, a program that allows you to configure, dial, and pass commands to the modem from your keyboard. Communications software, with your input, ensures that the signals sent from your computer, through the modem and telephone lines, will be understandable to the hardware setup on the remote system. The communications software supplied with Windows is called **Terminal**.

Using Terminal

Terminal

To start Terminal, choose (double-click on) its icon in the Accessories group. The window shown in Figure 8.11, at the top of the next page, will then open.

FIGURE 8.11   The Terminal Window

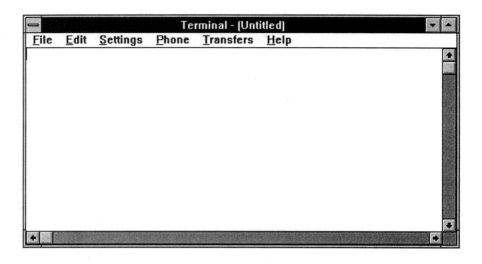

You can now use Terminal to establish a communications link with a remote computer. This process involves two basic steps; you must:

1. Configure (set up) Terminal properly, so that the remote computer will "understand" the signals it is sent. This step entails specifying numerous communications parameters.

2. Connect to the remote computer by dialing its modem's telephone number and *logging-on* to the system, providing any necessary identification codes.

Once the link is established, you can exchange information, view data, and/or transfer files between your computer and the remote system.

Configuring Terminal for the Connection

Before you can transmit data to another computer, you have to *configure* Terminal — specify a number of communications settings or *parameters*. The proper settings depend mostly on the system with which you're trying to communicate, so you may have to specify different parameters for each remote computer with which you want to connect.

Fortunately, many parameters can be left at their *default* values — those suggested by Windows. The others are usually prominently listed in your modem's user guide or in documentation available from the organization that runs the host system. If this documentation is not available, you may be able to call the host system (at its voice, not data, phone number) to get the required information.

Configuration parameters
All configuration parameters are selected from items on Terminal's Settings menu:

1. Phone Number specifies the telephone number for the remote computer.

2. Communications specifies the way that data will be transmitted.

3. Modem Commands tells Terminal the type of modem you have.

4. Terminal Emulation sets up your computer to act like a type of terminal with which the remote computer can communicate.

Let's take a look at these items, one at a time.

Phone Number When you choose Phone Number from the Settings menu, the Phone Number dialog box is displayed:

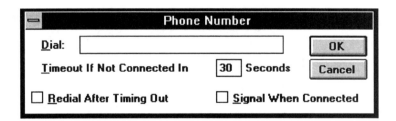

- Enter the phone number for the remote computer in the Dial text box. (This is the number that Terminal dials when you select Dial from the Phone menu.) Spaces, parentheses, and hyphens are ignored. Thus, (213) 555-1212 and 2135551212 will dial the same number.

    If you want the modem to pause in the dialing process (perhaps to wait for the dial tone on an "outside line"), place a comma at this point in the phone number. Typically, each comma inserts a two-second pause. For example, 9,,5551212 inserts a four-second pause after the 9 is dialed.

- In the Timeout box, the default value allows a reasonable amount of time for the connection to take place. If you are having trouble connecting, try a larger value.

- If the Redial box is selected, Terminal will automatically retry the number after a "timeout." If the Signal box is selected, a "beep" is sounded when the connection is made.

Communications   When you choose Communications from the Settings menu, the Communications dialog box, shown below, is displayed. This dialog box contains most of the key parameters needed to achieve a successful connection. If you cannot determine a particular setting from your modem's user guide and the host's documentation, leave that parameter at its default value.

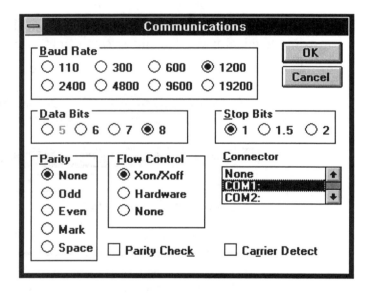

- The Baud Rate area in this dialog box specifies the rate at which the transmissions between the computers will take place. Roughly speaking, the **baud rate** gives the number of bits per second that are sent across the phone lines. Set this parameter at the maximum value specified for your modem. If the host computer cannot handle this baud rate, the two systems will usually automatically settle on a lower rate.

- The number of Data Bits defines the size of the basic packet of information transmitted. Most systems use either 7 or 8 data bits. Check the host's documentation for the required value.

- To separate one character from another, the modem pauses slightly between transmitted characters. This is the number of Stop bits. This parameter is determined by the host system.

- Parity refers to a simple kind of error checking. This value is also determined by the host system.

- The method of Flow Control determines which computer turns the flow of information off (and then, back on) if your computer cannot receive more data at any given time.

- The Connector area specifies which serial port, usually COM1 or COM2, is assigned to your modem.

- Leave the Parity Check and Carrier Detect check boxes deselected.

Modem Commands   To configure Terminal to work with your modem, choose Modem Commands from the Settings menu. The Modem Commands dialog box will open:

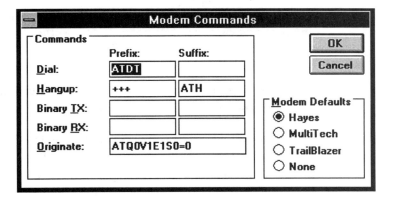

The key area in this dialog box is Modem Defaults. When you select the option button for one of the three modems listed, Terminal automatically determines the commands necessary to perform basic operations, such as having the modem dial a number.

Terminal Emulation   The remote system may expect your computer to act like (emulate) a specific type of terminal. Check the host's documentation for the proper emulation. Then, choose Terminal Emulation from the Settings menu, select the appropriate option button in the dialog box, and choose OK.

If you are planning to connect to the same remote computer at some time in the future, you should *save* the set of parameters you've just specified by choosing Save As from the File menu. (Choose Save if you have modified an existing settings file and want to replace the old one.) The usual Save As dialog box will open (see Section 4.4), allowing you to select a drive, directory, and file name for the settings file. Use a meaningful name; for example, you might select CS for CompuServe settings. (Windows will add a TRM extension, saving this file as CS.TRM.)

The next time you want to call this remote computer, choose Open from the File menu. The usual Open dialog box will be displayed (see Section 4.4), allowing you to select the file that contains the proper settings for this connection.

Connecting to the Remote Computer

After you have configured Terminal to work with your modem and the remote computer (by specifying the required Phone Number and Communications, Modem Commands, and Terminal Emulation parameters), establishing a communications link to the remote computer is a simple two-step process:

1. Dial the number specified in the Phone Number dialog box by choosing Dial from the Phone menu. A dialog box will be displayed showing the number called and counting down the seconds until the timeout value specified in the Phone Number dialog box. (If you have not yet entered a number in the Phone Number dialog box, it will be displayed, allowing you to enter a phone number at this time.)

2. When the remote computer "answers," you will normally have to go through a *log-on* process, giving your account or identification number and perhaps a password. The text sent by the remote computer and your responses will appear in the Terminal window.

Because of the number of parameters involved, setting up and establishing a link to a remote computer can be a tricky business. Here are a few trouble-shooting tips:

- If the modem doesn't dial when you choose Dial from the Phone menu, check the cable connections and, if you have an external modem, that it's turned on. Also, make sure you've selected the proper model in the Modem Commands dialog box and specified the correct serial port in the Communications dialog box.

■ If the modem dials and apparently connects with the host but the text that appears in the window is garbled, check the Communications settings. If you don't have documentation from the host, change each of the following, one at a time, and try to connect again: select a lower baud rate (1200 almost always works); change the data bits from 7 to 8, or vice-versa; change the parity; and increase the stop bit number.

Using the Remote Computer

After you have logged onto the remote computer, you will have access to specific applications and/or data on this system. Access is often provided in the form of menus or queries sent by the host and displayed in the Terminal window. Some systems also allow you to type commands to access information. These, too, appear in the window as you type them.

The scroll buffer

Terminal stores all text sent and received in a special area of RAM called the *scroll buffer*. If you have sent and/or received more text than can fit in the window, you can review text that is not visible by using the scroll bars to move through the scroll buffer. If you want to clear all previous text from the buffer, including the text in the window, choose Clear Buffer from the Edit menu.

Printing text

Text can be *printed* in two ways:

1. You can print incoming text as you receive it by choosing Printer Echo from the Settings menu. The Printer Echo option remains in effect until you choose it again. A check mark next to this menu item indicates that it is in effect.

2. You can print any or all text in the scroll buffer by copying it to the Clipboard (see Section 2.4), pasting it into a word processor such as Write, and then printing it from this application. (The Select All item on the Edit menu may be useful here; it selects all the text currently in the scroll buffer.)

Transferring Files

To transfer text, data, and programs between your computer and the host, you can *send* files to the remote computer or *receive* files from it. Terminal can send or receive two types of files:

■ In a *text file transfer*, the file must consist entirely of **ASCII characters**; roughly speaking, those that can be typed at the keyboard. Text files cannot contain any other symbols or formatting commands, such as you might find in a program file or spreadsheet.

■ In a *binary file transfer*, the symbols in the file are transmitted as a sequence of bits — zeros and ones. Any file, including text files, can be transmitted as a binary file.

Before sending or receiving a file, you must decide which of the two forms of file transfer to use. Since text file transmission is faster, you should use it whenever you can; for example, for electronic mail and word processing files in ASCII form (those with no special formatting codes). Program files, spreadsheet files, and graphics must be sent in binary form. If you try to transmit a binary file using a text transfer method, an error message will be displayed or the transmission will be garbled.

Sending a File   To *send* a file to the remote computer:

1. Signal the remote computer (usually by selecting an option from a menu) that you want to transmit a file to it. Sending a *text* file is usually treated the same way as typing the text at the keyboard, so this step may not be necessary for text files.

2. Choose either <u>S</u>end Text File or Send <u>B</u>inary File, as appropriate, from the <u>T</u>ransfers menu. The corresponding dialog box will open. For example, if you choose <u>S</u>end Text File, the following dialog box is displayed. (The Send Binary File dialog box looks almost the same.)

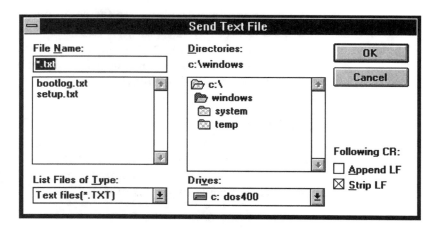

3. Sending a file is analogous to *opening* your file on the remote computer, and the Send dialog boxes work the same way as the Open dialog box discussed in Section 4.4: Select the drive and directory in which the file is stored from the Dri<u>v</u>es and <u>D</u>irectories lists, respectively. Then, double-click on the File <u>N</u>ame, or select it and choose the OK button, to send the file.

When you send a text file, the following *status bar* will appear at the bottom of the Terminal window:

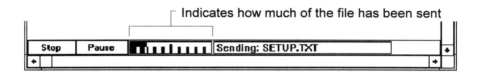

You can use the Pause or Stop buttons to temporarily pause the transmission or stop it completely. If the transmission is paused, the Pause button becomes a Resume button, which allows you to resume sending the file. (The status bar for sending a binary file does not have a Pause button.)

Receiving a File   To receive a file from the remote computer:

1. Choose either <u>R</u>eceive Text File or Receive Binary <u>F</u>ile, as appropriate, from the <u>T</u>ransfers menu. The resulting dialog box, which resembles the Save As dialog box discussed in Section 4.4, will then open.

2. Select the drive, directory, and file name under which you want to save the incoming file and than choose the OK button.

3. Give the remote computer the required command (it varies from host to host) to start transmission.

A status bar, similar to the one for sending a file, will appear at the bottom of the window.

It is usually not necessary to set parameters for a file transfer prior to attempting it; the default values usually work. However, if you are unable to send or receive a file, you may have to change a default value by choosing either Te<u>x</u>t Transfers or <u>B</u>inary Transfers from the <u>S</u>ettings menu. This will display either the Text Transfer or Binary Transfer dialog box.

If a text transfer is giving you trouble, check the host's documentation for the proper settings. For a binary transfer, simply select the currently deselected option button (XModem or Kermit) and try again.

Terminating Your Session

When you are done working with the remote computer:

1. Execute the host's *log-off* procedure. This usually consists of choosing an exit command from the main menu or typing bye at a command prompt.

2. Break the connection by choosing Hangup from the Phone menu. (If you hang up before exiting on an on-line information service, your account might be charged for some additional time.)

3. You can then quit Terminal using any of the methods for exiting a Windows application; for example, double-clicking on its Control menu box, pressing Alt+F4, or choosing Exit from the File menu.

Customizing Terminal

After using Terminal for a while, you may want to arrange the Terminal window more to your liking. You can do this with the help of a few of the options on the Settings menu. We will briefly describe these options below; for more information, see the chapter on Terminal in the Windows *User's Guide*.

Terminal Preferences   Choosing Terminal Preferences from the Settings menu displays the Terminal Preferences dialog box, which allows you to change the way information is displayed in the Terminal window. For example, you can specify the text font and size, the shape of the cursor, and whether or not the scroll bars are visible.

Function Keys   Some aspects of using a modem can require a lot of tedious typing. For example, to log on to a remote computer, you might have to type something like this:

```
^$C^$D08^MSVenit^Mec3zzy^M
```

Terminal allows you to assign any string of characters (any *command*) to

FIGURE 9.3   Types of Memory

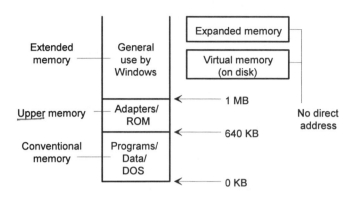

portions of upper memory to store small programs, such as device drivers, and for other special purposes.

- **Extended memory** is the term used to describe all memory in locations above 1 MB. An *extended memory manager* allows programs to use this memory without conflicting with one another. Windows makes extensive use of extended memory with the help of a built-in memory manager, which is called HIMEM.

- **Expanded memory**, unlike the types just described, does not refer to memory in a specific location. Rather, it is a system of memory management, developed before Windows became popular, that allows DOS programs to access more RAM than just conventional memory. To make use of expanded memory, your system must include an *expanded memory manager* and either a 386 class processor (or better) or a 286 processor together with a special circuit board. (See the Introduction to this text for a discussion of processors.) Windows and Windows applications do not use expanded memory, but Windows can provide expanded memory to DOS programs through a built-in expanded memory manager, which is called EMM386.

- **Virtual memory** is hard disk space that is used by the computer system as if it were additional RAM. Windows makes use of virtual memory through the use of a *swap file*, which allows it to run more applications simultaneously than the amount of available RAM would otherwise permit.

Terminal to dial a phone number, pause for eight seconds, and then send a carriage return character, the string "SVenit", a carriage return, the string "ec3zzy", and finally, another carriage return. (For a complete list of codes, see the Terminal chapter in the Windows *User's Guide*.)

Using the function keys

You can have Terminal carry out the command assigned to a given function key in the following way:

1. Choose Show <u>F</u>unction Keys from the <u>S</u>ettings menu. Function key buttons are then displayed at the bottom of the Terminal window (and this menu item turns into Hide <u>F</u>unction Keys):

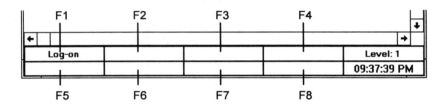

2. To change the level, choose the Level button (which reads "Level: 1" in the diagram above).

3. To carry out the command assigned to F1 through F8, click on the appropriate button. (You can also carry out the command assigned to Fn by pressing the Ctrl+Alt+Fn key combination.)

The function key display has one other useful feature: by choosing T<u>i</u>mer Mode from the <u>S</u>ettings menu, you can turn the clock into a timer that keeps track of how long you are connected to the remote computer. (Many on-line information services charge for the amount of time that you're connected.) Choosing T<u>i</u>mer Mode again restores the clock function.

Hands-On

8.5

Start up Windows and Terminal (if necessary) and try the following exercise. To create a printed copy of your work, see Appendix B.

1. For a remote computer to which you have access, specify the appropriate Phone Number, and the proper Communications and Terminal Emulation parameters in their respective dialog boxes.
2. Determine the type of modem you are using and specify it in the Modem Commands dialog box.
3. Turn on Printer Echo.
4. Dial and log-on to the remote computer. Turn off Printer Echo.

5. If possible, transfer a file to or from the remote computer.
6. Log-off the remote computer and exit Terminal.

8.6   Additional Accessories

Windows supplies three additional, relatively specialized, accessories. We will describe each of them very briefly in this section.

1. **Media Player** allows you to play multimedia files and control multimedia devices, such as CD-ROM drives. **Multimedia** is a catch-all term applied to the creation or display of documents that make use of sound, sophisticated graphics, and/or video components. As an example, a computer-generated multimedia presentation might combine graphics and sound stored on a CD-ROM to simulate television-like images.

2. **Sound Recorder** allows you to record and play sound files. To use Sound Recorder, you must have the proper hardware installed on your computer.

3. **Object Packager** allows you to embed icons (*packages*) that represent pictures, text, or sound in a document. When the icon is activated, it "plays back" the embedded object. For example, using Object Packager, you can embed an icon in a text document that, when double-clicked, plays back a prerecorded message.

Chapter Summary

Key Terms   ASCII characters [page 332]   Baud rate [328]

Calculator [297]   Calendar [309]

Cardfile [301]   Character Map [299]

Clock [296]   Communications software [325]

Database [302]   Database manager [301]

Macro [317]   Media Player [337]

Modem [325]   Multimedia [337]

Object Packager [337]   Recorder [317]

Sound Recorder [337]   Terminal [325]

Topics Covered

Clock

To select a mode	Choose Analog or Digital from the Settings menu.
To hide or display the seconds/date/title bar	Choose Seconds/Date/No Title from the Settings menu.
To keep the clock visible	Choose Always on Top from the Control menu.

Calculator

To select a mode	Choose Scientific or Standard from the View menu.
To enter a digit or operation	Click on the corresponding calculator key.

Character Map

To change the font	Select a font from the Font list.
To copy a character to the Clipboard	Double-click on the character (or select it with the Arrow keys and choose the Select button) and choose the Copy button.

Cardfile

To add a card	Choose Add from the Card menu and fill in the index line and information area.
To select a card (bring it to the front)	Click on it; or use the scroll arrows (or Page Up/Page Down keys) until the desired card is selected; or choose List from the View menu and choose the desired index line.
To search for a card (and bring it up front)	Choose Go To from the Search menu to search for text on the index line; or choose Find from the Search menu to search for text in the information area.
To delete a card	Select it and choose Delete from the Card menu.

To edit a card	Select it and choose Index from the Edit menu to change index line text; or select it and delete text or type new text in the information area.
To print a card *or* the entire card file	Select the card and choose Print from the File menu *or* choose Print All from the File menu.

Calendar

To select Day view or Month view	Choose Day or Month from the View menu (or press F8 or F9, respectively).
To select a date in Day view	Click on the scroll arrows; or choose Previous or Next from the Show menu; or choose Date from the Show menu (or press F4) and type the desired date in the dialog box.
To alter the listed appointment times	Choose Day Settings from the Options menu to change the time interval; or choose Special Time from the Options menu (or press F7) to add a particular time to the list.
To enter an appointment	Click on the appropriate time and type the text.
To set an alarm	Click on the desired time and choose Set from the Alarm menu (or press F5).
To select a month in Month view	Use the scroll arrows; or press Page Up/Page Down; or type a date in the Date dialog box.
To select a date in the current month	Click on it; or highlight it with the Arrow keys.
To mark a date in Month view	Select a date, choose Mark from the Options menu (or press F6) and choose a symbol from the dialog box.

Recorder

To define a macro	Switch from the target application to Recorder, choose Record from the Macro menu, fill in the dialog box options and choose Start, record the desired keystrokes and mouse actions, and press Ctrl+Break to stop recording.

To play back a macro	Ensure that the macro is listed in the Recorder window. Then, press the macro's shortcut key; or double-click on the macro's name in the Recorder window; or select the macro in the window and choose Run from the Macro menu.
To change a macro's properties	Select the macro in the Recorder window, choose Properties from the Macro menu, and change the desired settings in the dialog box.

Terminal

To configure Terminal	Choose Phone Number, Communications, Modem Commands, and Terminal Emulation from the Settings menu and specify parameters in the dialog boxes.
To connect to the remote computer	Choose Dial from the Phone menu and log-on.
To print text	Choose Printer Echo from the Settings menu to print all incoming text; or copy text from the window to a word processor and print it.
To send a file	Signal the remote computer (if necessary) and choose Send Text File or Send Binary File from the Transfers menu.
To receive a file	Choose Receive Text File or Receive Binary File from the Transfers menu and signal the remote computer to send the file.
To define function keys	Choose Function Keys from the Settings menu and type key names and commands in the dialog box.
To display function keys	Choose Show Function Keys from the Settings menu.

Chapter Exercises

Short Answer   Complete each statement in Exercises 1 through 20.

1. If you want Clock to be Always on Top, select this option from its
_____ menu.

2. If Clock's menu bar is not visible in the window, you can display it by _____ anywhere in the Clock window.

3. Clicking on Calculator's Back key erases the _____ digit in the display.

4. To magnify a character displayed by Character Map, point at it and _____ .

5. In Cardfile, the cards are sorted according to the text on their _____ .

6. To view the text in the information area of a card, Cardfile must be in _____ view mode.

7. To search for a card in a card file that contains the word *house* on its index line, choose _____ from the Search menu.

8. To print an entire card file, choose _____ from the File menu.

9. In Calendar, to enter an appointment for the day after the current one, click on the _____ to bring up that day's appointments.

10. To set an alarm in Calendar, position the cursor at the desired time and choose _____ from the Alarm menu.

11. In Calendar, to enter an appointment at 7:35, you must first list this time by choosing Special Time from the _____ menu.

12. If Calendar's Day view mode is in effect, to see the calendar for the current month, switch to _____ view.

13. The Recorder accessory defines and plays back _____ .

14. Using Recorder, you can play back previously-recorded keystrokes and mouse actions by pressing a _____ .

15. To define a macro that maximizes any application window, select the _____ Application option from the Record Macro dialog box.

16. A _____ is a device that can translate computer data into signals that can be sent over telephone lines to another computer.

17. In Terminal, to change the baud rate, the number of stop bits, and the parity, choose _____ from the Settings menu.

18. To connect to a remote computer using Terminal, choose _____ from the Phone menu and log-on.

19. To use Terminal to print a copy of all text received from the remote computer, choose _____ from the Settings menu.

20. To keep track of the amount of time you are connected to a remote computer, choose Timer Mode from the _____ menu.

In Exercises 21 through 35, determine whether each statement is true or false.

21. When Clock is reduced to an icon, it continues to display the time.

22. The number shown in the Calculator display can be copied to the Clipboard.

23. Character Map only displays the characters in the Symbol font.

24. Whenever a card is added to a card file, it is placed in the proper alphabetical order.

25. You can delete a card from a card file by selecting it and then pressing the Delete key.

26. To merge two card files, open the first, open the second, and then save the result.

27. In Calendar, you can enter appointments in either Day view or Month view.

28. In Calendar, if an alarm is set for a 4 pm appointment, you can have it go off at 3:50 pm by using the Controls option on the Alarm menu.

29. In Calendar's Month view, you may mark a single day with up to five symbols.

30. Ctrl+Alt+Shift+F1 is a valid Recorder shortcut key.

31. To play back a Recorder macro, it must be listed in the Recorder window.

32. Each Recorder macro must be saved in its own file.

33. To tell Terminal the kind of modem you are using, choose Modem Commands from the Settings menu.

34. A binary file contains only ASCII characters.

35. The Terminal scroll buffer contains only incoming text, not the text you have typed.

In Exercises 36 through 45, choose the correct answer.

36. To display Clock's menu bar, if it is hidden:

    a. Choose No Title from the Settings menu.
    b. Click on the Clock window.
    c. Double-click on the Clock window.
    d. Press the Enter key.

37. To change the Calculator number display from 8 to 0:

    a. Click on the C button.
    b. Click on the CE button.
    c. Click on the Back button.
    d. Perform any of the above actions.

38. You cannot select a card (bring it to the front) in Cardfile by:

    a. Clicking on it.
    b. Typing its index line text in the Index dialog box.
    c. Double-clicking on its index line in List view.
    d. Clicking on a scroll arrow until the card appears in front.

39. A card in a card file contains the word *dog* in its information area. To search for this card:

    a. Type dog in the Go To dialog box and choose OK.
    b. Type dog in the Find dialog box and choose OK.
    c. Type dog in the information area of a blank card and choose Duplicate from the Card menu.
    d. Type dog in the information area of a blank card and choose Go To from the Search menu.

40. Calendar appointment times:

    a. Must be spaced at one-hour intervals.
    b. Must start with 7:00 am.
    c. Can include 7:35 am, if you want.
    d. Are always preceded by an alarm symbol.

41. To set an alarm for 7:00 am in Calendar, you must first:

    a. Type 7:00 am in the Special Time dialog box.
    b. Choose Controls from the Alarm menu.
    c. Highlight the day of the appointment in Month view.
    d. Move the insertion point to this appointment time in Day view.

42. To define a Recorder macro, in the Record Macro dialog box:

    a. You must type a name for the macro.
    b. You must select a shortcut key for the macro.
    c. You must select either a name or a shortcut key.
    d. You need not do any of the above.

43. To play back a previously-defined Recorder macro:

    a. Recorder must be the active window.
    b. Recorder must be reduced to an icon.
    c. Recorder must not be running.
    d. The macro must be listed in the Recorder window.

44. To use Terminal to connect to another computer:

    a. The baud rate must be set properly.
    b. A function key must be set up for the log-on process.
    c. Your computer must be set up as a black-and-white terminal.
    d. You must do all of the above.

45. To receive a graphics file from a remote computer:

    a. You must use a text file transfer.
    b. You must use a binary file transfer.
    c. You may use either a text or binary file transfer.
    d. Graphics files cannot be sent from a remote computer.

Hands-On Start up Windows, if necessary, and perform the indicated tasks. To create a printed copy of your work, see Appendix B.

46. a. Start Clock.
    b. Turn on the date display and the Always on Top option, if either one is not already selected.
    c. Reduce Clock to an icon. Are both the time and date displayed?
    d. Restore Clock and turn off the date display.
    e. Reduce Clock to an icon again. Is the date displayed now?
    f. Switch to Program Manager and maximize it. Is the Clock icon still visible?
    g. Restore Clock and exit it.

47. a. Start Calculator and then Character Map.
    b. Select the Times New Roman font in Character Map.
    c. Select the characters 5, +, and 9, in that order.
    d. Copy these characters to the Clipboard by choosing the Copy

button.

e. Select the font that was active when you started Character Map.

f. Switch to Calculator and select the Standard mode, if necessary.

g. Paste the data on the Clipboard into the number display. What number is pasted into the display?

h. Exit Calculator and Character Map.

48. a. Start Calendar.

b. Change the date to January 4, 1994.

c. Enter the following appointments on this day:
   - 1:00 PM: Lunch
   - 2:35 PM: Meeting with the boss (Use the Special Time feature to set this appointment.)

d. Set an alarm for the 2:35 appointment.

e. Switch to Month view.

f. Mark January 4, 1994 with a box symbol.

g. Insert a header with your name, your class, and the date, all on one line.

h. Print the appointments for January 4, 1994. Does the box symbol or the alarm symbol appear on the printout?

i. Remove the alarm and the special time.

j. Exit Calendar without saving the changes.

49. a. Maximize Program Manager (if necessary) and start Recorder.

b. Define a macro that will start the Terminal application from Program Manager. In the Record Macro dialog box:
   - Name the macro "Start Terminal".
   - Assign the shortcut key Ctrl+Shift+T to this macro.
   Choose the Start button to start recording.

c. In Program Manager, select the Accessories window and start Terminal by double-clicking on its icon. Then, press Ctrl+Break to stop recording.

d. Exit Terminal and test the macro by switching to Program Manager and pressing Ctrl+Shift+T. Did the macro work properly?

e. Exit Terminal, restore the Program Manager window, and resize it so the Accessories group window is no longer visible.

f. Test the macro again. According to the message displayed, why didn't it work this time?

g. Return the Program Manager window to its original size and exit Recorder.

50. a. Start Cardfile.

b. Insert the Lab Projects diskette in its drive and open the

ADDRESS.CRD file in its root directory.

c. Search for a card that contains a "4" in its information area. Change each 4 to a 6.

d. Search for other cards that contain a "4". How many are there?

e. Edit the index line of the "Baker, Joan" card so that it reads "Smith, Joan". When you close the dialog box, is the card automatically inserted in the correct order?

f. Add a card with AAA on its index line and your name and class in the information area.

g. Insert a header with the date (and nothing else) centered on the page and delete the default footer.

h. Print the card file.

i. Exit Cardfile without saving the changes.

Creative Writing

51. Start each of the following accessories and, with the aid of Windows on-line help system, describe in your own words (in one paragraph) the function of:

a. Object Packager.
b. Sound Recorder.
c. Media Player.

52. Windows does not supply a personal Telephone Directory accessory (although you could create one using Cardfile). Suppose you are in charge of designing such an accessory. List its menus and describe its menu items (in one sentence each). Describe or draw a picture of its icon.

53. Which Windows accessories would you place in the StartUp group? In one or two paragraphs, justify your answer.

54. Suppose that your computer is equipped with a modem and that you have a subscription to an on-line information service, whose communication settings are contained in the file ONLINE.SET. Further suppose that all information on this service resides in text files that can be accessed by selecting menu items and that you want to read an encyclopedia article on Thomas Jefferson. If you have just started Windows, describe the process by which you would call and use the on-line service to obtain a copy of this article.

 **9**

Advanced Topics

OVERVIEW   The basic philosophy of Windows is to provide a user-friendly, yet powerful environment that shields you from the technical aspects of using a computer. Nevertheless, to get the most out of Windows, it is sometimes necessary to understand its inner workings. In this chapter, we will discuss some advanced Windows features. You will learn about:

1. Object linking and embedding (OLE).

2. Types of memory and how memory is used by Windows.

3. Windows' modes — Standard and 386 Enhanced.

4. Program information files (PIFs).

5. Using PIF Editor.

9.1   Object Linking and Embedding

The Windows Clipboard (Section 2.4) provides an easy way to transfer information from one application to another. However, once that data has been placed in the target application, it may not be easy to edit it. If changes need to be made, you may have to delete the existing information and then reinsert a modified version of it. Object Linking and Embedding provides a better way to transfer and edit information. In this section, we will discuss the embedding, linking, and editing processes.

What is OLE?

Object Linking and Embedding (OLE, pronounced "olay") allows you to transfer information from one document (the *source*) to another (the *destination*), in such a way that it can be edited from within the latter. In Windows parlance, the information to be transferred is called an **object**. An object can be text produced by a word processor, pictures drawn in a graphics program, data contained in a spreadsheet, or any other piece of information created by a Windows application. For example, you could use OLE to copy a drawing object, created in Paintbrush, into a Write document. Then, if the graphic needs to be modified, just double-click on it in Write and it will be displayed in the Paintbrush window, ready for editing.

Not all Windows applications can use linking and embedding. If an application can *create* embedded and linked objects, it is called an **OLE server**; if it can *receive* these objects, it is called an **OLE client**. Paintbrush is an example of an OLE server; Write is an OLE client. Some applications can function as both a server and a client.

Difference between linking and embedding   Although linking and embedding are usually mentioned together, they are really two different processes. When an object is **embedded**, a copy of it is inserted in the destination document. Then, when this object is edited, the copy is altered, not the original version; the source document remains unchanged.

On the other hand, when you **link** an object, an image of it is inserted in the destination document and information *about* the original object (for example, in which file it can be found) is also stored in the destination file. We say that a link, or reference, to the source object has been established. When you edit a linked object, the original document file is changed and the link is *updated*. Figures 9.1 and 9.2 illustrate the two processes.

FIGURE 9.1   Creating an Embedded or Linked Object

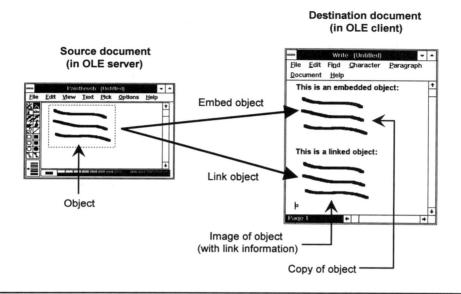

FIGURE 9.2   Editing an Embedded or Linked Object

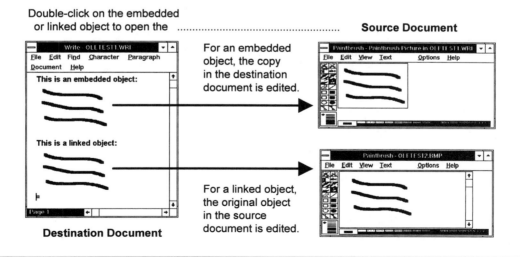

Linking and embedding accomplish the same thing: they transfer an object from one document to another and provide easy editing of the image. So, which should you use? Generally speaking, we usually *embed* an object when that object is needed in just one destination document. An embedded object is a little easier to edit than a linked one, and the resulting document file is a little smaller. On the other hand, if you want to use the same object in several documents, it makes sense to *link* it to them. Then, to update the object's image in all documents, you need only edit it once (in the source file).

To illustrate the embedding, linking, and editing processes, we will use Paintbrush (Chapter 7) as the OLE server and Write (Chapter 6) as the OLE client. Thus, in what follows, our source is a Paintbrush drawing and our destination is a Write document. The procedures described here work in a similar way for all clients and servers.

Embedding and Editing an Object

You can embed a Paintbrush drawing object in a Write document in two ways: starting from Write or starting from Paintbrush. We will discuss the latter method because it more closely resembles the usual Clipboard-based technique for transferring information between applications. To embed a drawing *starting from Paintbrush*:

Embedding an object

1. In Paintbrush, create the drawing or open an existing drawing. Then, use the Scissors tool or Pick tool to select the part of the drawing to be transferred. This is our drawing *object*.

2. Choose Copy from the Edit menu to place the object on the Clipboard.

3. Switch to Write, or start it if necessary.

4. Position the cursor where you want to insert the object.

5. Choose Paste from the Edit menu, or press Ctrl+V, to insert the object into the Write document.

Once an object is embedded in a document, it can be edited from within that document. To edit an object embedded in a Write document:

Editing an
embedded
object

1. In Write, double-click on the object (or select it and choose Edit Paintbrush Picture Object from the Edit menu). This will open the Paintbrush window and display the object within it.

2. Use Paintbrush to edit the object in any way you like.

3. Choose Update from the File menu to transfer the changes to the embedded object in the Write document.

4. To close the Paintbrush window, choose Exit and Return from the File menu, press Alt+F4, or double-click on the Control menu box.

Linking and Editing an Object

To create a link between a Paintbrush drawing and a Write document, the drawing must be saved in a file before it can be linked. Otherwise, the process is very similar to that used to embed an object. To transfer a linked object from Paintbrush into Write:

Linking
an object

1. In the Paintbrush window, open the file containing the object to be linked or create that object.

2. Save the object to be linked, if it has not yet been saved. (If you want to link part of the drawing, select that part and save it with the Copy To command on the Edit menu.)

3. Select the object to be linked using the Scissors or Pick tool.

4. Choose Copy from the Edit menu to place the object on the Clipboard.

5. Switch to Write, or start it if necessary.

6. Position the cursor where you want to insert the object.

7. Choose Paste Link from the Edit menu to insert the object into the Write document.

Once an object is linked to a source document, it can be edited from within the destination document. To edit an object in a Write document that is linked to Paintbrush:

Editing a
linked object

1. In Write, double-click on the object (or select it and choose Edit Paintbrush Picture Object from the Edit menu). This will open the Paintbrush window and display the object within it.

2. Use Paintbrush to edit the object in any way you like.

3. Choose <u>S</u>ave from the <u>F</u>ile menu to save the edited drawing. This action will automatically update the image of the Paintbrush object in the Write document.

4. Exit Paintbrush, if you want, in the usual way; for example, choose E<u>x</u>it from the <u>F</u>ile menu, double-click the Control menu box, or press Alt+F4.

Creating multiple links

If the same drawing is used in several Write documents, you may want to link it to all these documents. To do so, you can either:

■ Repeat the linking procedure with each Write document.

or

■ In the Write document containing the linked image, select it, copy it to the Clipboard, and paste it into the other documents. This copies the image *and* its link to all these documents.

Now, if you edit the object in the source document and then *save it*, the linked image will be updated in all destination documents.

Modifying a link

After you have created a linked object, Windows allows you to change the nature of the link, break the link, or repair a broken link. To perform any of these operations, choose Lin<u>k</u>s from the client's (Write's) <u>E</u>dit menu, which displays the Links dialog box:

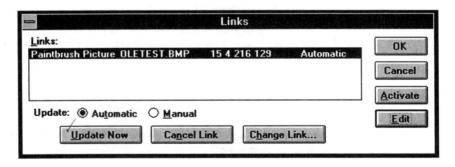

The <u>L</u>inks box lists all links for the current document. You can modify any of these links in the ways described below; all changes will go into effect when you choose the OK button in this dialog box.

■ If a link is updated *automatically* (the default), the image of the object in the destination document is changed whenever the edited source object is saved. To prevent this from occurring — to require a link to be updated *manually* — select it in the <u>L</u>inks list and click the Manual option button. To update a manual link, you must open the Links dialog box, choose the Update Now button, and then choose OK.

- When you *break* a link, the object's image remains in the destination document, but it can no longer be edited. To break a link, select it in the Links list and choose the Cancel Link button.

- Sometimes a link is inadvertently broken by changing the file name of the source document. If you then try to edit that object's image, Windows can no longer find the source document. To *repair* (reestablish) the link, select the object in the Write document, then open the Links dialog box and choose the Change Link button. In the Change Link dialog box that appears, double-click on the new file name for the Paintbrush document in the File Name list (or select the name and choose OK). You will be returned to the Links dialog box, and the repaired link will now appear in the list.

Hands-On 9.1

Start up Windows and Paintbrush and try the following exercise.

1. In Paintbrush, create a simple graphic, such as a filled circle, and save it to a floppy disk.
2. Select your graphic with the Pick tool and copy it to the Clipboard.
3. Start Write and choose Paste from the Clipboard to embed the drawing object in the Write document.
4. Now, choose Paste Link from the Edit menu to insert a linked image of the drawing object in the document. Is there any difference in the appearance of the embedded and linked objects?
5. Print the Write document.
6. Double-click on the linked object and, when Paintbrush opens, edit it (for example, change it to a filled square).
7. Save the new image to the floppy disk and exit Paintbrush. Is the object automatically changed in Write?
8. Print the Write document and exit Write.

9.2   Windows' Use of Memory and Modes

One of Windows' most important "hidden" features is its ability to manage memory in a way that enables you to run several large programs at the same time. In this section, we will discuss types of memory and how

Windows makes use of them. We will also describe the difference between Windows' two operating modes — Standard and Enhanced.

Types of Memory

When we use the term *memory* in referring to a personal computer, we usually mean its Random Access Memory, or RAM. In a broader sense, however, memory is any medium for storing information. From this perspective, every computer system contains several types of memory:

- Random Access Memory (RAM) for storing programs and data while they are in use.

- Read-Only Memory (ROM) for permanently storing information used by the operating system.

- Mass storage — hard and floppy disks, magnetic tape, CD-ROM disks, and the like — for storing data and programs semi-permanently.

- Memory used by certain hardware, such as printer memory to temporarily store data sent to the printer and video memory to store the contents of the screen.

(For more information concerning these computer components, see the Introduction to this text.)

Recall that memory is measured in *bytes*; each byte can hold one character of information. One *kilobyte* (KB) is 1,024 bytes and one *megabyte* (MB) is 1,024 KB, or about one million bytes. To access memory, each byte is assigned an *address* — a number designating its storage location. (An address is really the "logical" location of a byte; physically, it resides on a chip or chips on the motherboard or on an adapter board.)

Memory is also classified according to its storage location or the way it is used. (Figure 9.3 illustrates this in a pictorial fashion.)

- **Conventional memory** refers to the first 640 KB of RAM. This is the memory used by DOS and its applications. All programs run by DOS must reside partly or wholly in this address space.

- **Upper memory** has addresses ranging from 640 KB to one MB. This region was originally reserved for memory used by hardware devices (such as the video adapter) and ROM. Nowadays, a type of system software called a **memory manager** can make use of unused

→ B34

a function key. You can then choose that function key instead of typing the required characters. This not only speeds up the process of communicating with the remote computer, but also takes some of the frustration out of it.

To assign a sequence of characters to a function key:

1. Choose Function <u>K</u>eys from the <u>S</u>ettings menu. The following dialog box will be displayed:

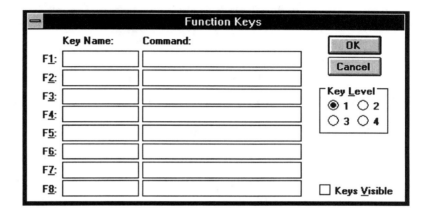

2. Select a Key <u>L</u>evel option button. On each of the four levels, you can assign commands to eight function keys.

3. For any function key, F<u>1</u> to F<u>8</u>:

    ■ Type a label in the Key Name box that will remind you of the function of that key; for example, Log-on. These labels can be displayed on function key buttons in the Terminal window, as described shortly.

    ■ Type the corresponding character string in the Command box.

4. When you're done, choose the OK button.

The "commands" can be ordinary text or contain special *command codes*, such as:

^M sends a carriage return character;
^$C dials the number specified in the Phone Number dialog box;
^$D*n*, where *n* is a two-digit number, inserts a pause of *n* seconds in the transmission.

For example, the command   ^$C^$D08^MSVenit^Mec3zzy^M   instructs

Windows' Operating Modes

Windows 3.1 has two modes of operation — **Standard mode** and **Enhanced mode**. When Windows starts up, it automatically chooses (based upon your computer hardware) one of these modes under which to run. If Windows is currently running, and you're curious which mode is being used, choose About Program Manager from its Help menu; the resulting dialog box provides (among other things) the mode of operation.

Standard mode is normally used with relatively low-level systems — those with a 286 class processor or less than two megabytes of RAM. Enhanced mode, which is sometimes called *386 Enhanced mode*, is used on more powerful systems. It has the following advantages over Standard mode. In Enhanced mode:

Advantages of Enhanced mode

1. You can run most DOS — non-Windows — applications in a window (see Section 2.5). Running a DOS application in a window provides it with these features:

   ■ You can change the size of its screen font.

   ■ You can transfer selected information between it and the Clipboard.

2. Windows can simulate expanded memory for those non-Windows applications that require it.

3. DOS applications can run at the same time as Windows applications, sharing system resources with them. We will discuss this **multitasking** feature in more detail shortly.

4. Windows sets up a **swap file**, a special section of the hard disk, to use as virtual memory. If you are running more applications than can fit into the available RAM, Windows will copy, or "swap," one of them to disk to provide more memory for the active application. We will discuss swap files later in this section.

Multitasking   As you know, Windows can run several applications at the same time. It accomplishes this by having the computer's processor switch among the running applications many times per second, giving each a *slice* of its processing time. This is done so quickly that it is usually not noticeable; while working on the active (*foreground*) application, you will normally be unaware that the processor is also serving the inactive (*background*) applications.

Multitasking can be extremely useful at times. For example, while the Terminal communications program (Section 8.5) is receiving a large data file from a remote computer *in the background*, you can use (say) a word processor to simultaneously work on another project *in the foreground*. The file transfer will take longer this way, but you probably won't notice any difference in the way the word processor performs.

In Enhanced mode, Windows can multitask DOS programs as well as Windows applications. However, because DOS applications are not written to run under Windows, this process sometimes needs a little fine-tuning. For example, a DOS program normally assumes that it has the sole use of the computer's resources and its program code may contain nonstandard "tricks" to take advantage of this fact. Running this program simultaneously with other applications may lead to display or printer problems, or even a program *crash* — a sudden, unexpected termination of the program.

386 Enhanced

If you encounter a problem multitasking DOS and Windows programs, you can sometimes cure the problem by using the 386 Enhanced utility or the PIF Editor. (We will discuss PIF Editor in Section 9.3.) To start the **386 Enhanced utility** program, open the Control Panel window from the Main group and choose the 386 Enhanced icon. The following dialog box will be displayed:

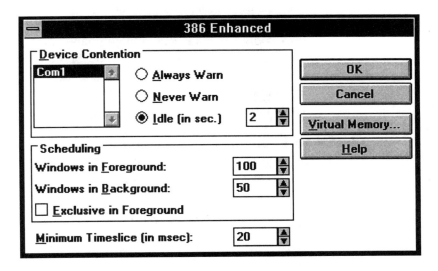

Although the default values for the Device Contention and Scheduling parameters usually work satisfactorily, you can easily change them to solve problems or improve system performance.

Device contention

■ With multitasking, it is possible that two applications will try to access the same device (say, a printer or modem) at the same time.

If both programs were written to run under Windows, this will not cause a problem. However, if one of the programs is a DOS application, Windows must be told how to handle the situation. To do so, select a Device Contention option button for each communications port listed:

1. If you select Always Warn, a message will appear on the screen informing you of the contention and asking you to decide which application can use the device.

2. If you choose Never Warn, contention can occur and cause problems. Do not select this option.

3. The default option, Idle, forces an application to wait for the specified period of inactivity (two seconds is the default) before it tries to use a communications port. This option almost always prevents contention without your intervention.

Scheduling
■ Recall that when applications are multitasked, each one gets a slice of the processing time. All Windows applications are supplied with one time slice and each DOS application receives a slice of its own. The Scheduling options in the 386 Enhanced window, combined with similar options in the PIF Editor, determine how the processor time is divided among the running applications. We will discuss how this works in Section 9.3. It should be noted here, however, that if the Exclusive in Foreground check box is selected and a Windows application is active, all DOS programs in the background will be temporarily halted.

Swap Files Recall that when Windows is running in Enhanced mode, it can use a swap file on your hard disk to serve as additional "RAM." Windows can set up either a temporary swap file or a permanent swap file:

■ If a *temporary swap file* has been set up, it is created every time you start Windows. This kind of swap file grows and shrinks, as needed, and is automatically deleted when you exit Windows.

■ A *permanent swap file* is a hidden file of fixed size that takes up a continuous section of disk space, even when Windows isn't running.

To determine the kind (temporary or permanent) and size of the swap file Windows is using:

1. Open Control Panel by choosing its icon from the Main group.

386 Enhanced

2. Choose the 386 Enhanced icon in the Control Panel window. The 386 Enhanced dialog box will be displayed.

3. Choose the Virtual Memory button in the 386 Enhanced dialog box. The following dialog box will then appear:

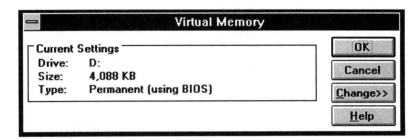

To change the current settings for Drive, Size, or Type:

1. Choose the Change button, which will expand the Virtual Memory dialog box.

2. In the expanded dialog box, select the desired Drive, Type, and New Size for the swap file.

3. Choose the OK button. A dialog box will be displayed asking you if you want to restart Windows to put the changes into effect.

4. Choose the Restart button to put the changes into effect.

A permanent swap file yields slightly better performance than a temporary one, because it reserves a contiguous section of disk space, which in turn results in faster disk access. You can also improve performance by placing the swap file on your fastest hard disk drive, if you have more than one.

On the other hand, if your hard disk is almost full, you might want to sacrifice some performance to maximize the available disk space. In this case, select Temporary or None for the swap file type. "None" prevents Windows from creating a swap file, which limits the storage space for programs and data to actual RAM. In particular, you will not be able to run as many programs simultaneously as you could while using virtual memory.

Hands-On

9.2

Try the following exercise. To create a printed copy of your work, see Appendix B.

1. If Windows is running, exit it. At the DOS prompt, type MEM and press the Enter key. How much conventional, extended, and expanded memory is available on your system?

2. Start Windows (type WIN and press Enter) and the 386 Enhanced utility program. What option is set for Device Contention? Are Windows applications set to run exclusively in the foreground?

3. Open the Virtual Memory dialog box. What are the current settings for the swap file drive, type, and size?

4. Choose the Change button. What is the swap file size recommended by Windows?

5. Choose Cancel twice to exit the 386 Enhanced utility; then exit Control Panel.

9.3   Program Information Files and PIF Editor

Windows applications, those written specifically to run under Windows, follow its guidelines for using RAM, the video display, printers, and so on. When running a DOS program, Windows determines how this application uses system resources by reading a **program information file**, or **PIF**. In this section, we will discuss program information files and how to modify them using the Windows PIF Editor.

The PIF Editor

Many developers of DOS applications supply a program information file with their software. When the command is given to start the DOS application, Windows reads the PIF and allocates resources accordingly. If Windows cannot find a program information file for a DOS application, it uses a generic PIF, located in the WINDOWS directory and named _DEFAULT.PIF. Unfortunately, the default PIF doesn't always work — the DOS program may not run properly, if at all. In this case, a new PIF must be created for this application using the PIF Editor.

PIF Editor is a Windows utility that allows you to create a custom program information file for a DOS application. Using PIF Editor, you specify the command that starts the application, the amount of memory it needs to run, the type (if any) of graphics it uses, and many other para-

PIF Editor

meters. This information can usually be found in the application's user guide, but it also helps to have had some experience using the program.

Depending on how Windows was set up, PIF Editor resides in either the Main or Accessories group. When you choose its icon, the PIF Editor window opens. Figure 9.4 shows the window that is displayed if Windows is running in 386 Enhanced mode.

FIGURE 9.4   The PIF Editor Window (Enhanced Mode)

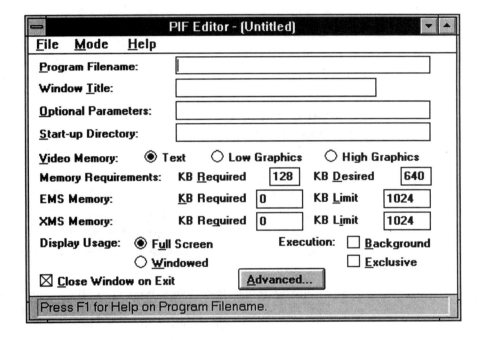

To use PIF Editor to create or edit a program information file, follow these general steps:

1. If you want to edit an existing PIF, choose Open from the File menu, which displays the usual Open dialog box (see Section 4.4). The existing PIFs in the WINDOWS directory will be listed in the File Name box. Double-click on the file to be opened, or select it and choose the OK button.

2. Fill in and/or make changes in the requested information in the PIF Editor window.

3. Choose Save <u>A</u>s from the <u>F</u>ile menu and save the PIF in the same way you would save any file. Or choose <u>S</u>ave from the <u>F</u>ile menu to save a modified PIF under the same name. (See Section 4.4 for information about saving a file.) In naming the PIF, use the application's program file name with the extension PIF; if you don't type an extension, Windows will add the extension PIF.

4. Exit PIF Editor as you would any other Windows application; for example, double-click on its Control menu box, or press Alt+F4, or choose E<u>x</u>it from its <u>F</u>ile menu.

Basic PIF Options

We will now provide information about the options in the PIF Editor window shown in Figure 9.4.

Start-up Options   The first four text boxes supply information to Windows about starting the DOS application.

- In the <u>P</u>rogram Filename box, type the full path name of the file that starts the application; for example: c:\wp51\wp.exe. (This particular command starts the WordPerfect word processor.)

- Type a short, but meaningful, description of the application in the Window <u>T</u>itle box; for example: WordPerfect. This name or phrase will appear under the application's icon and on the title bar of its window.

- In the <u>O</u>ptional Parameters box, type the parameters (if any) that you would normally type after the application's program file name, if you were starting it from the DOS prompt. For example, if you use the command c:\wp51\wp/m-layout to start your word processor, then type /m-layout in this text box.

- In the <u>S</u>tart-up Directory box, type the full path name of the directory that you want to be the current directory when the application starts.

Start-up Screen Mode   The <u>V</u>ideo Memory option buttons specify the screen mode used by the application when it starts up. This, in turn, tells Windows how much video memory to reserve for it. Here, Text refers to text mode (no graphics), Low Graphics is usually CGA graphics mode, and High Graphics refers to EGA or VGA graphics. If the application switches video modes once it is running, Windows will make more or less video memory available, as appropriate.

The default for <u>V</u>ideo Memory is Text, which can sometimes cause display problems if an application normally starts in another screen mode. Selecting High Graphics guarantees that there will be enough memory available regardless of the start-up screen mode, but also means that less memory is available for other applications.

Even if you select High Graphics, you may encounter display problems after start up. If the application switches to a lower resolution mode, Windows will free some of the video memory for use by other applications. If your application now switches back to a high graphics mode, there might not be enough memory available and the application may partially or completely disappear from the screen. To prevent this from happening, choose the <u>A</u>dvanced button and select the Retain Video <u>M</u>emory check box (see Figure 9.5 on page 365).

Use of RAM PIF Editor allows you to specify the amounts of conventional, extended, and expanded memory to be used by the application. These values are listed in the Memory Requirements, EMS Memory, and XMS Memory text boxes, respectively. The "KB Required" values specify the minimum amount of memory of each type that must be *free* before Windows attempts to start the application. Leave these figures at their default values. The default values for "KB Desired" and "KB Limit" are usually satisfactory, as well, but:

- If the application can run using less than 640 KB of conventional memory, change the KB Desired to a lower value to free memory for use by other applications.

- If the application benefits from using more than 1024 KB (1 MB) of either expanded (EMS) or extended (XMS) memory, you could increase the appropriate KB Limit. However, this may decrease the memory available to other applications.

- If you want to prevent Windows from supplying EMS or XMS memory to the application, set the corresponding KB Limit to 0.

Other Basic PIF Options

- If you want the application to start in window mode, select the

<u>W</u>indowed option button; otherwise, select the F<u>u</u>ll Screen option button.

- If the <u>B</u>ackground check box is not selected, execution of the application will be suspended when you switch to another application. On the other hand, if the <u>E</u>xclusive check box is selected, all other applications are suspended when this one is active.

- Deselect (clear) the <u>C</u>lose Window on Exit check box if you do not want the application's window to immediately disappear from the screen when you exit it. To close the window if this option is deselected, open the application's Control menu (by clicking on it or by pressing Alt+Spacebar) and choose <u>C</u>lose.

Advanced PIF Options

You can access additional PIF options by choosing the <u>A</u>dvanced button from the PIF Editor window (Figure 9.4). This will display the dialog box shown in Figure 9.5. To return to the PIF Editor window after you have made the desired changes, choose the OK button to accept these changes or the Cancel button to cancel them.

The options in the Advanced Options dialog box can usually be kept at their default settings. We will discuss those that occasionally need to be changed to prevent problems or increase performance.

Multitasking Options   These options determine the percentage of processor time that this application will receive while operating in the foreground (when it's active) or background (when it's not). You may set values from 0 to 10000 in the <u>B</u>ackground Priority and <u>F</u>oreground Priority check boxes, but these figures are only meaningful in relation to those set for the other applications running.

For example, suppose that this application is running in the background using the default priority value of 50. Further suppose that the active program is a Windows application with a foreground priority of 125 (as set in the 386 Enhanced option of Control Panel) and another inactive DOS program has a background priority of 25. (There may be other inactive *Windows* applications, but they do not enter into the computation; all Windows applications are given one time slice to share.) To compute the time slice provided to our application, divide its background priority by the sum of these figures: $50 / (50 + 125 + 25) = 50 / 200 = 0.25$. Thus, our application will receive 25% of the processor time.

FIGURE 9.5   The PIF Editor Advanced Options Dialog Box

```
┌─────────────────────────────────────────────────────────────────┐
│ ▬                        Advanced Options                        │
├─────────────────────────────────────────────────────────────────┤
│ ┌─Multitasking Options──────────────────────────┐  ┌─────────┐  │
│ │ Background Priority:  [50]   Foreground Priority: [100]│  │   OK    │  │
│ │            ⊠ Detect Idle Time                  │  └─────────┘  │
│ └───────────────────────────────────────────────┘  │ Cancel  │  │
│ ┌─Memory Options─────────────────────────────────────────────┐  │
│ │      □ EMS Memory Locked        □ XMS Memory Locked        │  │
│ │      ⊠ Uses High Memory Area    □ Lock Application Memory  │  │
│ └────────────────────────────────────────────────────────────┘  │
│ ┌─Display Options────────────────────────────────────────────┐  │
│ │ Monitor Ports:   □ Text    □ Low Graphics   □ High Graphics│  │
│ │            ⊠ Emulate Text Mode    □ Retain Video Memory    │  │
│ └────────────────────────────────────────────────────────────┘  │
│ ┌─Other Options──────────────────────────────────────────────┐  │
│ │ ⊠ Allow Fast Paste            □ Allow Close When Active    │  │
│ │ Reserve Shortcut Keys:  □ Alt+Tab  □ Alt+Esc   □ Ctrl+Esc │  │
│ │                         □ PrtSc    □ Alt+PrtSc □ Alt+Space│  │
│ │                         □ Alt+Enter                        │  │
│ │ Application Shortcut Key:   [None                     ]     │  │
│ └────────────────────────────────────────────────────────────┘  │
├─────────────────────────────────────────────────────────────────┤
│ Press F1 for Help on Priority.                                   │
└─────────────────────────────────────────────────────────────────┘
```

Reserving Shortcut Keys   Normally, if a shortcut key defined within an application conflicts with one used by Windows, the Windows key takes precedence. If you want to have Windows ignore one of the listed shortcut keys while the application is running in the foreground, select the corresponding Reserve Shortcut Keys check box. For example, if you select the Alt+Tab box, pressing this key combination while our application is active will *not* cause a switch to a new application. Instead, the action (if any) defined for this key in the active application is carried out.

Hands-On

9.3

Start up Windows and PIF Editor, if necessary, and try the following exercise. To create a printed copy of your work, see Appendix B.

1. Choose Open from the File menu and display the existing PIFs in the WINDOWS directory. How many are there?
2. Open DOSPRMPT.PIF. What program does this PIF start?

    3. Use PIF Editor's Help system to determine:
- The function of the <u>M</u>ode menu.
- The meaning of the entry -1 in the Memory Requirements text boxes.

    4. Choose the <u>A</u>dvanced button. What shortcut keys, if any, does this PIF reserve?

    5. Exit PIF Editor.

Chapter Summary

Key Terms

386 Enhanced utility [page 357]	Conventional memory [354]
Embed an object [348]	(386) Enhanced mode [356]
Expanded memory [355]	Extended memory [355]
Link an object [348]	Memory manager [354]
Multitasking [356]	Object [348]
Object linking and embedding [348]	OLE [348]
OLE client [348]	OLE server [348]
PIF [360]	PIF Editor [360]
Program information file [360]	Standard mode [356]
Swap file [356]	Upper memory [354]
Virtual memory [355]	

Topics
Covered

Object Linking and Embedding (OLE)

To embed an object	Copy the object to the Clipboard, and in the destination document, choose <u>P</u>aste from the <u>E</u>dit menu.
To edit an embedded object	Double-click on the object, edit it in the source document, and choose <u>U</u>pdate from the source's <u>F</u>ile menu.
To link an object	Save the object in the source document, copy it to the Clipboard, and in the destination document, choose Paste <u>L</u>ink from the <u>E</u>dit menu.

| To edit a linked object | Double-click on the object, edit it in the source document, and save the source document to update the linked image. |
| To modify a link | Choose Links from the client's Edit menu and make the desired changes in the Links dialog box. |

Types of Memory

Conventional memory (0 KB - 640 KB)	Stores programs and data while they are in use.
Upper memory (640 KB - 1 MB)	Stores ROM and adapter memory; also used by memory managers to provide additional RAM.
Extended memory (Above 1 MB)	Used by Windows and extended memory managers to provide additional RAM.
Expanded memory	Used by an expanded memory manager to provide additional RAM for DOS programs.
Virtual memory	Disk space used by Windows as additional RAM.

Windows' Modes

| Standard mode | Used with 286 processors and systems that have less than 2 MB of RAM. |
| (386) Enhanced mode | Provides benefits when running DOS programs; also provides more effective use of virtual memory. |

The 386 Enhanced Utility Program

To start	Open the Control Panel window in the Main group and choose the 386 Enhanced icon.
Multitasking options	Can fine-tune the way Windows applications multitask with DOS programs (device contention and scheduling).
Virtual memory options	Provides control over the type, size, and location of swap files.

The PIF Editor Utility Program

| To start | Choose the PIF Editor icon from the Main or Accessories group. |

To use	Open the PIF to be edited, make the desired changes (from the basic and advanced options), and save the modified PIF.
Basic options	Specify how to start the DOS program (including screen mode and required RAM).
Advanced options	Include multitasking options and the use of certain shortcut keys.

Chapter Exercises

Short Answer Complete each statement in Exercises 1 through 10.

1. An application that can create linked and embedded objects is called an OLE _____ .

2. To edit a linked or embedded object, _____ on that object in the destination document.

3. You can break a link between an object and its image by choosing the Cancel Link button in the _____ dialog box.

4. The RAM used by Windows with addresses above 1 MB is called _____ memory.

5. On a computer with 4 MB of RAM and a 486 processor, Windows will normally start in _____ mode.

6. The 386 Enhanced utility is started by choosing its icon from the _____ window.

7. Windows uses virtual memory by creating a _____ on your hard disk to use as additional RAM.

8. A _____ file tells Windows how to start a DOS program and how to allocate system resources to it.

9. You use the _____ utility to modify a program information file.

10. If you start a program from the DOS prompt with the command line C:\TP\TURBO/M, then in PIF Editor, type _____ in the Program Filename text box and _____ in the Optional Parameters text box.

In Exercises 11 through 20, determine whether each statement is true or false.

11. When you edit an embedded object, you can change it without altering the original (in the source document).

12. A single object in a source document can be linked to images in several destination documents.

13. To prevent Windows from automatically updating a linked object every time the source document is saved, select the Manual Update option button in the Links dialog box.

14. Random Access Memory (RAM) is the only place a computer system can store information for later retrieval.

15. Virtual memory is RAM located in addresses above 1 MB.

16. When operating in Standard mode, Windows sets up a permanent swap file to supply additional "RAM."

17. When operating in 386 Enhanced mode, Windows can supply expanded memory to those DOS applications that request it.

18. Every Windows application must be associated with a program information file.

19. If Windows cannot find a PIF for a DOS program, it uses a file named GENERIC.PIF to start that application.

20. If the shortcut key Alt+Tab has been reserved for the active DOS program, then you cannot use this key to switch from this application to another.

In Exercises 21 through 26, choose the correct answer.

21. To embed an object in a Write document, copy it to the clipboard, switch to Write, and:

    a. Choose Paste from the Edit menu.
    b. Choose Embed from the Edit menu.
    c. Choose Copy from the Edit menu.
    d. None of these actions will embed the object.

22. To edit a linked object, double-click on it in the destination document, edit it in the source document, and:

    a. Choose Update from the File menu.
    b. Choose Save from the File menu.

    c.   Choose Copy from the Edit menu.

    d.   Choose Paste from the Edit menu.

23. The memory that occupies the first 640 KB of address space is:

    a.   Conventional memory.

    b.   Virtual memory.

    c.   Expanded memory.

    d.   Extended memory.

24. Using the Virtual Memory dialog box, you can change:

    a.   The kind (permanent, temporary, or none) of the swap file.

    b.   The size of the swap file.

    c.   The location (disk drive) of the swap file.

    d.   All of the above.

25. Using PIF Editor, you can change:

    a.   The start-up information for a Windows application.

    b.   The start-up information for a DOS application.

    c.   The way you quit a Windows application.

    d.   All of the above.

26. When applications are multitasked:

    a.   The foreground application may be given all the processor time.

    b.   The slice of processor time given to Windows applications can be adjusted using the 386 Enhanced utility.

    c.   The slice of processor time given to a DOS application can be adjusted in its program information file.

    d.   All of the above are true.

Hands-On   Start up Windows, if necessary, and perform the indicated tasks. To create a printed copy of your work, see Appendix B.

27. a.   Start Write, insert the Lab Projects diskette in its drive, and open the OLETEST.WRI document in its root directory.

     b.   Double-click on the embedded object to edit it.

     c.   In the Paintbrush window, use the Eraser tool to erase the bottom curve.

     d.   Update the embedded object and Exit and Return to OLETEST.

     e.   Print the OLETEST.WRI document.

     f.   Exit Write, saving the changes in the document.

28. a. Start Write, insert the Lab Projects diskette in its drive, and open the OLETEST.WRI document in its root directory. (If a dialog box appears, update the link.)

   b. Start File Manager and rename the OLETEST.BMP file in the root directory of the Lab Projects disk as OLENEW.BMP.

   c. Switch to Write and double-click on the *linked* object in the document. What message is displayed?

   d. Select the linked object, open the Links dialog box, and repair the broken link by supplying the new name of the BMP file.

   e. Edit the linked object by using the Eraser tool to delete the bottom curve. Save the Paintbrush document to update the link.

   f. Exit Paintbrush and print the Write document.

   g. Exit Write (saving the changes) and File Manager.

29. a. Insert the Lab Projects diskette in its drive. In the root directory is a DOS application called DOSPROG.EXE.

   b. Start PIF Editor and create a PIF for this application by:
   - Typing the proper Program Filename. (Don't forget the floppy drive designation!)
   - Leaving the other parameters at their default settings.
   - Saving the PIF to the floppy drive as DOSPROG.PIF.

   c. Exit PIF Editor and start File Manager.

   d. Select the floppy drive and double-click on DOSPROG.PIF.

   e. Exit DOSPROG by following the on-screen instructions.

   f. Exit File Manager.

30. a. Start the 386 Enhanced utility from the Control Panel window.

   b. Open the Virtual Memory dialog box. What is the type, size, and location of the swap file? If it is a permanent swap file, carry out parts c through f.

   c. Start up File Manager and select the root directory of the drive on which the swap file is located.

   d. Choose By File Type from the View menu, select the Show Hidden/System File check box, and choose the OK button.

   e. A permanent swap file is named 386SPART.PAR. Is the size of this file the same as the size listed for the swap file in the Virtual Memory dialog box? (Remember that one kilobyte is 1,024 bytes.)

   f. Deselect the Show Hidden/System Files check box in the By File Type dialog box and exit File Manager.

   g. Exit the 386 Enhanced utility.

Installing
Windows 3.1

Before using the Windows operating environment, you have to *install* it — copy the files from the Windows distribution diskettes to your hard disk and set up Windows to work with your hardware. In this appendix, we will discuss the installation process.

System Requirements

To use Windows, your computer system must meet certain minimum requirements. In order to run, Windows needs:

- An IBM-compatible personal computer with a 80286, 80386, 80486, or Pentium processor, running under the DOS operating system, version 3.1 or higher.

- At least one megabyte of RAM to run Windows in Standard mode and at least two megabytes of RAM to run it in Enhanced mode. (See Section 9.2 for a discussion of Windows' modes.)

- From seven to ten megabytes of free hard disk space, depending on the installation you choose.

- A 3½-inch or 5¼-inch floppy disk drive.

- A monitor and video display adapter supported by Windows.

- A mouse supported by Windows, although not required, is highly desirable.

■ A printer supported by Windows, if you want to be able to print your documents.

Although Windows will run on almost all systems that meet the minimum requirements just described, it may run sluggishly or lack certain features. To improve performance, a 386 (or better) processor and at least 4 MB of RAM are highly recommended. Moreover, because Windows applications tend to be very large, a correspondingly large hard disk — at least 120 MB — should be considered a necessity. Finally, Windows puts great demands on the video adapter and display, so a fast video adapter, capable of 800 x 600 resolution, and a color monitor with a 15 inch or larger screen, will certainly add to the enjoyment of using Windows.

Windows Setup

Installing Windows is really very easy. In most cases, the only information that you have to provide is your name, the type of printer you will be using, and the port to which it's connected. A program called Setup and the Windows 3.1 distribution diskettes do the rest. To run Setup to install Windows:

1. Turn on the computer and wait for the DOS prompt (usually `C:\>`) to appear.

2. Insert Windows Disk 1 into the appropriate floppy disk drive, type the drive's designation (either `A:` or `B:`), and press the Enter key.

3. Type `SETUP` and press the Enter key. A screen will appear that provides a short description of the installation process.

4. After you've read the information on the screen, press the Enter key.

Express Setup versus Custom Setup

5. You will now be asked whether you want to use Express Setup or Custom Setup.

■ If you choose Express Setup, Windows will carry out the installation process almost automatically. You will have to do little more than periodically insert diskettes in the floppy drive and press the Enter key.

■ If you choose Custom Setup, you will have more control over the installation process, but also have to make more decisions.

You will have to, among other things, decide in which directory to install the Windows files, provide or verify information about your system's hardware, and determine which Windows components to install.

Express Setup is the more commonly used installation option; we will describe it in the next section. However, regardless of which option you choose, Windows provides detailed on-screen instructions to guide you through installation.

If you need additional help at any time during the installation process, press the F1 function key. This will activate the Windows Help system, described in Section 1.5. When you have located the information you were seeking, press the Escape key to return to installation.

If you want to abort the installation process at any time, press the F3 function key. Setup will exit to DOS and return your system to the state it was in when the process began, except that files already copied to your hard disk will not be erased. To install Windows after you have aborted the process, you will have to start again from the beginning.

Express Setup

Express Setup is not only easier to use than Custom Setup, but, in the vast majority of cases, it also produces a completely satisfactory installation. When you are presented with the Express Setup/Custom Setup decision, press the Enter key to choose Express Setup. Then, the following actions will take place:

1. If this is a new installation, Windows will create the C:\WINDOWS directory and begin copying files to it. If you are upgrading from Windows 3.0, you will be asked to specify the directory in which to install Windows 3.1. To accept the default (your previous Windows directory), press the Enter key; Windows will then begin copying files, updating your old ones in the process.

2. After a while, you will be prompted to insert another disk into the floppy drive. Remove the current disk, insert the specified one, and press the Enter key. Windows Setup will then go back to work. (You will have to repeat this step several times during the installation process.)

3. At some point, the Setup program will switch out of the text-based DOS mode and begin to run under Windows. You will notice the difference in the look of the screen.

4. After Setup enters Windows mode, you will be given the opportunity to try the Windows on-screen Tutorial. It consists of two parts: using the mouse and performing basic operations. If you start the Tutorial, you can exit it at any time by pressing the Escape key. (You can run the Tutorial any time *after* Windows has been installed by choosing <u>W</u>indows Tutorial from the Program Manager <u>H</u>elp menu.)

5. A dialog box will appear, asking you to type your name and company. (This information will be displayed in the About Program Manager dialog box, which opens when you select this item from its <u>H</u>elp menu.) After typing the text, press Enter or click on the OK button to continue.

6. Eventually, you will be asked to select a printer from the list displayed by Setup. Follow the instructions to install your printer and to specify the port (usually LPT1) to which it is connected.

7. Toward the end of the process, Setup will search your hard disk for applications. Those it recognizes will be installed in Program Manager groups. DOS (non-Windows) applications will be installed in the Applications group.

8. When installation is complete, a dialog box will be displayed asking you if you want to <u>R</u>eboot the computer or Return to MS-<u>D</u>OS. Press the Enter key to reboot and put all changes to your system into effect.

If, at any time in the future, you want to change the hardware configuration or Windows components set up in the installation process, you can run the Setup program from within Windows. To do so, choose (double-click on) the Windows Setup icon in Program Manager's Main group. For additional information, see Section 5.6.

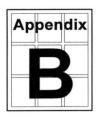

Appendix B

Printing Your Solutions to Exercises

You can use the Windows Write accessory, with occasional help from the Clipboard, to produce a printed copy of your answers or solutions to the exercises in the text. In this appendix, we will demonstrate how to do this. (The material presented here will be more easily understood if you have already completed Chapter 2.)

Using Write to Type Your Answers

To start Write:

Write

1. Switch to Program Manager, if necessary, by holding down the Alt key and pressing the Tab key until the words "Program Manager" appear in a box on the screen; then, release both keys.

2. Open the Accessories window, if necessary, by double-clicking on its icon. If neither the Accessories icon nor its window is visible on the screen, you can open the Accessories window by choosing this group from Program Manager's Window menu.

3. Start the Write application by double-clicking on its icon in the Accessories group. The Write window (Figure 1 on the next page) will open.

You can then quickly switch between Write and any other running application by repeatedly pressing Alt+Tab (as described in step 1 above) until the title of the desired application appears in a box on the screen; then release both keys. (See Section 2.4 for more information on switching among applications.)

FIGURE 1   The Write Window

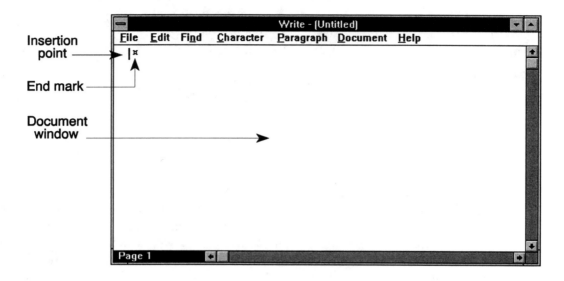

Insertion point

End mark

Document window

Once you have started Write, you can type whatever you want at the keyboard; the corresponding text will appear in the document window and be stored in RAM. The *insertion point*, the blinking vertical bar, indicates where the next character you type will appear on the screen. The *end mark* (see Figure 1) indicates the end of the document.

When you reach the end of a line, just keep typing; the text will automatically *wrap* to the beginning of the next line. If you want to start a new line manually, press the Enter key and the insertion point will move to the beginning of the next line. To skip a line, press Enter again.

For example, if you type your name, your class, and the date, pressing the Enter key after your name and class, the three entries will appear on separate lines. Moreover, if you press Enter twice after the date, your document will have the form shown in Figure 2.

If you make a typing error, you can erase the character just to the left of the insertion point by pressing the Backspace (or ←) key; to delete the character just to the right of the insertion point, press the Delete (or Del) key. If you notice a mistake elsewhere on the screen, you can use the Arrow keys (or other special keys) to move the insertion point to this location, or just click on the location with the mouse. (See "Working within a Window" in Section 1.3.)

FIGURE 2   Entering Text in the Write Window

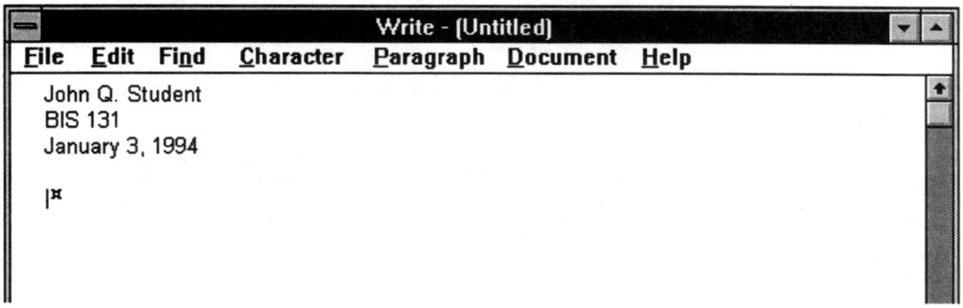

Capturing Screens

For the Hands-On exercises, you may have to "capture" the active window or the entire screen as part of the solution. For example, if the instructions ask you to "Move the Main window to the bottom of the screen," you can demonstrate that you've successfully performed this task by placing an image of the entire screen in your Write document. To capture screens and windows, you make use of the Windows Clipboard (see Section 2.4):

- To place an image of the *entire current screen* at the insertion point of your Write document:

  1. Press the Print Screen key to copy the screen to the Clipboard.

  2. Switch to the Write application (and your document) by repeatedly pressing Alt+Tab until the application's title appears in a box on the screen.

  3. Choose Paste from Write's Edit menu.

- To place an image of the *active window* at the insertion point of your Write document, follow the same procedure but press Alt+Print Screen instead of Print Screen in step 1.

For example, suppose the instructions to a Hands-On exercise ask you to "Choose Run from the File menu, and in the resulting Run dialog box, type A:SETUP and select the Run Minimized check box." As part of your solution to this exercise, you perform the indicated task, capture the Run dialog box (by pressing Alt+Print Screen), and insert it into your Write document. The latter would now resemble the one in Figure 3.

FIGURE 3   The Write Window with the Captured Screen

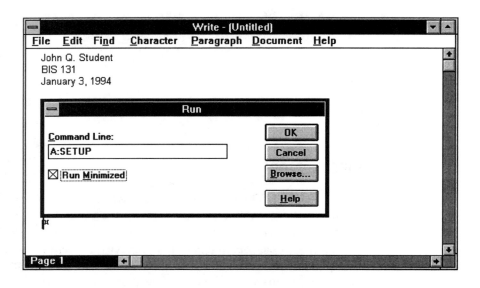

Saving Your Document

Whenever you finish an assignment, it is wise to save a copy of it to disk. (When you exit Write, the document will be erased from RAM.) To *save* the document you have created to a floppy disk:

1. Insert your disk into the appropriate drive.

2. Switch to Write, if necessary.

3. Choose <u>S</u>ave from the <u>F</u>ile menu.

    ■ If the document has been saved previously, this newer version will be saved under the same name, replacing the former version. The <u>F</u>ile menu will close and you can skip to step 7.

    ■ If this document has not been saved before, the Save As dialog box (Figure 4) will open and you will have to complete all the remaining steps.

FIGURE 4   Write's Save As Dialog Box

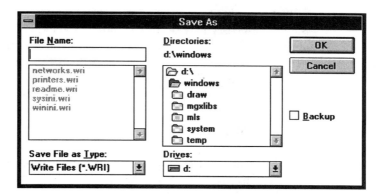

4. Open the Dri<u>v</u>es drop-down list box (by clicking on it) and select the appropriate drive (a: or b:).

5. Select the File <u>N</u>ame text box and type a valid file name for your document. The file name will be valid if you use a combination of up to eight letters and numerals, beginning with a letter, and having no spaces in between. For example, Ch2Ex41 is a valid file name. (For more information about file names, see Section 3.1.)

6. Choose the OK button. The Save As dialog box will close.

7. Remove your floppy disk from its drive.

Printing Your Document

Once you have finished the assignment, it is a simple matter to make a printed copy of your Write document. Follow these steps:

1. Make sure that the printer connected to your computer is ready to receive information from it.

2. Switch to Write, if necessary.

3. Choose <u>P</u>rint from the <u>F</u>ile menu. The Print dialog box will appear.

4. Choose the OK button or press the Enter key.

Quitting Write

When you have completed the assignment, you can exit Write in the same manner you exit most applications running under Windows. The quickest ways are to double-click on the Control menu box, or press Alt+F4, or choose Exit from the File menu. (For more information on quitting an application, see Section 2.6.)

For More Information ...

The following sections of the text contain information that pertains to the material discussed in this appendix:

- Section 1.3 describes how to move around in a document window.

- Sections 2.3 and 2.6 discuss starting applications and quitting applications, respectively.

- Section 2.4 demonstrates how to switch among several applications and how to transfer information (text and graphics) between applications.

- Section 3.1 discusses files and directories in general and file names in particular.

- Section 4.4 provides a general discussion on working with documents.

- Chapter 6 covers all facets of the Write word processor.

Appendix C

Answers to Selected Exercises

Introduction

1. hardware
3. eight
5. tape *or* CD-ROM
7. applications
9. DOS
11. ENIAC
13. 1975
15. Apple Macintosh
17. true
19. true
21. false
23. true
25. true
27. true
29. false
31. d
33. b
35. b
37. a
39. a

Chapter 1

1. WIN
3. Alt+E
5. active
7. maximize
9. dotted rectangle
11. Glossary
13. false
15. true
17. true
19. false
21. false
23. false

25. A - Control menu box   B - Title bar
     C - Minimize button   D - Maximize button
     E - Menu bar   F - Horizontal scroll bar
     G - Vertical scroll bar

27. c   29. a
31. d   33. d

Chapter 2

1. applications; documents   3. Main
5. Ctrl (Control)   7. Shift key
9. StartUp   11. Clipboard
13. DOS *or* non-Windows   15. Ctrl+Alt+Del
17. true   19. false
21. false   23. false
25. false   27. true
29. a   31. c
33. a   35. c

Chapter 3

1. subdirectory   3. Map.Dwg; C:\Windows\Draw
5. Tree and Directory   7. View
9. Ctrl   11. Shift
13. formatted   15. false
17. false   19. false
21. false   23. true
25. true   27. b
29. c   31. c
33. b   35. b

Chapter 4

1. New   3. Run Minimized
5. associated   7. File
9. Save; Save As   11. Pause
13. false   15. false
17. false   19. true
21. false   23. false
25. b   27. d
29. d   31. a

Chapter 5

1.	Main	3.	luminosity
5.	screen saver	7.	Keyboard
9.	(scalable) fonts	11.	(Windows) Setup
13.	false	15.	true
17.	true	19.	false
21.	true	23.	false
25.	false	27.	d
29.	a	31.	d
33.	b		

Chapter 6

1.	Accessories	3.	Ctrl+End
5.	Cut	7.	Fonts
9.	Document	11.	(left-aligned) tab stops
13.	Object Linking and Embedding *or* OLE	15.	&p
17.	true	19.	false
21.	true	23.	false
25.	false	27.	false
29.	false	31.	b
33.	a	35.	d
37.	d	39.	d

Chapter 7

1.	View Picture	3.	foreground
5.	Paint Roller	7.	Scissors
9.	Shift	11.	Copy To
13.	Backspace	15.	header
17.	false	19.	true
21.	false	23.	true
25.	false	27.	false
29.	false	31.	b
33.	a	35.	a
37.	c	39.	b

Chapter 8

1.	Control	3.	right-most
5.	index lines	7.	Go To
9.	right scroll arrow	11.	Options
13.	macros	15.	Any
17.	Communications	19.	Printer Echo
21.	true	23.	false
25.	false	27.	false
29.	true	31.	true
33.	true	35.	false
37.	d	39.	b
41.	d	43.	d
45.	b		

Chapter 9

1.	server	3.	Links
5.	Enhanced *or* 386 Enhanced	7.	swap file
9.	PIF Editor	11.	true
13.	true	15.	false
17.	true	19.	false
21.	a	23.	a
25.	b		

Index